Natural Law & Thomistic Juridical Realism

Natural Law & Thomistic Juridical Realism

Prospects for a Dialogue with Contemporary Legal Theory

Petar Popović

Foreword by F. Russell Hittinger

THE CATHOLIC UNIVERSITY OF AMERICA PRESS

Washington, D.C.

Cataloging-in-Publication Data available
from the Library of Congress
ISBN 978-0-8132-3550-9

To Professors Hervada (1934–2020) and Errázuriz,

to all the professors and students at the

Pontifical University of the Holy Cross in Rome,

and to my parents, with gratitude

Contents

Foreword

In one of his lectures on natural law at the University of Chicago during the winter term of 1958, Yves Simon paused to underscore what he took to be an "epoch-making event in the history of notions of law."[1] Over centuries, the primary meaning of the word "right" (*ius*) referred objectively to the thing itself that is right—*ipsa res iusta*. According to the jurisprudents, whether corporeal or incorporeal, the thing that belongs to another as his very "own" is the nub of a social relation of debt. The right thing and the correlative debt to recognize and fulfill the right of the other person constitute the object of the virtue of justice: "A constant and perpetual will to give to each what is his right" (*Iustitia est constans et perpetua voluntas ius suum cuique tribuendi*, D. 1.1.10).

Simon notes that in the eighteenth century, the primary meaning of "right" changed and came to mean "subjective rights," which is to say an individual's legally recognized claim or faculty to do this or not to do that. Subjective rights highlight personal capacities to create, cancel, or redirect one's own lines of conduct, especially in the face of social or political powers that would preemptively bind the individual. Of the claims to goods or actions

---

1. Yves R. Simon, *The Tradition of Natural Law: A Philosopher's Reflection* (New York: Fordham University Press, 1992), 120.

due by nature (*ius naturale*), those pertaining to individual freedoms and immunities are paramount in the modern tradition of subjective rights, which articulated rights as personal powers in contrast to what Locke would have called "absolute and arbitrary powers" of government. For critics of subjective rights, however, such freedoms and immunities convey the impression of morally untethered and inadequately specified rights that are not reliably correlated with obligations on the part of others.

Debates over which of these notions of right is primary or secondary are long standing. It is well to be reminded that even Justinian's *Digest* takes note of the fact that the word *ius* is "used in several senses" (D. 1.1.11). The question of the foundation of natural rights took on more urgency after World War II with the international efforts to formulate declarations and covenants on human rights, and those decades have been characterized as a time of "disillusioned sovereignty." Indeed, disordered institutions of sovereignty are the gifts that perennially give natural right doctrines renewed appeal. After the world wars and in the face of global struggles for decolonization, there was a strong presumption that just laws and institutions of law must be based on more than either procedural grounds or on titles and efficiencies required by state sovereignty.

This was also a lively and pressing issue for the Catholic tradition, which remained the institutional home of scholastic philosophy and that of objective right rooted in natural law. The church quickly gave support to the human rights project, notably in the papal encyclical *Pacem in Terris* (1963), which enumerated twenty-five discrete natural or human rights. In some three millennia of natural rights discourse, no one had attempted such a list. The church also began to define its own mission and competence in worldly affairs in reference to those rights. The 1983

Code of Canon Law, for example, reads: "It belongs to the Church always and everywhere to announce moral principles, even about the social order, and to render judgment concerning any human affairs insofar as the fundamental rights of the human person or the salvation of souls requires it."[2]

Regarding those "fundamental human rights," some neo-scholastic thinkers and perhaps most churchmen who still understood the distinction between objective right and subjective rights had to bend diplomatically in order to accommodate some aspects of subjective rights. After all, rights belong either to individual or corporate persons, and therefore rights have *bearers* who make or can make *claims* about what belongs to them in justice. That much of "subjectivity" seems unavoidable even under the discipline of ancient Roman law.

The neo-Thomist philosopher and diplomat Jacques Maritain famously contended in the late 1940s that human rights reflect a practical "creed" or "ideology" rather than a morality that is philosophically verified and affirmed in its proper grounding—a grounding to be achieved in dialogue and good will. This required Catholic authorities diplomatically to rely on circumlocutions as placeholders for a fully adequate grounding of human rights. Placeholders invoke an assent of sorts while leaving the depth of the issue, or even more likely the complication of meanings, to one side. The hard work, of course, comes in grounding rights in an adequate anthropology and in light of an objective and normative moral order, to wit, natural law, but to put rights back into the vicinity of natural law requires more exacting attention to the juridicity of right or rights.

With that brief and tendentious introduction, I am pleased to recommend the present volume, *Natural Law and Thomistic*

2. *Code of Canon Law* (January 25, 1983), can. 747 §2.

Juridical Realism: Prospects for a Dialogue with Contemporary Legal Theory. A doctor of canon law, Petar Popović is on the faculty of canon law at the Pontifical University of the Holy Cross (Rome). He is trained in the school of juridical realism developed and explicated by twentieth-century scholars like the French legal historian Michael Villey and the Spanish jurist and legal philosopher Javier Hervada. This work, however, represents the author's own synthesis of the juridical tradition of objective right and natural law.

The term "juridical realism" has two closely related meanings, each based on the Latin word *ius*, the root of right, justice, and jurisprudence. First, a juridical realist takes the principal meaning of *ius* to denote the "right thing"—the very thing that belongs to someone as their *suum* and which constitutes a debt in relation to others. Justice depends on discovering and then fulfilling—in the case of contracts and positive rights, determining this realistic kernel of the just thing. Second, juridical realists hold that the operations of justice have as their main *object* things attributed and allocated. To be sure, as justice is but one instance of moral virtue, human goods as divisible and allocatable are only one part of morality. What we call law directs actions toward human perfection and, ultimately, to a common good that is not itself, strictly speaking, a divisible thing. Yet the juridical domain is realistically distinct precisely because it must view some human goods under the aspect of yours, mine, and ours. This domain is not merely a set of lawyerly complications that intrude into our quest for eudaimonia. Rather, the juridical "goods" are distinct and ineliminable aspects of friendship and social happiness.

The ontological status of human goods does not in the first place depend on their juridical standing but rather on their being fundamental facets of human perfection. Life, physical integrity, nurturing and educating the young, knowing truth, and entering society according to a rational order are goods to which we are directed by precepts of natural law (*Summa Theologica* I-II 94.2, hereafter *ST*). Within that order, as a part to the whole, is a juridical domain that St. Thomas considers in considerable detail in his treatise on justice (*ST* II-II, 57-122). It is worth noting that this treatise is several times longer than the preceding treatise on law. Here St. Thomas discusses *ius naturale* as a distinct part of *lex naturalis*.

The goods already outlined by the precepts of natural law come into view as juridical goods and have three aspects. First those goods or actions are outwardly manifest (*res exteriores*). Indeed, the internal feelings and emotions are very profound and important, but they must be evidentially justiciable in the court of a social relation. Second, those goods have the note of alteriety or otherness, as goods or actions are apportionable and attributable to "other" persons as their very own (*suum*). Third, such things constitute a socially communicable, interpersonal relation of debt (*debitum*). Simply, for justice to be fulfilled, we must know *who* owes *what* to *whom*.

These three aspects of the juridical domain are marked by Thomas Aquinas at the beginning of his treatise, where he contends that the right (*iustum*) can be established by consent, testament, or contract—either public or private. Some things, however, are due *ex ipsa natura rei*, by virtue of nature, and this is called natural right (*ius naturale*) (*ST* II-II 57.2). The just thing or right is attributed to its titleholder within a relation of justice. The foundation and title is human nature, which each person possesses as his very own. Law is a rule and measure of human acts, directing them "according to an order of justice" (*ST* I-II 91.5). Popović explains:

If this claim is read with the natural law in view, the link between the legality of natural law and the order of juridical justice becomes clearer. When a precept of natural law is considered under the aspect of the attribution of certain natural human goods to persons as their titleholders and their obligatoriness in the relational perspective, which includes other determinate subjects as debtors regarding these goods, we may refer to this normative structure also as a natural norm that pertains to the order of juridical justice.[3]

It is the author's goal to show that human goods, beyond being understood as perfective of human beings in the moral domain, are also apportionable as outward and other-directed goods that belong to a person under the aspect of mine, yours, ours. The moral domain of law already contains the juridical domain. What are deemed objective goods are also the subject of objective rights. If this can be confirmed, we can bring together a synthesis of St. Thomas's two discussions of natural norms in the *Summa*. And from here, a dialogue with contemporary legal theory's notion of subjective rights can fruitfully begin.

F. Russell Hittinger
Professor Emeritus of Catholic Studies, University of Tulsa
Senior Fellow, Lumen Christi Institute

3. See p. 237.

Abbreviations

Dig.	*The Digest of Justinian*
ITC	International Theological Commission
Nic. Eth.	Aristotle, *Nicomachean Ethics*
Sent. Eth.	Thomas Aquinas, *Sententia Libri Ethicorum*
ST	Thomas Aquinas, *Summa Theologica*

Natural Law & Thomistic Juridical Realism

Introduction

This book proposes a new approach to the question of the juridical domain of natural law, albeit not one that adds to or otherwise revises the theory of natural law in its Thomistic formulation. Neither does it revise the Thomistic take on the essence of the juridical domain, "*ius.*"

Granted, the concepts of natural law and natural justice are quite old, almost as old as philosophical inquiry itself,[1] and their development from antiquity to the present day has yielded an enormous body of literature on the link between the natural law and the juridical phenomenon.

Nonetheless, I believe that my line of argument, even while operating with old, classical—Thomistic, if you will—conceptual tools, adds something substantially new to the intersection between the normative status of natural law and the essence of the juridical domain. To present this line of argument in a manner that fully reveals its novelty, I will address the juridical status of natural law in its contextual, traditional, and developmental aspects.

---

1. On the origins of the concept of natural law in Greek philosophical thought, see Helmut Koester, "ΝΟΜΟΣ ΦΥΣΕΩΣ: The Concept of Natural Law in Greek Thought," in *Religions in Antiquity: Essays in Memory of Erwin Ramsdell Goodenough*, ed. Jacob Neusner (Leiden: E. J. Brill, 1970), 521–41, and James L. Adams, "The Law of Nature in Greco-Roman Thought," *The Journal of Religion* 25, no. 2 (1945): 97–118.

Within the contextual aspect, I will present the contemporary *status quaestionis* of the juridicity of natural law by looking to the most relevant philosophical accounts of the "law-morality" intersection in the last half-century. Some of these accounts adopt a Thomistic position regarding the cognitive process of grasping the precepts of natural law and their ontological background. Their authors seek to interrelate this position with what they understand to be its juridical effects. Other authors, however, envision the connection between law and morality within a reduced or "minimalist" version of natural law, as they endorse a view on law and morality that contrasts deeply with the Thomistic conception of natural law. Whereas the advocates of the Thomistic position claim to have satisfactorily integrated the natural moral law within the juridical domain, legal positivists and advocates of minimalist natural law, as I will show, deny the existence of any juridically relevant substantive morality; in fact, they exclude the possibility of predicating juridicity of human nature in any necessary way.

These contrasting approaches, presented in the first chapter of this book, provide context for a clearer understanding of my contribution to the juridical status of natural law proposed in the ensuing chapters. Their mutual differences notwithstanding, both theoretical accounts reveal the existence of an unsolved problem, or at least a crucial question left unanswered at the very center of the contemporary treatment of the "law-morality" intersection. Regardless of their respective conclusions, both approaches focus on the question of whether morality has any necessary impact on the domain of positive law and, if so, what such impact is. They both take for granted the premise that to include substantive moral values within the juridical domain necessitates answering a further, more fundamental question. Instead of beginning with the question of how relevant morality is for the sphere of positive law, should we not first understand if and how juridicity, the quality of being juridical or the essence of the juridical phenomenon, is predicated on the moral domain itself? Although the central arguments of the theoretical accounts presented in the first chapter have been addressed elsewhere within the context of legal philosophy, they have not as yet been considered in light of the question of the immediate juridical status of moral values. My doing so will provide a fresh perspective on the arguments of their authors. In this manner, the first chapter will prefigure some of the elements that pertain to this new contribution to the understanding of the juridicity of natural law.

Subsequently, I will present the singular tradition that has, indeed, provided an illuminating answer to the question of the juridical status of natural law and which has emerged within the doctrinal context provided by a *realistic juridical conception of law and rights*, with respect to both the natural law and the positive law. Initially outlined in the classical works of Aristotle, the Roman jurists, and Thomas Aquinas, this conception gained new currency in the late twentieth century as it was interpreted anew by authors such as Michel Villey and Javier Hervada.

The authors within this tradition are as much interested in understanding the juridical status of law and rights as they are in grasping the normative structure of morality. Since Villey and Hervada have both made significant efforts to gather the classical arguments of juridical realism into a coherent juridical-philosophical doctrine, the thought of these two authors, as well as that of their sources—especially Aquinas—will ground my presentation of the realistic juridical tradition in the second chapter of this work.

The synthesis of Villey's and Hervada's realistic juridical conception of law and rights has rarely been studied in an integral way within the Anglo-Saxon world of legal philosophy.[2] Consequently, their doctrine on the concept of juridicity, which they claim to have fully inherited from Aristotle, the Roman jurists, and Aquinas, has not been given the attention it deserves. For the same reasons, the predominantly Thomistic tradition of the realistic juridical conception of law and rights has not as yet been sufficiently confronted with the numerous scholarly attempts to elaborate on the concept of natural law within the same tradition. This book seeks to reestablish this connection with regard to the question of the juridical status of natural law.

In my estimation, Villey's and Hervada's arguments on the juridical domain *inherent* in natural law represent a singular contribution to the natural-law theory as well as a unique approach to the law-morality intersection in juridical philosophy. Their arguments on the juridical status of natural law will be presented in the third chapter. To my knowledge, this is the first attempt to harmonize the two philosophers' respective lines of argumentation. In addition, since Villey and Hervada have not provided a fully developed account of all the aspects of the juridical status of natural law, I will occasionally complete their line of argumentation by bringing implicit or underdeveloped elements of their

2. For references to some aspects of Villey's theory, see Richard Tuck, *Natural Rights Theories: Their Origin and Development* (Cambridge: Cambridge University Press, 1979), 7–8, 22–23; Ralph McInerny, "Natural Law and Human Rights," *The American Journal of Jurisprudence* 36, no. 1 (1991): 1–3; Brian Tierney, "Villey, Ockham and the Origin of Individual Rights," in *The Idea of Natural Rights: Studies on Natural Rights, Natural Law and Church Law 1150–1625* (Atlanta: Scholars Press, 1997), 13–42; and Riccardo Saccenti, *Debating Medieval Natural Law: A Survey* (Notre Dame, Ind.: University of Notre Dame Press, 2016), 13–21. For a more complete presentation of Villey's thought, see John R. T. Lamont, "Conscience, Freedom, Rights: Idols of the Enlightenment Religion," *The Thomist* 73, no. 2 (2009): 198–235. For references to some aspects of Hervada's theory, see Carlos J. Errázuriz , *Justice in the Church: A Fundamental Theory of Canon Law*, trans. Jean Gray (Montréal: Wilson & Lafleur Ltée, 2009), 96–105.

ideas to their logical consequences. I will also occasionally high-light certain aspects of their respective arguments by comparing them with similar positions held by other contemporary natural-law theorists or by using original texts of Aquinas that Villey and Hervada may have insufficiently considered.

Given that Villey's doctrinal arguments, and even more so Hervada's, are largely unknown to Anglophone academic readers concerned with natural-law theory, and to legal philosophers in general, this might be an opportune moment to introduce these authors.

Michel Villey was born on April 4, 1914, in Caen, France.[3] After obtaining his doctoral degree in 1942, he was appointed professor of legal history at the School of Law in Nancy. His first works in legal history are dedicated to a doctrinal analysis of the concept of *ius* in Roman law and its influence on modern jurid-ical thought.[4] After his appointment as a professor at the School of Law in Strasbourg in 1949, Villey focused his research on the history of juridical philosophy, and this academic discipline re-mained the focus of his philosophical interest throughout his whole career. In 1959, he became the lead editor of the academic journal *Archives de philosophie du droit*, a position he held until

3. Michel Villey's biographical information was obtained from "Michel Villey: Repères biographiques et bibliographiques," in *Réflexions sur la philosophie et le droit: Les carnets de Michel Villey*, ed. Maria-Anne Frison-Roche and Christophe Jamin (Paris: Presses Universitaires de France, 1995), xiii–xv; Alfred Dufour, "In memoriam Michel Villey," *Persona y Derecho* 20 (1989): 284–88; F. Vallançon, "Réflexions biographiques sur Michel Villey," *Droits* 29 (1999), 119–24; and François Vallançon, "In memoriam," in *Michel Villey et le droit naturel en question*, ed. Jean-François Niort and Guillaume Vannier (Paris: Éditions L'Harmattan, 1994), 13–17.

4. Some of his first published works include Michel Villey, *Recherches sur la littéra-ture didactique du droit romain* (Paris: Les Éditions Domat-Montchrestien, 1945); Villey, "L'idée du droit subjectif et les systèmes juridiques romains," *Revue historique du droit français et étranger* 24 (1946): 201–28; and Villey, "Du sens de l'expression *jus in re* en droit romain classique," *Revue internationale des droits de l'Antiquité* 2 (1949): 417–36.

1985. He was the professor of the history of legal philosophy of the School of Law at Paris University II from 1961 to 1985. He died on July 24, 1988.

Javier Hervada was born on February 7, 1934, in Barcelona, Spain.[5] After obtaining his doctoral degree in 1958 at the Central University of Madrid, he also earned a doctorate in canon law at the University of Navarra in 1962. He was appointed Professor of Canon Law at the University of Zaragoza in 1964, and in 1965 became the Ordinary Professor of Canon Law at the University of Navarra. In 1981 he was nominated Ordinary Professor of Philosophy of Law and Natural Right at the same university. These two academic areas, namely, canon law and philosophy of law, continued to be his main points of interest throughout his career. He also taught various courses in these fields at the Pontifical University of the Holy Cross in Rome (at the time Roman Academic Center of the Holy Cross) between 1985 and 1990 and was awarded a doctorate *honoris causa* by this university on November 26, 2002. He served as the editor-in-chief of the academic journals *Ius Canonicum* from 1970 to 1973 and *Persona y Derecho* from 1974 until 1992. He died in Pamplona on March 11, 2020.

The fourth chapter of this work further accentuates the need for a synthesis between the realistic juridical conception of law and rights and contemporary Thomistic natural-law theory. In this chapter, I will provide an outline of the basic aspects of a theory of the juridical domain of natural law, which I will henceforth refer to as "natural norms of justice." After the presentation of the essence of the concept of right in the second chapter, and

---

5. Javier Hervada's biographical information was obtained from "Extracto del *curriculum vitae* del profesor Javier Hervada," *Ius Canonicum: Escritos en honor de Javier Hervada: volumen especial* (1999): xxi–xxx; Juan I. Arrieta, "Laudatio al prof. Javier Herada Xiberta," *Ius Ecclesiae* 14, no. 3 (2002): 611–14; and Massimo Del Pozzo, *L'evoluzione della nozione di diritto nel pensiero canonistico di Javier Hervada* (Roma: EDUSC, 2005), 23–28.

its status regarding the norms of natural law in the third chapter, we will be fully equipped for a better understanding of the natural norms of justice as *juridical* norms constituted in view of certain concrete natural rights understood as *natural juridical goods*.

In the fifth and final chapter of this work, the results of my analysis will be re-contextualized within the dialogue with congenial or competing contemporary perspectives on the law-morality intersection presented in the first chapter.

The outline of this work bears some resemblance to the structure of Thomas Aquinas's article in his *Summa Theologica*.[6] The main *quaestio* of my study, therefore, is, roughly speaking, whether we may validly predicate a specifically juridical domain of natural law. The first chapter amounts to a series of objections against an affirmative answer to the above question, since, as we will see, each contemporary theoretical account of the law-morality intersection actually denies that there is a juridical domain inherent to natural law. The second chapter, and parts of the third, constitute a *sed contra* argument, since they make explicit a traditional line of argument in support of an affirmative answer to the main question of my study. Furthermore, parts of the third chapter, together with the fourth, might be considered as the main *corpus* of this work, the *respondeo dicendum* part of the argumentation. These parts of the text should provide the elements that underlie the doctrine of the natural norms of justice as I elaborate on my affirmative answer to the main question of this study. In the fifth chapter, as well as in other instances throughout the text, I will provide some responses to the objections from the first chapter.

The difference in length between a standard Thomistic article and this work is obvious and has several causes. The first is

---

6. On the classical structure of Aquinas's argument in the *Summa Theologica*, see Otto Bird, "How to Read an Article of the *Summa*," *The New Scholasticism* 27, no. 2 (1953): 129–59.

that Aquinas was an almost unmatchable master of synthesis. Although Aquinas's approach, in both style and content, remains a model that continues to inspire, I do not presume to be able to match Thomas in his capacity for synthesis, originality, and precision of insight. The second cause arises from the fact that Aquinas did not explicitly dedicate a separate article in his *Summa Theologica* to the topic that constitutes the main question of my present study. As we will see over the course of this work, he did leave valuable doctrinal elements scattered throughout various loci of his texts, all of which are pertinent to the establishment of a juridical domain of natural law. Nonetheless, he never specifically and comprehensively addressed this topic. Therefore, when treating the main question of this study, one is necessarily confronted with an enormous body of academic literature regarding various positions on the juridical significance of natural law, within the broader question of the law-morality intersection. The attempt to answer the main *quaestio* of my present analysis according to a decisively Thomistic point of view thus entails taking into consideration not only Thomas's relevant texts on the topic but also those pertinent aspects gathered from all of the tradition that followed.

Hence, the attempt to address the concept of natural law within these doctrinal coordinates—namely, the contemporary juridical-philosophical context of the law-morality intersection and the predominantly Thomistic tradition of a realistic juridical conception of law and rights—is immediately confronted with a more modest and, really, more "realistic" scope. Certain reductions will have to be made, and some arguments will have to be left for future study. The narrow scope of this study is, therefore, to argue for a substantial and valid answer to the elements of the main *quaestio* outlined by the title of this work. How exactly is the juridical domain of natural law constituted according to the realistic juridical conception of law and rights? How is it doctrinally situated within the broader context of other dominant juridical-philosophical perspectives of the law-morality intersection (not all of which are sympathetic to the Thomistic account of natural law)?

The translations of Villey's and Hervada's original French and Spanish texts found in this work, as well as all other translations from these and other languages into English, are my own. Therefore, the responsibility for their correct translation to English, as well as for eventual shortcomings regarding these translations, is completely mine. On occasion, I found it necessary to distance myself from certain translation choices found in the published English translations of Villey's or Hervada's texts when they unintentionally reduced the intended effect of the original text. This was most frequently the case regarding translations of the terms "law" and "right."

I am fully aware that, in the English language, an objectivist meaning of the various manifestations of the juridical phenomenon is usually conveyed by the term law, whereas the term right is reserved almost exclusively for the modern subjectivist concept of individual rights. In the course of this study, we will see how Villey's and Hervada's realistic conceptions of right and juridicity instead both presuppose and repropose a contemporary restatement of the ancient and medieval concept of *ius*. The premodern concept of *ius* denotes a meaning of right that cannot be reduced to the law (when by law we understand the legal norm, the legal order, or even law as an institution) or to modern and contemporary meanings of subjective rights understood as individual powers to advance claim-rights.

For this reason, throughout this study, I will use the term right primarily in the sense that corresponds to this premodern realistic conception, namely, as *something that, in itself, objectively represents that which is just.* Throughout this work, especially in the second chapter, I will further present various necessary nuances and constitutive criteria concerning the precise significance of "something" or the "thing" that "in itself objectively represents that which is just." I will argue that this meaning of right may be used interchangeably with the concept of juridical good. As we will see, the conceptual link between the right and the juridical good is very useful for the correct understanding of how the right may be predicated on a thing. It is my opinion that the English term right may, indeed, be adequate to designate not only the subjectivist sense of right but also this objectivist sense. In most other European languages, the objectivist sense of *ius* is included within the meaning of terms such as *droit* (French), *derecho* (Spanish), or *diritto* (Italian), sufficiently differentiated from the terms law, *loi* (French), *ley* (Spanish), and *legge* (Italian).[7] Thus, throughout this study, I will insist on the terms "right" (henceforth without

7. For the difficulties in harmonizing the legal terminology of the European continental tradition with the Anglo-Saxon tradition with regard to the translations of the concept of *ius* in the translations of Hervada's texts, see Carlos J. Errázuriz M. and Petar Popović, "Presentation of the Second English Edition," in Javier Hervada, *Critical Introduction to Natural Right*, 2nd ed., trans. Mindy Emmons (Montréal: Wilson & Lafleur Ltée, 2020), xiii–xiv, originally published as *Introducción crítica al derecho natural* (Pamplona: EUNSA, 1981). See also William L. Daniel, translator's introduction to *What Is Law? The Modern Response of Juridical Realism: An Introduction to Law*, by Javier Hervada, trans. William L. Daniel (Montréal: Wilson & Lafleur Ltée, 2007), xi–xvi, originally published as *Qué es el derecho? La moderna respuesta del realismo jurídico: una introducción al derecho* (Pamplona: EUNSA, 2002). For the same issue regarding translations of Villey's texts, see Guillaume Voilley, translator's introduction to "Epitome of Classical Natural Law (Part I)," by Michel Villey, trans. Guillaume Voilley, *Griffith Law Review* 9, no. 1 (2000): 75. See also Stewart R. Shackleton, "La pensée juridique de Michel Villey dans le monde Anglophone," in Niort and Vannier, *Michel Villey et le droit naturel en question*, 108; Gaëlle Demelemestre, "La réception de l'interprétation française des théories du droit naturel dans le monde anglo-saxon," *Archives de philosophie du droit* 58 (2015): 387–422; and Anthony Lisska, "Human Rights Theory Rooted in the Writings of Thomas Aquinas," *Diametros* 38 (2013): 137–39.

quotation marks) and "juridicity," as well as the adjective "juridical," precisely to denote the doctrinal possibility that envisions
the concept of right according to a realistic perspective of "that
which is just," rather than "that which is in one's legal power to
claim," "that which is the consequence of the legal norm," or "that
which constitutes part of the legal order."[8]

8. This present book, besides providing context for terminological differences and discontinuities between the European continental tradition and the Anglo-Saxon tradition, should also contribute, in a collateral way, to a clarification of doctrinal elements underlying certain aspects of conceptual inconsistencies. A paradigmatic example of these inconsistencies, which actually highlights them as a doctrinal problem, may be found in the following text: "The words '*droit*,' '*diritto*,' and '*Recht*,' used by continental jurists, have no simple English translation and seem to English jurists to hover uncertainly between law and morals, but they do in fact mark off an area of morality (the morality of law) which has special characteristics. It is occupied by the concepts of justice, fairness, rights, and obligation." See H. L. A. Hart, "Are There Any Natural Rights?" *The Philosophical Review* 64, no. 2 (1955): 177–78.

1

The Juridical Domain of Natural Law in Contemporary Legal Philosophy—*Status Quaestionis*

Any contemporary presentation examining points of contact between the juridical domain of rights and positive law, on the one hand, and the natural-law theory, on the other, is bound to require a preliminary question. We may paraphrase this question from the title of Alasdair MacIntyre's 1988 *magnum opus*:[1] "Whose *concept of justice*? Which *natural law*?"

According to Thomas Aquinas's classical definition, the natural law is "the participation of the eternal law in the rational creature," whereby the rational creature "has a natural inclination to

1. Alasdair MacIntyre, *Whose Justice? Which Rationality?* (Notre Dame, Ind.: University of Notre Dame Press, 1988).

its proper act and end."[2] This participation is "impressed"[3] in the order of being and order of knowledge of the rational creature, and has, in Aquinas's view, the following basic structure:

All those things to which man has a natural inclination are naturally apprehended by reason as being good, and consequently as objects of pursuit, and their contraries as evil, and objects of avoidance. Wherefore according to the order of natural inclinations is the order of the precepts of the natural law.[4]

This is the basic normative structure according to which natural law is situated within Aquinas's general definition of law: "an ordinance of reason for the common good, made by him who has the care of community, and promulgated."[5] Contemporary Thomists have further developed this chain of arguments by claiming that natural law is "the communication of moral necessities to a created intellect,"[6] which both has a "legal character"[7] and comprehensively determines the structural role of all three foci around which the answer to the question of "what is natural law?" traditionally coalesces: human reason, human nature, and divine reason.[8]

2. *ST* I-II, q. 91, a. 2. For the English translation of the texts from Aquinas's *Summa Theologica*, I will be using Thomas Aquinas, *Summa Theologiae: First Complete American Edition in Three Volumes*, trans. Fathers of the English Dominican Province (New York: Benziger Brothers, 1947–1948).

3. *ST* I-II, q. 90, a. 4, ad 1; I-II, q. 91, a. 2; I-II, q. 91, a. 3, ad 2; and I-II, q. 93, a. 5.

4. *ST* I-II, q. 94, a. 2.

5. *ST* I-II, q. 90, a. 4.

6. Russell Hittinger, *The First Grace: Rediscovering the Natural Law in a Post-Christian World* (Wilmington, Del.: ISI Books, 2003), xxiii.

7. Stephen L. Brock, *The Light That Binds: A Study in Thomas Aquinas's Metaphysics of Natural Law* (Eugene, Ore.: Pickwick Publications, 2020).

8. For a brief overview of the three so-called traditional foci of natural law, and for a categorization of natural-law theories according to the inclusion of some of the foci as their central theoretical feature, see Russell Hittinger, introduction to *The First Grace*, xvi, xviii–xxiii; Hittinger, "Natural Law and Catholic Moral Theology," in *The First Grace*, 4–12; and Hittinger, "Authority to Render Judgment," in *The First Grace*, 95–98.

Over the course of the history of legal philosophy, this concept of natural law has mutated into a kaleidoscope of contrasting theories, each gravitating toward only one or two of the three foci. Since modern philosophy has abandoned the classical Aristotelian-Thomistic metaphysics, legal philosophy has been developed largely within the reductive ontological framework in which the terms *nature* and *law*, when predicated together, essentially belonged either "to a physical state of affairs" or "only to mental constructs"[9] expressed through purely human conventions.[10] The vast majority of legal philosophers from the last half-century, having inherited this framework, opted for the latter view, placing a clear focus on the claim that theories of laws and rights may not be founded on a single, natural, comprehensive viewpoint on the substantive content of morality prior to law. Some of these authors, however, have continued to employ the term natural law despite having thoroughly reconstructed the very essence of this

9. Hittinger, introduction to *The First Grace*, xxii.

10. A well-known example of the claim that the term natural law has become unintelligible outside of the context of natural science, as well as for the claim that the content traditionally ascribed to natural law has in fact always and exclusively been an object of human convention, can be found in Margaret MacDonald's writings in legal philosophy, inspired by the German philosopher Karl R. Popper. "There is no end set for the human race by an abstraction called 'human nature.' There are only ends which individuals choose, or are forced by circumstances to accept. There are none which they must accept.... In short, natural rights are the conditions of a good society. But what those conditions are is not given by nature or mystically bound up with the essence of man and his inevitable goal, but is determined by human decisions.... Assertions about natural rights, then, are assertions of what ought to be as the result of human choice." See Margaret MacDonald, "Natural Rights," *Proceedings of the Aristotelian Society* 47 (1946–1947): 237–38, 242. "By saying that some systems of laws can be improved, that some laws may be better than others, I rather imply that we can compare the existing normative laws (or social institutions) with some standard norms which we have decided are worthy to be realized.... Nature consists of facts and of regularities and is in itself neither moral nor immoral. It is we who impose our standards upon nature, and who introduce in this way morals into the natural world, in spite of the fact that we are part of this world." See Karl R. Popper, *Open Society and Its Enemies*, vol. 1, *The Spell of Plato* (London: Routledge, 1945), 52.

concept. This state of affairs explains why authors who strongly oppose the Thomistic formulation of the theory of natural law, such as H. L. A. Hart,[11] Ronald Dworkin,[12] or even John Rawls,[13] subscribe to forms of so-called "natural-law inclusive" theories.[14]

In light of such terminological confusion, other authors who continue to be inspired by the Thomistic natural-law theory consider the term natural law to be almost irreparably contaminated by radically contrasting meanings and, therefore, rendered almost unintelligible for the general public. They propose instead a terminological shift, suggesting potential new terms—such as "higher law"[15] or "human ecology"[16]—for the content that has classically been categorized under natural law.

In this chapter, I will present a variety of positions that situate the concept of natural law at some structural locus within the intersection between law and morality. Some of these authors, like Hart, Dworkin, Rawls, and Joseph Raz, develop a "minimalist" natural-law theory or argue for merely procedural or system-

11. As we will see over the course of this chapter, Hart is prepared to adopt a "minimum content of natural law." See H. L. A. Hart, *The Concept of Law*, 3rd ed. (Oxford: Oxford University Press, 2012), 193–200.

12. See, for example, Dworkin's famous claim that, "if … any theory which makes the content of law sometimes depend on the correct answer to some moral question is a natural law theory, then I am guilty of natural law." See Ronald Dworkin, "'Natural Law' Revisited," *University of Florida Law Review* 34, no. 2 (1982): 165.

13. "Thus, justice as fairness has the characteristic marks of a natural rights theory. Not only does it ground fundamental rights on natural attributes, but it assigns rights to persons by principles of equal justice." See John Rawls, *A Theory of Justice* (Cambridge, Mass.: Belknap Press of Harvard University Press, 1971), 505, n. 30.

14. For a more complete overview of these "minimalist" natural-law theories, see Russell Hittinger, "Varieties of Minimalist Natural Law Theory," *The American Journal of Jurisprudence* 34, no. 1 (1989): 133–70; Russell Hittinger, "Liberalism and the American Natural Law Tradition," *Wake Forest Law Review* 25 (1990): 429–99; and Steven A. Long, *Minimalist Natural Law: A Study of the Natural Law Theories of H. L. A. Hart, John Finnis and Lon Fuller* (PhD diss., The Catholic University of America, 1993).

15. See Hittinger, "Natural Law and Catholic Moral Theology," 34–37.

16. See Erika Bachiochi, "Safeguarding the Conditions for an Authentic Human Ecology," *Position Papers*, February 2017, 21–22.

ic points of contact between law and morality. Their theoretical accounts will be evaluated in reference to the central question of whether and how they attribute juridical status to the moral sphere. I will then present other authors who, conversely, claim to offer a contemporary restatement of the Thomistic approach to natural law and develop arguments to explain the passage from the moral domain of human action toward the constitution of the juridical obligation linked to the concepts of law and rights.

A presentation of this broad palette of theoretical accounts should provide a closer focus on the main cluster of problems regarding the connection between the moral domain of natural law and its specifically juridical domain. It should also facilitate a clearer grasp of the eventual shortcomings or theoretical voids of these accounts.[17]

Debates on the Question of the Juridical Status of Morality

H. L. A. Hart and the "No Necessary Connection" Thesis

Beginning in the late 1950s, Oxford professor of jurisprudence Herbert Lionel Adolphus Hart (1907–1992) elaborated a highly influential body of work in legal philosophy that is still considered absolutely essential for any contemporary analysis of the general theory of law and rights.[18] A distinguished member of

17. For a detailed analysis of the conceptions of law and rights of some of these authors (like Finnis, Dworkin, and Rawls), see Petar Popović, *The Goodness of Rights and the Juridical Domain of the Good: Essays in Thomistic Juridical Realism* (Roma: EDUSC, 2021).

18. In the preface to the third edition (published in 2012) of Hart's most famous work, *The Concept of Law* (originally published in 1961), Leslie Green affirms that quickly after its publication, it "became the most influential book in legal philosophy ever written

the British intelligence services during World War II,[19] Hart was one of the most prominent voices in the postwar debate over the connection between morality and law, which was catalyzed by a broader philosophical evaluation of jurisprudential questions in light of the tragic experiences of war, genocide, and the various totalitarian perversions of the rule of law. Hart had joined the postwar movement of philosophical reconsideration and critique of the possibility of a pure legal positivism, a movement that was, for many of his colleagues, frequently accompanied by an embrace of natural-law theory. However, although he sympathized with his fellow jusnaturalist legal scholars, who were firsthand witnesses of the terrors of totalitarianism, writing of them as ones who "have descended into hell, and ... brought back a message for human beings,"[20] his vision of the law-morality intersection diverged significantly from theirs.

Throughout his writings, Hart establishes a *via media* position between a pure "no-point-of-contact" positivistic approach to the law-morality intersection (which, in his view, "few, if any," ever truly supported)[21] and the "necessary-connection" approach of the natural-law theory.

Hart's critique of the natural-law approach to the law-morality intersection rests on the philosophical premise that the passage from "law as it is and law as morally it ought to be" must not be bridged by "various forms of the claim that there are *conceptual necessary* connections, not *merely contingent* ones, between law

---

in English" and adds that "scholars in law, in philosophy and in political theory continue to develop, build on, and criticize its arguments," while it also serves as "a widely used introduction to its subject and is ... read by students ... around the globe" (xi).

19. Nicola Lacey, *H. L. A. Hart. The Nightmare and the Noble Dream* (Oxford: Oxford University Press, 2004), 83–111.

20. H. L. A. Hart, "Positivism and the Separation of Law and Morals," in H. L. A. Hart, *Essays in Jurisprudence and Philosophy* (Oxford: Oxford University Press, 1983), 72.

21. Hart, *The Concept of Law*, 185.

and morality."[22] He is careful enough to clarify that this central claim of his theory is not entirely dependent on the adherence to post-Humean cognitive theories that evaluate the validity of moral judgments according to their capacity to escape the "razor" of the "is-ought" naturalistic fallacy.[23] His account of the intersecting points between morality and law, therefore, is not predicated primarily on moral theory but rather on specifically juridical grounds.[24]

It does not follow that because … a decision [is] intelligently reached by reference to some conception of what ought to be, we have a junction of law and morals. We must, I think, beware of thinking in a too simple-minded fashion about the word "ought." This is not because there is no distinction to be made between law as it is and ought to be. Far from it…. The word "ought" merely reflects the presence of some standard of criticism; one of these standards is a moral standard but not all standards are moral.[25]

Hart is, therefore, convinced that there are, indeed, important points of contact between the moral and juridical domains,

22. Hart, introduction to *Essays in Jurisprudence and Philosophy*, 8. Emphasis added.

23. "None the less I think (though I cannot prove) that insistence upon the distinction between law as it is and law as it ought to be has been, under the general head of 'positivism,' confused with a moral theory according to which statements of what is the case ('statements of fact') belong to a category or type radically different from statements of what ought to be ('value statements'). It may, therefore, be well to dispel this source of confusion" (Hart, "Positivism and the Separation of Law and Morals," 82).

24. "The only difference which the acceptance of this ['cognitive'] view of the nature of moral judgments [according to which, in contrast to a 'noncognitive' view, the drastic distinction in type between statements of what is and what ought to be is inexistent] would make would be that the moral iniquity of such laws would be something that could be demonstrated…. But the demonstration of this would not show the rule not to be (or to be) law. [Such] proof … leaves untouched the fact that there are laws which may have any degree of iniquity or stupidity and still be laws. And conversely there are rules that have every moral qualification to be laws and yet are not laws" (Hart, "Positivism and the Separation of Law and Morals," 84).

25. Hart, "Positivism and the Separation of Law and Morals," 69.

but throughout his writings, he forcefully denies that such points of contact are necessary and essential for the constitution of the juridical domain (paradigmatically embodied in his concept of "law" as a system of legal norms). We could label this thesis as a juridical extension of Hart's version of "moral agnosticism," which his colleague John Finnis describes as the double bind between positions reducible to the following claims: "you are blind" and "you are seeing ghosts."[26] Hart claims that even when moral values do, in fact, enter into deliberation for the constitution of the juridical domain, they are built into it as no more than contingent standards:

> I argue in this book [*The Concept of Law*] that though there are many different contingent connections between the content of law and morality, there are no necessary conceptual connections between the content of law and morality; and hence morally iniquitous provisions may be valid as legal rules or principles.[27]

> Again, though this proposition [that a legal system *must* exhibit some specific conformity with morality or justice, or *must* rest on a widely diffused conviction that there is a moral obligation to obey it] may, in some sense, be true, it does not follow from it that the criteria of legal validity of particular laws used in a legal system must include, tacitly if not explicitly, a reference to morality or justice.[28]

26. See John Finnis, "On Hart's Ways: Law as Reason and as Fact," in *Collected Essays*, vol. 4, *Philosophy of Law* (Oxford: Oxford University Press, 2011), 254. "In the vast literature from Plato to the present day which is dedicated to the assertion, and also to the denial, of the proposition that the ways in which men ought to behave may be discovered by human reason, the disputants on one side seem to say to those on the other, 'You are blind if you cannot see this' only to receive in reply, 'You have been dreaming'" (Hart, *The Concept of Law*, 186). The same juridical aspect of moral agnosticism seems to be operative in Hart's introductory remark to the chapter "Laws and Morals": "There are many different types of relation between law and morals and there is nothing which can be profitably singled out for study as *the* relation between them" (Hart, *The Concept of Law*, 185).

27. H. L. A. Hart, postscript to *The Concept of Law*, 268.

28. Hart, *The Concept of Law*, 185.

[One of the] main themes of [my] essay [entitled "Positivism and the Separation of Law and Morals" is] my denial that there are any important necessary connections between law and morality.[29]

Hart develops this argument within his explicit critique of the classical natural-law theory, which, by contrast, holds that the moral domain of human (personal and social) ontology and action is, in a certain way, essentially and necessarily connected with the juridical domain of those same realities. He quite effectively, if only in synthesis, defines the classical theory of natural law as the belief that "there are certain principles of human conduct, awaiting discovery by human reason, with which man-made law must conform if it is to be valid."[30] Elsewhere, he will restate this definition by affirming that "the doctrine of natural law in its various traditional forms" embodies the thesis that "the criteria which distinguish good law from bad do not merely reflect human preferences, tastes, or conventions ... rather, they are determined by certain constant features of human nature and the natural environment."[31]

Hart's criticism of the classical natural-law theory is elaborated on three discrete levels. First, on a philosophical-epistemological level, he claims that the natural-law theory generally involves "ob-

---

29. To this argument he immediately adds the following claim: "I hope that I am not simply blinded by natural obstinacy or by age in still adhering to these now much criticized positions" (Hart, introduction to *Essays in Jurisprudence and Philosophy*, 6).

30. Hart, *The Concept of Law*, 186. According to Hart, the "Thomist tradition of natural law" offers the clearest formulation of the claim that "between law and morality there is a necessary connection" (156). Hart occasionally attributes to the classical natural-law theory certain arguments that are either too harsh, or downright false. For example, he claims that "in the teleological view of the world, man, like other things, is thought of as tending toward a specific optimum state or end which is set for him and the fact that he, unlike other things, may do this consciously, is not conceived as a radical difference between him and the rest of nature" (190).

31. H. L. A. Hart, "Problems of the Philosophy of Law," in Hart, *Essays in Jurisprudence and Philosophy*, 111.

scurities and metaphysical assumptions" that are "unacceptable to most modern secular thought"[32] and are in themselves, according to Hart, "debatable"[33] and ultimately "disputable."[34] Next, from the perspective of political philosophy, he attributes great importance to the fact that persons "may profoundly disagree" about certain properties of human conduct and moral excellence when confronted with proposals of the natural-law theory. Finally, on a specifically juridical level, and within his broader argument for the essential separation of law and substantive morality, Hart denies the claim that juridicity is necessarily predicated on the moral domain, their respective contingent points of contact notwithstanding:

[Natural-law theorists] often confuse their important arguments concerning the principles by which law and social institutions should be judged with arguments designed to show that a reference to morality or justice must be introduced into the definition of law or legal validity.[35]

Hart precludes any "necessary" inclusion of moral values into the definition of law or into essential requirements of validity of legal norms. In his view, even in a hypothetical situation of the absence of epistemological or socio-pluralistic dissensus, morality does not contain, by any criteria whatsoever, the essential and necessary properties of juridicity. Rather, his conception of law is exemplified by his thesis on the need for a separate treatment of questions regarding the invalidity of law from those concerning its possible immorality. In favor of this conception of law, Hart invokes the radical case of totalitarian and manifestly immoral laws:

32. Hart, "Problems of the Philosophy of Law," 111.
33. Hart, *The Concept of Law*, 191.
34. Hart, *The Concept of Law*, 192.
35. Hart, "Problems of the Philosophy of Law," 111.

A concept of law which allows the invalidity of law to be distinguished from its immorality, enables us to see the complexity and variety of these separate issues; whereas a narrow concept of law which denies legal validity to iniquitous rules may blind us to them. It may be conceded that [for example, those] who for selfish ends procured the punishment of others under monstrous laws, did what morality forbad; yet morality may also demand that the state should punish only those who, in doing evil, did what the state at the time forbad. This is the principle of *nulla poena sine lege*. If inroads have to be made on this principle in order to avert something held to be a greater evil than its sacrifice, it is vital that the issues at stake be clearly identified.[36]

Hart thus establishes that law, as well as legal rights and obligations derived thereof, should remain the exclusive focal points of juridicity even outside of the question whether "there is some moral ground for asserting their existence"; this claim is, in his view, "one aspect of this form of separation of law from morality."[37] One of Hart's most famous intellectual disciples and the author of his intellectual biography, Neil MacCormick, highlights that at the center of Hart's legal philosophy lies the rejection of any theory which "suggests or implies that whatever is 'law' properly so-called is conclusive of the moral question what I am to do."

Law is indeed morally relevant. But it is never, and should never, be deemed morally conclusive. What has been done in the name and "in the forms" of law has often been appalling moral iniquity. The least unreliable way of opening human eyes to the possibility of such iniquity, and of keeping them open to and alert against its occurrence or recurrence, is to teach that "laws" get their name because of the structural and functional properties of the system to which they belong. They do

36. Hart, *The Concept of Law*, 211.
37. Hart, postscript to *The Concept of Law*, 268–69.

not get it because they are or can be presumed to be demands of an enlightened morality.[38]

This conception of the law-morality intersection—the "simple positivist doctrine that morally iniquitous rules may still be laws"[39]—represents, in Hart's view, a helpful theoretical tool for overcoming possible dilemmas related to extreme cases of immoral laws. For Hart, the correct juridical solution in the case of valid but deeply immoral positive legal norms always involves the preference for a clear separation between law and morality rather than direct legal application of morality by the courts or the enactment of new laws with retroactive effects to correct the consequences of past iniquitous laws.

At the same time, Hart never really abandons the claim that law does, indeed, overlap with morality at various important, though contingent, points of contact. As evidenced before, he concedes that certain social facts and moral values enter into deliberation for the creation of positive law. He situates this nonessentialist conception of the law-morality intersection, however, within a broader evaluative framework that he labels "critical morality," which denotes the assemblage of general moral principles used in critically evaluating actual social institutions. In his view, "critical morality" also includes the so-called "positive morality," which is "the morality actually accepted and shared by a given social group."[40]

Anyone who raises, or is willing to debate, the question whether it is justifiable to [legally] enforce morality, accepts the view that the actual institutions of any society, including its positive morality, are open to

38. Neil MacCormick, *H.L.A. Hart*, 2nd ed. (Stanford, Calif.: Stanford University Press, 2008), 197.

39. Hart, *The Concept of Law*, 212.

40. H. L. A. Hart, *Law, Liberty and Morality* (Oxford: Oxford University Press, 1963), 20.

criticism. Hence, the proposition that it is justifiable to enforce morality is, like its negation, a thesis of critical morality.[41]

This sequence of arguments renders the Hartian concept of law absolutely autonomous from any account of the necessary moral foundations of law and relatively autonomous from the ultimately contingent dynamics between positive and critical morality in the evaluation of both law-as-it-is and law-as-it-ought-to-be. At the same time, the domain of social morality is itself understood as an open-source structure susceptible to internal criticism. More adequate social facts and moral values may be considered for inclusion into the content of legal norms provided that they are perceived within a nonessentialist, contingent realm of moral influence.

In his effort to restate "in an acceptable form the claim that there are certain objective and rationally determined criteria for the evaluation and criticism of law,"[42] Hart identifies certain nonessential normative clusters of values at the intersection of law and morality. The first of these clusters consists of certain substantive values that Hart labels as the *minimum content of natural law*. At the heart of his argument, he is convinced that certain "simple contingent facts"[43] (such as human vulnerability) point to some "common sense" truisms regarding values that we could label "natural necessities."[44] These values are, however, disentangled from a full-scale natural-law teleology. They represent "basic conditions of social life"[45] that are found at "the lowest stratum"[46] of a more complex and debatable natural-law theory. This "lowest

41. Hart, *Law, Liberty and Morality*, 82.

42. Hart, "Problems of the Philosophy of Law," 112.

43. Hart, *The Concept of Law*, 191. Among these, he enumerates "human vulnerability," "approximate equality," "limited altruism," "limited resources," and "limited understanding and strength of will" (194–99).

44. Hart, "Positivism and the Separation of Law and Morals," 80.

45. Hart, "Problems of the Philosophy of Law," 112.

46. Hart, *The Concept of Law*, 191.

stratum" certainly falls below the level of natural-law teleology of the "purposes men have for living in society,"[47] which is in Hart's theory, "too conflicting and varying to make possible much extension of the argument that some fuller overlap of legal rules and moral standards is 'necessary' in this sense."[48]

These *minimum natural-law* truisms about values are natural in the sense that they are differentiated from "mere conventions or human prescriptions,"[49] because they represent certain "common-sense" ends that men generally desire, not in the sense that would entail their positioning at some higher, teleologically more engaging stratum above mere contingency. As nonessential "natural necessities," they are juridically relevant since they point to rules of conduct which "any social organization must contain if it is to be viable,"[50] and which are "so fundamental that if any system did not have them there would be no point in having any other rules at all."[51] With regard to the law-morality intersection, according to Hart, we may claim only that these rules constitute a "common element,"[52] a mere nonessential "factual overlap."[53]

Aside from "substantive" laws,[54] another "overlap" between the legal and moral standards is the cluster of rules that concern the so-called procedural[55] "principles of natural justice"[56] that

47. Hart, "Positivism and the Separation of Law and Morals," 81.

48. Hart, "Positivism and the Separation of Law and Morals," 81.

49. Hart, *The Concept of Law*, 190.

50. Hart, *The Concept of Law*, 193.

51. Hart, "Positivism and the Separation of Law and Morals," 80. See also Hart, "Problems of the Philosophy of Law," 112.

52. Hart, *The Concept of Law*, 193.

53. "Such [legal] rules overlap with basic moral principles vetoing murder, violence and theft; and so we can add to the factual statement that all legal systems in fact coincide with morality on such vital points, the statement that this is, *in this sense*, necessarily so" (Hart, "Positivism and the Separation of Law and Morals," 80–81). Emphasis added.

54. Hart, "Problems of the Philosophy of Law," 112.

55. Hart, "Problems of the Philosophy of Law," 112, 114–16.

56. Hart, *The Concept of Law*, 206–7.

represent the minimum demands of certain procedural issues in the creation and administration of the law.[57] In Hart's opinion, they "might well be called natural,"[58] in the sense that they make possible "*more efficient* pursuit of [persons'] aims."[59] They do not, however, condition law's substantive content to the degree that they would influence this content in any necessary way.

In a famous debate with Hart, American legal scholar Lon L. Fuller claimed that these procedural principles of natural justice constitute a necessary and substantive "inner morality of law."[60] Hart develops his response to Fuller in two steps. First, he concedes that if a necessary connection between law and morality amounts exclusively to the procedural principles of natural justice, then "we may accept it."[61] Second, Hart notes that the mere existence of procedural principles of natural justice does not constitute the necessary point of contact with substantive morality. These principles are only procedural, and, hence, "neutral"[62] and "compatible with very great iniquity."[63]

Surely, Hart's doctrine on the "minimum content" of natu-

---

57. Among these procedural requirements or principles of natural justice, Hart enumerates, for example, the generality of rules of law, the clarity with which they are phrased, the publicity given to them, as well as impartiality in the application of law, etc. See Hart, *The Concept of Law*, 206–7; Hart, "Positivism and the Separation of Law and Morals," 81; and Hart, "Problems of the Philosophy of Law," 114–16.

58. Hart, *The Concept of Law*, 206.

59. Hart, "Positivism and the Separation of Law and Morals," 113. Emphasis added.

60. Fuller's contributions to the debate can be found in Lon L. Fuller, "Positivism and Fidelity to Law: A Reply to Professor Hart," *Harvard Law Review* 71, no. 4 (1958): 630–72; Lon L. Fuller, *The Morality of Law*, 2nd ed. (New Haven, Conn.: Yale University Press, 1969).

61. Hart, *The Concept of Law*, 207.

62. "[Lon L. Fuller] takes me seriously to task for having said that respect for the principles of legality is unfortunately 'compatible with great iniquity'; but I cannot find any cogent argument in support of his claim that these principles are not neutral as between good and evil substantive aims." See H. L. A. Hart, "Lon L. Fuller: The Morality of Law," in Hart, *Essays in Jurisprudence and Philosophy*, 351.

63. Hart, *The Concept of Law*, 207.

ral law—which is, in his own words, "a modest empirical counterpart to the more ambitious teleological doctrine of natural law"[64]—falls within the conceptual scope of what I have previously referred to as the minimalist natural-law theory. The non-essential legal reference to a minimum content of natural law and the merely procedural character of the principles of natural justice have led John Finnis to affirm that Hart's minimum might "equally well have been 'The Minimum Content of Positive Law.'"[65]

For the immediate context of this present study, it is important to highlight once more that Hart's theory denies a necessary and essential predication of juridicity on the moral domain of goodness inherent in human nature and action. Under the rubric of the law's "goodness," Hart permits only a contingent set of values that should (but do not necessarily) constitute the nucleus of every legal system. Upon becoming the law, these values remain connected to the moral realm only as coincidental "factual overlaps." The moral content included in the legal norm takes on a separate and autonomous juridical life of its own. Questions of the validity or the inherent dynamics of change of the juridical domain are absolutely independent from any necessary point of contact with the moral sphere. Hence, in Hart's account, the reasons behind the possible alteration of legal content in light of considerations regarding "what law ought to be" are established exclusively in the metajuridical framework of critical morality, not at the conceptual level of law's ontology.

64. Hart, "Problems of the Philosophy of Law," 113.
65. John Finnis, "Hart as a Political Philosopher," in *Collected Essays*, vol. 4, *Philosophy of Law*, 262.

Joseph Raz and the Systemic Moral Value of Law as an Institution

A somewhat different but equally influential attempt to discuss points of contact between morality and law in terms of law's goodness is provided by another legal philosopher from the University of Oxford, Joseph Raz (1939).

Raz develops his line of argument through a peculiar nonlinear methodological process marked by an upward spiral development of fundamental ideas, diachronically scattered throughout his books. Consequently, his account of the points of contact between morality and law is complex[66] but nonetheless coherent. He has confessed to be aware of his idiosyncratic approach.

[All my books] feel like stages in a journey. They develop and sometimes bring to completion, not the proper treatment of a subject, but my treatment of it.... There is never a terminus; there are merely temporary resting points along a never-ending route.[67]

Continuing the debate generated largely by Hart's *The Concept of Law*, Raz seeks to restate the central question of the law-morality intersection: "Should we, as is common, make the question 'is there a necessary connection between law and morality?' a litmus test for the basic orientation of different theories of law?"[68] He regards this particular formulation of the question—which

66. One of Raz's frequent critics and interlocutors in the debate on precisely this subject, Ronald Dworkin, has admitted that "Raz's argument for [his] bold propositions is complex." See Ronald Dworkin, "Thirty Years On," review of *The Practice of Principle: In Defense of a Pragmatist Approach to Legal Theory*, by Jules Coleman, *Harvard Law Review* 115, no. 6 (2002): 1665.

67. Joseph Raz, preface to *The Authority of Law*, 2nd ed. (Oxford: Oxford University Press, 2011), v.

68. Joseph Raz, "About Morality and the Nature of Law," in *Between Authority and Interpretation: On the Theory of Law and Practical Reason* (Oxford: Oxford University Press, 2009), 167.

we have seen to be crucial for a clear identification of Hart's central thesis—as more misleading than helpful.[69] Nonetheless, he maintains that the general question on the relationship between the moral and legal spheres is truly central to legal philosophy.[70] Therefore, he proposes an alternative formulation of this central question, one he believes from his "arch-positivist"[71] viewpoint will cut to "the backbone of the version of positivism I would like to defend" since it is "far more successful in getting at the common core of the positivist tradition."[72] At the same time, interestingly enough, his alternative formulation of this central question "need not conflict with the natural lawyer's view con-

69. "A theory belongs to legal positivism tradition if and only if it maintains that the necessary features of the law can be stated without the use of any moral concepts. By this thesis, my writings on the nature of law do not belong to the legal positivist tradition.... I do not care whether my views are classified with legal positivism, as they commonly are, or not. I believe that the classification of legal theories as legal positivist or non-legal positivist ... is unhelpful and liable to mislead." See Joseph Raz, "The Argument From Justice, or How Not to Reply to Legal Positivism," in *Law, Rights and Discourse: Themes from the Legal Philosophy of Robert Alexy*, ed. George Pavlakos (Portland, Ore.: Hart Publishing, 2007), 20. Another version of this argument can be found in the following remarks: "According to that [austere and rigorous] conception of legal positivism ... the universe of human thought is necessarily divided into two mutually exclusive camps, such that anyone who admits any moral minimum to be essential to the existence of law belongs outside the positivist camp and in that of its rival.... Believers in this two-way-minded universe of jurisprudence assign to the category of 'natural law' any theory that fails their austere test for positivism.... In truth, such dichotomies are rarely revealing of any important truth." See Neil MacCormick, *Institutions of Law: An Essay in Legal Theory* (Oxford: Oxford University Press, 2007), 278.

70. "To be sure, clarifying the relations between law and morality is rightly seen as central to the explanation of the nature of law" (Raz, "About Morality and the Nature of Law," 168). "Given the importance of law there is little surprise that the problem of the relation of law and morals has always been regarded as one of the central concerns of legal theory." See Joseph Raz, *Practical Reason and Norms*, 2nd ed. (Oxford: Oxford University Press, 1999), 162.

71. According to some notable legal scholars, Raz is "usually regarded as an arch-positivist." See Jeremy Waldron, "Jurisprudence for Hedgehogs," New York University Schools of Law, Public Law and Legal Theory Research Paper Series, Working Paper No. 13–45, July 5, 2013, 16, http://dx.doi.org/10.2139/ssrn.2290309.

72. Raz, "The Argument from Justice, or How Not to Reply to Legal Positivism," 22.

cerning ... the relation between law and morality."[73] The alternative framework for describing the law-morality intersection should contain the following claim: "Determining what the law is does not necessarily, or conceptually, depend on moral or other evaluative considerations about what the law ought to be in the relevant circumstances."[74]

The difference between his alternative framework and its "no necessary connection" antecedents is highly subtle and may not be readily discerned at first sight, but it should become clearer once we know that Raz would have been more inclined—if left only with the first, original central thesis—to situate his own theory within the orbit of the natural-law tradition, for reasons that will soon become clear. In the context of the alternative formulation of that thesis, however, he is far more prepared to subscribe to what he calls the "moderate"[75] version of "theories within the tradition of legal positivism."[76]

In clear contrast to Hart, Raz is convinced that "there can be no doubt that there are necessary connections between law and morality."[77] He holds that "even if all the law's essential features can be stated without the use of moral concepts," the very fact that the law possesses those essential features "entails that it has some moral merit."[78] To cast aside any shadow of doubt regarding possible essentialist interpretations of the claim on "law as [morally] good in its very nature,"[79] Raz is always careful to

---

73. Joseph Raz, "Legal Positivism and the Sources of Law," in Raz, *The Authority of Law*, 39.

74. Raz, "The Argument from Justice, or How Not to Reply to Legal Positivism," 22. The formulation of the thesis is originally from Andrei Marmor, *Positive Law and Objective Values* (Oxford: Oxford University Press, 2001), 71.

75. Raz, "Legal Positivism and the Sources of Law," 39.

76. Raz, "The Argument from Justice, or How Not to Reply to Legal Positivism," 22.

77. Raz, "About Morality and the Nature of Law," 168.

78. Raz, "The Argument from Justice, or How Not to Reply to Legal Positivism," 20.

79. Raz, "About Morality and the Nature of Law," 167.

emancipate the very concept of law from all extralegal appeals to broader metaphysical resources that are classically adopted by Thomistic natural-law theorists. Rather than directly engaging the substance of natural-law theories, he opts for an alternative route of critique—to show that the theories of natural law are incapable of defending their claims to uniqueness in providing adequate ultimate foundations of positive law. Among his angles of attack is one that takes as its starting point the use of normative language—the phenomenon that, in his view, lies at the heart of the problem of the normativity of law.[80]

In analyzing how it is that "many people who do not accept the natural-law view of the necessary morality of law"[81] raise no objection whatsoever to the application of normative language to the law, Raz arrives at a threefold conclusion. First, he asserts, "if natural-law theories are to explain the use of normative language in [legal] contexts, they must show not only that all law is morally valid but also that this is generally known and thus accounts for the application of normative value to law."[82] This assumption, according to Raz, cannot be demonstrated.

Second, Raz proposes instead that the motivational claims of those who endorse a natural-law position be situated within the so-called belief-based approach to normativity, wherein the adherents of the natural-law theory express the "belief that they provide the best explanation of the normativity of law."[83]

Third, since the key to the problem of the normativity of law, in Raz's view, is "not that laws *are* valid reasons" for action but that "people *believe* that [laws] are [valid reasons],"[84] Raz ad-

80. Raz, *Practical Reason and Norms*, 169.
81. Raz, *Practical Reason and Norms*, 169.
82. Raz, *Practical Reason and Norms*, 170.
83. Raz, *Practical Reason and Norms*, 169.
84. Raz, *Practical Reason and Norms*, 170.

vocates the claim that "belief-based explanations are nearer the truth than validity-based explanations"[85] for the correct justification of normative language in a legal context. He thus draws the conclusion that laws establish a discrete set of *exclusionary reasons for action*. These exclusionary reasons do not necessarily overlap with valid moral reasons for action; in fact, they always trump appeals to extra-legal substantive moral goods on all occasions where the relevance of these goods might be applicable.[86]

Thus, since laws constitute valid exclusionary reasons for action even if their content is not fully harmonized with the realm of substantive morality (a realm that includes the natural-law approach to morality), Raz's alternative understanding of the necessary point of contact between law and morality is also situated on a level emancipated from issues of substantive morality.[87] This point of contact is connected precisely with the fact that laws are constituted as valid reasons for action to the "exclusion" of all other types of reasons—even moral reasons. The necessary aspect of law's goodness that Raz has in mind is somehow already present in *what the law is*, again without any necessary conceptual reference to *what the law ought to be* in terms of its underlying substantive moral *ratio*.

The fact that other people follow … norms [in a legal context] and that institutions enforce them may itself become a reason for people who do not believe in the validity of the norms or systems concerned.… That is the background for the widespread use of statements accord-

---

85. Raz, *Practical Reason and Norms*, 170.

86. See Raz, *Practical Reason and Norms*, 36–84, 182–94.

87. "The question is whether the identifying features of legal systems or the conditions necessary for them to be in force entail that such systems always possess some moral worth. One does not have to be a moral objectivist to accept the possibility that they do, since nothing is implied about the 'epistemological status' of the moral views" (Raz, *Practical Reason and Norms*, 166).

ing to law—the fact that even people who do not endorse them have a practical interest in what is required by law.[88]

According to Raz, there is one architectonic moral value built into the very concept of law. If we can identify the possibility or likelihood of at least one necessary connection between law and morality in the form of a "specific moral task" that law has "by its nature," this should be, in Raz's view, sufficient to establish at least some minimalist common ground between legal positivism and natural-law theories on the juridical status of morality.[89] Raz locates this "specific moral task" of law in what he calls the *systemic moral feature of the law*.

The case for the moral character of the law, understood as the quest for its systemic moral properties, rather than for the moral properties of each and all its binding standards, is the moral case for having legal authorities, of the law-making and law-applying qualities.[90]

For what it is worth, however, let me state, rather briefly and dogmatically, what task I can see for the law. It arises out of the law's character as a structure of authority, that is a structured, coordinated system of authority.... *The law's task, put abstractly, is to secure a situation whereby moral goals which ... would be unlikely to be achieved without it ... are realized.*[91]

According to Raz, then, the law possesses this inbuilt architectonic "systemic moral feature": it is a morally valuable institution only because of the unique processes and functions that it actualiz-

---

88. Raz, *Practical Reason and Norms*, 177.

89. See Raz, "About Morality and the Nature of Law," 176–78.

90. At this point, Raz again attempts to establish a dialogue with natural-law theory by adding to the above-quoted sentence the claim that "there is such a case ... it is a Thomist case." In a corresponding footnote, he then quotes John Finnis's theory as a paradigmatic example of the Thomist tradition (Raz, "About Morality and the Nature of Law," 172–73).

91. Raz, "About Morality and the Nature of Law," 178. Emphasis in original.

es from the perspective of the legal system as a whole—not because of any actual relationship between individual legal norms and substantive moral values. The law, then, claims to have an "essential [systemic] feature," which Raz terms *legitimate authority*.[92] This claim is, in his view, "a moral claim," to the extent that it includes "the assertion of a right to grant rights and impose duties in matters affecting basic aspects of people's life and their interactions with one another."[93] Raz is careful enough to distinguish law's moral claim to legitimate authority from its putative "claim to moral correctness," since, in line with his already-established account of laws as "exclusionary" reasons for action, it is "in the very nature of authoritative rules that they are binding even if not correct."[94]

Finally, it is necessary to address Raz's account of the inclusion of substantive moral values in positive law, as well as to assess the status of this inclusion in his overall position on the intersecting points between law and morality.

Indeed I have endorsed, under the name of the "source thesis" in *The Authority of Law*, a stricter thesis [than the one according to which determination of what the law is as necessarily, or conceptually, dependent on moral or other evaluative considerations about what the law ought to be], namely, that the identification of law never requires the use of moral arguments or judgments about its merit.[95]

<hr>

92. Raz, "The Argument from Justice, or How Not to Reply to Legal Positivism," 20.

93. Raz, "The Argument from Justice, or How Not to Reply to Legal Positivism," 19. This passage of Raz's account of the law's essential systemic moral feature of legitimate authority includes yet another of his confessions of the upward spiral development of his thought through various stages: "In *Practical Reason and Norms* I argued (reformulating the point in a way that I now find clearer and more accurate)" (Raz, "The Argument from Justice, or How Not to Reply to Legal Positivism," 20).

94. Raz, "The Argument from Justice, or How Not to Reply to Legal Positivism," 32. The argument on the essential feature of legitimate authority of the law as a moral claim "relies on the systemic moral qualities of the law, from which an obligation to obey laws, including bad ones, can be derived" (Raz, "About Morality and the Nature of Law," 173).

95. Raz, "The Argument from Justice, or How Not to Reply to Legal Positivism," 22.

According to this argument, it would seem, then, that Raz's adherence to the thesis on the necessary connection between law and morality does not include any substantive moral values that would be incorporated into the process of identification of law or evaluation of its merit. Under the name of this *source thesis*, Raz builds an argument that, in a sense, overlaps with his thesis on the systemic moral feature of the law.[96] However, the focus of his source thesis revolves around the premise that the identification of the law—what constitutes valid and thus applicable law in a given political community—is a matter of social fact. This focus also includes the question of whether one must necessarily resort to substantive moral arguments in order to identify the law.[97] At least two fundamental claims of the source thesis fall within the scope of this question. The first is the claim that a law has a *source*—the relevant facts that are socially recognized to give rise to valid juridical obligations and make possible their interpretation—if its existence and content can be determined *without* using moral arguments. A law is source-based if its existence and content can be identified by reference to social facts alone, without resort to any evaluative argument.[98]

The second claim is that even if a rule referring to morality has been, to a certain extent, incorporated into the law, this does not imply that the moral dimension to which it refers is thereby incorporated into the concept of law.[99] Many legal rules cannot escape determining issues that are necessarily related to various aspects of morality. Besides, people's moral views and intentions

96. "The main justification of the social thesis [later to be renamed as the 'source thesis'] lies in the character of law as a social institution" (Raz, "Legal Positivism and the Sources of Law," 42).

97. See Raz, "Legal Positivism and the Sources of Law," 37–52.

98. Joseph Raz, "Authority, Law and Morality," in *Ethics in the Public Domain: Essays in the Morality of Law and Politics* (Oxford: Oxford University Press, 1994), 211.

99. See Raz, "Legal Positivism and the Sources of Law," 46.

may be taken into juridical consideration for the purposes of law's interpretation,[100] and judges are often expected to resort to moral arguments (for example, when, as Raz says, they "break new ground" in developing the law).[101] In all these cases, once the moral argument has been incorporated into law, the claim to legitimate authority of the corresponding legal norm as an exclusionary juridical reason for action is entirely rooted in its being a source of law. For the purposes of its identification and application *as law*, this legal norm is structurally cut off from the fact that the moral argument it contains also constitutes a substantive moral reason for action: "Even if a certain social fact entails certain moral consequences, it can still be a source of law. It is a source of law as the social fact it is, and not as a source of moral rights and obligations."[102]

Thus, in both directions—from the law to its potential moral sources and from the moral sources to the question of the identification of the law—the necessary points of contact between law and morality in Raz's source thesis are separated from substantive moral values. The juridical domain is thus autonomous from the necessary appeals to identify the law and establish the criteria for its validity on the basis of its moral content and merit.[103]

Raz acknowledges that the systemic moral nature of law is rather abstract in one sense; namely, it does not automatically include the certainty that its historical manifestations (i.e., the con-

100. Raz, "Legal Positivism and the Sources of Law," 47.

101. Raz, "Legal Positivism and the Sources of Law," 48–49.

102. Raz, "Authority, Law and Morality," 235.

103. Hart himself seems to embrace the basic postulates of the source thesis when he claims that "the existence and content of law can be identified by reference to the social sources of the law (e.g., legislation, judicial decisions, social customs) without reference to morality except where the law thus identified has itself incorporated moral criteria for the identification of the law" (Hart, postscript to *The Concept of Law*, 269). Raz explicitly acknowledged Hart's adherence to the source thesis. See Joseph Raz, "Legal Reasons, Sources and Gaps," in *The Authority of Law*, 53.

tent of particular laws) will be morally valuable.[104] In his view, the concrete "identification of the moral tasks" is "left to a more extended and substantial discussion in political philosophy."[105]

Raz's writings in political philosophy should, then, provide further information on the status of substantive moral values in concrete laws, of course, always within the doctrinal coordinates of his source thesis. These writings reveal at least two fundamental properties of the content of concrete laws with regard to their substantive moral value. The first is that the social function of a law must not be "closely tied to any particular moral and political principles as to be of no use to anyone who does not completely and exclusively endorse them."[106] The second property is equally architectonic for the status of substantive moral values in state laws: Raz calls it *the principle of personal autonomy*, and he develops it throughout his texts in political philosophy, within the framework of his *perfectionist* form of liberalism.

So far I have tried to draw a picture of perfectionist liberalism.... One of the virtues of this form of liberalism is that its doctrine of freedom is moored in a wider conception of the good person and the good society, rather than being cut off from them as is the case with liberal doctrines of moral neutrality.[107]

The argument of the book [*The Morality of Freedom*] so far ... maintains that it is the function of governments to promote morality. That means that governments should promote the moral quality of the life of those whose lives and actions they can affect.[108]

---

104. Raz, "About Morality and the Nature of Law," 179.

105. Raz, "About Morality and the Nature of Law," 178.

106. Joseph Raz, "The Functions of Law," in *The Authority of Law*, 166–67.

107. Joseph Raz, "Liberalism, Scepticism, and Democracy," in *Ethics in the Public Domain*, 121.

108. Joseph Raz, *The Morality of Freedom* (Oxford: Oxford University Press, 1986), 415.

It would initially seem that Raz's perfectionist liberalism does not fully respect his previous claims for *in abstracto* separation of law from its potential moral sources, namely, his own source thesis. He frames a similar objection in the form of a question: "Does not this concession amount to a rejection of the harm principle … as being a curtail to freedom of government *to enforce morality*?"[109] His form of perfectionist liberalism, as well as his rather strong formulation of the principle of personal autonomy, however, prove to be fully coherent with his arguments on the law-morality intersection.

I wish to propose a different understanding of [the harm principle] according to which it is a principle about the proper way to enforce morality. In other words, I would suggest that the principle is derivable from a morality which regards personal autonomy as an essential ingredient of the good life, and regards the principle of autonomy … as one of the most important moral principles.[110]

The autonomy principle is a perfectionist principle.[111]

The autonomy principle means that, beyond providing the conditions for the availability of an adequate range of diverse and valuable options, the government must "leave individuals free to make of their lives what they will."[112] Citizens, in turn, "choose their own lives for themselves."[113] Thus, in Raz's perfectionist liberalism, the abstract good that is prefigured by the principle of autonomy becomes further specified in the sphere of each individual's moral life. The individual choice of substantive moral values *in concreto* does not alter the status of law's merely systemic goodness and its separation from substantive morality established

---

109. Raz, *The Morality of Freedom*, 415. Emphasis added.
110. Raz, *The Morality of Freedom*, 415.
111. Raz, *The Morality of Freedom*, 417.
112. Raz, "Liberalism, Scepticism, and Democracy," 120.
113. Raz, "Liberalism, Scepticism, and Democracy," 120.

by the source thesis *in abstracto*. In Raz's view, a government should not attempt to make its citizens good through its positive laws beyond the scope circumscribed both by the moral value of the systemic feature of the law and the principle of personal autonomy. For him, these are sufficient to create all essential conditions for the autonomous life and personal flourishing of citizens.

In sum, the juridical status of moral values—the issue of law's goodness—is reduced to the sole question of the systemic moral feature of the law as a social institution. Even though the principle of personal autonomy is the substantive architectonic moral value pertinent to the concrete content of legal rules, Raz's source thesis structurally bars it from constituting a necessary point of contact between law and morality. If the principle of personal autonomy, as the architectonic moral value, does not possess an inherent juridical domain, then neither do all other substantive moral values. A more comprehensive dialogue with the natural-law theory would necessarily require a theoretical openness on Raz's part not only to a necessary connection between the juridical domain and substantive morality but also to metaphysical and teleological resources broader than the overarching principle of personal autonomy alone.[114]

114. This is why I am more reserved in the evaluation of the compatibility of Raz's account with natural-law theory than are some contemporary theorists of natural law. The substantive moral value of the principle of autonomy, when set against the theoretical backdrop of law's systemic moral features and the source thesis, is hardly compatible with the Thomistic jusnaturalist claim for law's goodness. Thomistic natural-law theory, certainly, values personal autonomy, but not as an exclusive and architectonic moral value. The value of personal autonomy is, in fact, the only explicit substantive moral value that Raz presents as foundational for the content of the law. He envisions this value also as the guiding perfectionist standard for the juridical recognition of "valuable" (as opposed to "really immoral and ignoble") ways of life. See Raz, "Liberalism, Scepticism, and Democracy," 123. Therefore, I tend to be more favorable to Robert P. George's recognition that "Raz himself is interested in grounding liberal political theory in a notion of autonomy that can be exercised immorally" than to Martin Rhonheimer's claims that Raz's concept of personal autonomy implies "a politically relevant rejection of moral

Ronald Dworkin's Minimalist Natural-Law Account of Law's Goodness

Ronald Dworkin (1931–2013), one of the most influential American legal philosophers of the last half-century, calls the question of the relationship between law and morality the "hottest of the chestnuts burning lawyers' fingers for centuries" in his final book on jurisprudential issues.[115] He argues for a paradigm shift that would affect both his own approach to that question and how it is traditionally approached. In what Dworkin deems the "old" paradigm of the law-morality intersection, the central argument is based on a presupposition that law and morality are two different collections of norms. Philosophers of law, himself included, have all adhered to "this orthodox two-systems picture,"[116] and it is from this perspective that they have subsequently addressed the crucial question of how these two systems interact, or of "how far is morality relevant in fixing what the law requires on any particular issue."[117]

There is a flaw in the two-systems picture. Once we take law and morality to compose separate systems of norms, there is no neutral standpoint from which the connections between these supposedly separate systems can be adjudicated.[118]

------

relativism and skepticism." See Robert P. George, "The Unorthodox Liberalism of Joseph Raz," *The Review of Politics* 53, no. 4 (1991): 666; Martin Rhonheimer, "The Liberal Image of Man and the Concept of Autonomy: Beyond the Debate between Liberals and Communitarians," in *The Common Good of Constitutional Democracy: Essays in Political Philosophy and on Catholic Social Teaching* (Washington, D.C.: The Catholic University of America Press, 2013), 68.

115. Ronald Dworkin, *Justice for Hedgehogs* (Cambridge, Mass.: Belknap Press of Harvard University Press, 2011), 400.

116. Dworkin, *Justice for Hedgehogs*, 402.

117. Dworkin, *Justice for Hedgehogs*, 401.

118. Dworkin, *Justice for Hedgehogs*, 402–3.

Over the course of his career, Dworkin has gradually come to the understanding that a possible solution to this "apparently insoluble problem"[119] must be found by refuting this two-systems picture. The old paradigm, he claims, must be replaced with a fresh, "one-system picture": "we now treat law as a *part of political morality*."[120]

We are taught from the early days of law school about a potential conflict between law and justice. I try to describe law, not as something to be set beside morality and studied in conjunction with it, but as a branch of morality.... But in the end I argue that the alleged conflict disappears once we understand the way in which law can sensibly be treated as a branch of political morality.[121]

Before we analyze what this paradigm shift means, it should be noted that his approach in *Justice for Hedgehogs*, although solemnizing his new views on the subject matter, has precedents not only in explicit claims from his previous works[122] but also implicitly in the entirety of his thought. Dworkin himself suggests that his novel perspective on the law-morality intersection ought to serve as a hermeneutical key for all his previous works, and is, in fact, "meant to supplement my books ... not substitute

119. Dworkin, *Justice for Hedgehogs*, 403.

120. Dworkin, *Justice for Hedgehogs*, 405. Emphasis added.

121. Ronald Dworkin, "Justice for Hedgehogs: Keynote Address," *Boston University Law Review* 90, no. 2 (2010): 472–73.

122. "I want now to suggest that this traditional understanding, which encourages us to chart relations between two different intellectual domains [namely, law and morality] is unsatisfactory. We might do better with a different intellectual topography: we might treat law not as separate from but as a department of morality.... We might treat legal theory as a special part of political morality distinguished by a further refinement of institutional structures." See Ronald Dworkin, *Justice in Robes* (Cambridge, Mass.: Belknap Press of Harvard University Press, 2006), 34–35. Another famous legal scholar, Jeremy Waldron, has affirmed that the challenging shift in emphasis professed by Dworkin in *Justice for Hedgehogs* was, indeed, "adumbrated in *Justice in Robes*, albeit in a way that many readers missed (including this reader)." See Waldron, "Jurisprudence for Hedgehogs," 4–5.

for them."[123] It seems that an adequate understanding and assessment of the originality of Dworkin's contribution to the debate on the law's goodness entails a reading of the crucial arguments from his entire body of work through the lens of the new paradigm.

In sum, the main argumentative line of Dworkin's work is the thesis that "the law includes not just enacted rules ... but justifying principles as well."[124] This thesis is usually called "interpretivism."[125]

Interpretivism ... denies that law and morals are wholly independent systems. It argues that law includes not only the specific rules enacted in accordance with the community's accepted practices but also the principles that provide the best moral justification for those enacted rules. The law then also includes the rules that follow from those justifying principles, even though those further rules were never enacted.[126]

In his earlier writings, Dworkin formulates this thesis by developing "a theory of law out of a theory of adjudication,"[127] as his harsh critic Joseph Raz puts it. Dworkin maintains that lawyers and judges, in their role as ministers of law, appeal not only to specific "black-letter" legal rules "of the sort that appear in statutes or are set out in bold type in textbooks" but also to the so-called justifying legal principles.[128] These principles are standards that should be observed because they are "requirements

123. Dworkin, *Justice for Hedgehogs*, 400, n. 1.

124. Dworkin, *Justice for Hedgehogs*, 402.

125. "If lawyers and laymen take up the integrated, one system theory of law in place of the dead-end two-systems model ... the substance of the old confrontation between positivism and interpretivism would remain, but ... in a political rather than conceptual form" (Dworkin, *Justice for Hedgehogs*, 401–2).

126. Dworkin, *Justice for Hedgehogs*, 402.

127. Joseph Raz, "The Problem about the Nature of Law," in *Ethics in the Public Domain*, 202.

128. Ronald Dworkin, *Taking Rights Seriously*, 2nd ed. (Cambridge, Mass.: Harvard University Press, 1978), 46.

of justice or fairness or some other dimension of morality."[129] Judges decide the so-called "hard cases"[130] by appealing to these principles, which then figure as the "best justification of settled law."[131] This process of justification necessarily "includes a moral dimension,"[132] although not in the sense that legal principles are always sound or correct moral principles. Instead, according to Dworkin, legal principles are "always moral principles *in form* (whether they are sound or unsound, compelling or despicable as moral arguments)."[133]

What exactly does Dworkin mean when he claims that the law includes a moral dimension by way of the necessary appeal to legal principles that are moral principles in form? First, it means that justifying legal principles are, of themselves, structural carriers of moral content. This fact alone already renders them moral in form, regardless of the substantive moral qualification of their content *in concreto*. Secondly, it also seems to mean that the substantive moral standards to which lawyers and judges appeal through legal principles are not arbitrary or partisan but rather summoned in the process of justification on political grounds—"on the ground that certain legal principles of political morality are right."[134] Thirdly, justifying legal principles are nec-

---

129. Dworkin, *Taking Rights Seriously*, 22.

130. "Hard cases" are, in Dworkin's terminology, the "cases in which no explicit rule in the rule book firmly decides the case either way"; at the same time, "contrary moral principles directly in point are each compatible with the rule book." See Ronald Dworkin, *A Matter of Principle* (Cambridge, Mass.: Harvard University Press, 1985), 13, 17.

131. Dworkin, *Taking Rights Seriously*, 346.

132. Dworkin, *Taking Rights Seriously*, 346.

133. Dworkin, *Taking Rights Seriously*, 343. Emphasis added. Through the lens of Dworkin's paradigmatic shift of perspective, this argument of his thesis can now be read in the following fashion: "Just because law is a branch of morality, it does not follow that what the law requires is morally perfect or never morally regrettable" (Waldron, "Jurisprudence for Hedgehogs," 23–24).

134. Dworkin, *A Matter of Principle*, 9.

essarily moral because of the subject matter to which they refer: they make claims about the rights and duties of citizens,[135] and they justify a political decision by showing that it respects or secures those rights and duties.[136] Dworkin gives the example of an argument in favor of antidiscrimination statutes. The claim "that a minority has a right to equal respect and concern," he asserts, "is an argument of principle" that justifies those statutes.[137]

Hence, the adequate justification of legal rules is provided within the domain of *political morality*.[138] In this domain, justification is provided on *moral* grounds in the following fashion:

If two justifications provide an equally good fit with the legal materials, one nevertheless provides a better justification than the other if it is superior as a matter of political or moral theory; if, that is, it comes closer to capturing the rights that people in fact have.[139]

Propositions of law are true if they figure in or follow from the principles of justice, fairness, and procedural due process that provide the best constructive interpretation of the community's legal practice.[140]

Does Dworkin offer any substantive specification of the content of these justifying legal principles of political morality, beyond just their moral value in form? This question becomes considerably more urgent in light of his claim that "if … any theory which makes the content of law sometimes depend on the correct

---

135. Dworkin, *Taking Rights Seriously*, 343.

136. Dworkin, *Taking Rights Seriously*, 82.

137. Dworkin, *Taking Rights Seriously*, 82.

138. See Dworkin, *A Matter of Principle*, 143; Dworkin, *Taking Rights Seriously*, 340–41.

139. Dworkin, *A Matter of Principle*, 143.

140. Ronald Dworkin, *Law's Empire* (Cambridge, Mass.: Belknap Press of Harvard University Press, 1986), 225. This work includes Dworkin's well-known effort to highlight the difficulty of providing the best moral justification of legal rules through legal principles, in which he introduces an imaginary judge with "superhuman intellectual power and patience," whom he names Hercules (239).

answer to some moral question is a natural-law theory, then I am guilty of natural law."[141] Dworkin is, at first sight, surely more inclined than Hart or Raz to include an evaluative reference to moral elements in the very concept of law. In the same textual locus where he pleads guilty to some of his critics' accusations of adherence to a natural-law theory, Dworkin summarizes his main thesis on interpretivism (therein referred to as *naturalism*):

According to naturalism, judges should decide hard cases by interpreting the political structure of their community in the following, perhaps special way: by trying to find the best justification they can find, in principles of political morality, for the structure as a whole, from the most profound constitutional rules and arrangements to the details of, for example, the private law of tort or contract.[142]

He then adds, "Suppose this is natural law, ... what in the world is wrong with it?"[143] Granted, this nominal adherence does not necessarily mean that Dworkin endorses anything more than a "minimalist" version of natural-law theory. On several occasions, he contrasts his theory not only with positivism but also with what he labels the "orthodox natural-law theory,"[144] which is, in his words, supported by the "most extreme of the natural lawyers, who say that there can be *no difference* between principles of law and principles of morality,"[145] and deny "the difference between legal and moral arguments in hard cases."[146]

Dworkin's argument on justifying legal principles of political

141. Dworkin, "'Natural Law' Revisited," 165.

142. Dworkin, "'Natural Law' Revisited," 165.

143. Dworkin, "'Natural Law' Revisited," 165.

144. Dworkin, *Taking Rights Seriously*, 339

145. Dworkin, *Taking Rights Seriously*, 342. Emphasis added.

146. Dworkin, *Taking Rights Seriously*, 344. For a more detailed assessment of the debate between Dworkin and the proponents of what he calls the "strong" natural-law theory, see Popović, *The Goodness of Rights and the Juridical Domain of the Good*, 157–180.

morality does not exclude the possibility that judges might rely on controversial moral convictions while performing their institutional duties in complex pluralistic communities.[147] Such reference, however, must not be purely partisan.[148] Rather, it should be constructed according to the principles of political morality, which in Dworkin's system regulate the substantive content that may be deemed admissible for the justification of legal rules. These postulates can essentially be approximated to Raz's principle of personal autonomy.

Government must treat those whom it governs with … respect, that is, as human beings who are capable of … forming and acting on intelligent conceptions of how their lives should be lived. Government must not … constrain liberty on the ground that one citizen's conception of the good life of one group is nobler or superior to another's. These postulates, taken together, state what might be called the liberal conception of equality.[149]

Thus, after Hart and Raz, we encounter another intentionally underdetermined account of substantive morality in Dworkin's claim that the "liberal conception of equality" generates the cluster of moral values that constitute an overarching natural right to equal concern and respect.[150]

---

147. See Ronald Dworkin, "Rawls and the Law: Keynote Address," *Fordham Law Review* 72, no. 5 (2004): 1399. Thus, "background moral rights enter … into the calculation of what legal rights people have when the standard materials provide uncertain guidance, and some positivists' theses, that legal rights and moral rights are conceptually distinct, is therefore wrong" (Dworkin, *Taking Rights Seriously*, 326).

148. "A judge's intellectual biography is not a legal argument" (Dworkin, "Rawls and the Law," 1399).

149. Dworkin, *Taking Rights Seriously*, 272–73. "[According to] the main principles of liberalism based on equality … the government must treat people as equals in the following sense. It must impose no sacrifice or constraint on any citizen in virtue of an argument that the citizen could not accept without abandoning his sense of equal worth" (Dworkin, *A Matter of Principle*, 205).

150. Dworkin, *Taking Rights Seriously*, 180–83, 272–78.

The "nuanced difference"[151] between Raz and Dworkin concerning the necessary connection between law and morality is not, however, located in the sphere of substantive morality. Raz reduces the sphere of substantive morality to the principle of personal autonomy, whereas Dworkin reduces it to the liberal conception of equality. The real point of divergence between their accounts concerns Raz's recognition of the juridically relevant domain of morality only in the abstract moral features of the law as a system, versus Dworkin's claim that the liberal conception of equality is immediately juridically relevant precisely as a value of political morality. Granted, Dworkin posits the law-morality intersection only in terms of a minimalist natural-law axiology founded on the right to equal concern and respect. The fact remains that his argument on the juridical domain as a specific sphere of political morality is poles apart from Hart's and Raz's respective accounts of the "no necessary connection" thesis.

In the course of this book, it will become evident that Dwor-

151. Jeremy Waldron has attempted to locate the main difference between Raz's and Dworkin's understanding of the law-morality intersection. His attempt should appear manifestly accurate after the overviews of these authors' main theses. According to Waldron's synthesis, Raz "treats morality as a background field, relative to which law-making and the law that is made make a difference [in the sense] that there really is something, some *thing*—the law—which having been made displaces moral requirements." By contrast, in Dworkin's theory, "the law that makes a difference to what background morality requires must itself be understood in moral terms ... not just in regard to the moral significance of the events (like enactment) that generate it, but in its content." Through the lens of Dworkin's paradigmatic shift of perspective, "the difference that [the law] makes is now what morality, after all, requires." Waldron concludes his analysis by affirming that "it is remarkable that the distinction between the positions held by two jurists as diametrically opposed as Ronald Dworkin and Joseph Raz ... should come down to this nuanced difference." See Waldron, "Jurisprudence for Hedgehogs," 19. Dworkin has himself referred to Raz's version of what he calls "exclusive positivism" as a "Ptolemaic dogma: it deploys artificial conceptions of law and authority whose only point seems to be to keep positivism alive at any cost." Under the rubric of these "artificial conceptions of law and authority," Dworkin considered Raz's "personification" of "the law" in its claim to legitimate authority to be particularly problematic. See Dworkin, "Thirty Years On," 1656, 1666.

kin, in fact, rediscovers a model for a structural relationship between the moral and juridical domains that is quite similar to the claim of the juridical status of natural law as elaborated in a realistic conception of law and rights. It is true that Dworkin applies his model of this structural relationship to an underdetermined juridical anthropology, reducing it to the liberal conception of equality. Nonetheless, a version of the main intuition of his "paradigmatic" shift of perspective—juridical domain as a somehow distinct and specific part of morality—is, in fact, already embedded within the juridical strand of the natural-law tradition. There is the essential difference, however, that the latter tradition is equipped to include broader juridical-anthropological resources.

The Priority of Juridical Constructivism over the Ideas of the "Good" in John Rawls

American political philosopher John Rawls (1921–2002) contributed to the understanding of the juridical status of moral values, or, as he preferred to address them, the *ideas of the good*, from a rather different viewpoint compared to the authors I have so far presented. To be sure, Rawls never really wrote a treatise on legal philosophy, as he chose rather to work within the domain of political philosophy. More precisely, his research centered on the conditions of a theory of justice for contemporary society marked by a profound division among the religious, philosophical, and moral comprehensive doctrines of its citizens. At least one of his ideas, however, represents a genuine and decisive contribution to the discussion on the law-morality intersection, an idea that is, in Rawls's own words, an "essential element" of his particular conception of justice, which he calls "justice as fairness" or "political liberalism."[152] It is the idea of the priority of *right* over the ideas of the *good*. Rawls envisions this fundamental idea as a crucial element of his effort to "articulate a public basis of justification for the basic structure of a constitutional regime ... abstracting from comprehensive religious, philosophical and moral doctrines."[153]

Michael Sandel, in a critique of Rawls's theory, asserts that Rawls's concept of the priority of right over good is properly understood in a sense that is essentially connected with the juridical domain, namely, with rights: "The right is prior to the good in that the principles of justice that specify our rights do not depend for their justification on any particular conception of good life."[154] Sandel notes that Rawls's idea of the priority of right and justice over the good has "prompted the most recent wave of debate about Rawlsian liberalism ... under the somewhat misleading label of the liberal-communitarian debate."[155] A deeper look at the writings arising from this debate shows that its participants' arguments have only rarely addressed a specifically juridical level of analysis.[156]

In the course of positing his idea of the priority of right over good,[157] however, Rawls does, in fact, make a claim that proves

152. John Rawls, *Political Liberalism*, expanded ed. (New York: Columbia University Press, 2005), 173.

153. John Rawls, "The Priority of Right and Ideas of the Good," *Philosophy and Public Affairs* 17, no. 4. (1988): 261–62.

154. Michael J. Sandel, "A Response to Rawls's Political Liberalism," in *Liberalism and the Limits of Justice*, 2nd ed. (Cambridge: Cambridge University Press, 1998), 185.

155. Sandel, "A Response to Rawls's Political Liberalism," 185–86.

156. For example, see Alasdair MacIntyre. *After Virtue: A Study in Moral Theory* (Notre Dame, Ind.: University of Notre Dame Press, 1981); Charles Taylor, "Atomism," in *Philosophical Papers*, vol. 2, *Philosophy and the Human Sciences* (Cambridge: Cambridge University Press, 1985), 187–210; Michael Walzer, *Spheres of Justice* (New York: Basic Books, 1983); and Amy Gutmann, "Communitarian Critics of Liberalism," *Philosophy and Public Affairs* 14, no. 3 (1985): 308–22.

157. Rawls has confessed that his political theory underwent a systematic transformation from a comprehensive doctrine of justice as fairness to a political conception of

very pertinent to a juridical assessment of the law-morality intersection. He develops this claim not by means of the standard conceptual tools of legal philosophy (e.g., the "[no] necessary connection" thesis) but rather from within the discipline of political philosophy. Nonetheless, even while developing his main line of argument on the level of political philosophy, he makes a strong claim with immediate consequences in legal philosophy.

I will not reconstruct Rawls's understanding of the concepts of law and rights here.[158] My aim is, instead, to follow his primary theoretical focus, political philosophy, because it might prove easier to work out his central account of the juridical domain by proceeding from the idea of the priority of the right over the good

---

justice, which should be able to, in his view, accommodate conflicting reasonable comprehensive doctrines. See John Rawls, introduction to the paperback edition of *Political Liberalism*, xl–xlv. I have not noticed any essential transformational shifts in his texts regarding the fundamental idea of the priority of right over good that would be pertinent for the connection of that idea to the juridical domain. Instead, in his body of work, it is possible to perceive a deep continuity and linear development of those aspects of the idea of the priority of right over good that are the focus of my present study. I will, therefore, freely quote his arguments in favor of this idea, taken from various parts of his body of work.

158. For my critical analysis of Rawls's concept of law and rights, see Popović, *The Goodness of Rights and the Juridical Domain of the Good*, 181–207. Few authors have attempted to expound a concept of rights arising from Rawls's political philosophy. Their studies, however, remain at the margins of the secondary literature on Rawls's work and thus bear witness to the fact that Rawls himself touches on the question of the concept of rights only incidentally. I will suggest that Rawls, instead, makes the decisive claims regarding the law-morality intersection within a framework that structurally precedes the strictly juridical level of argumentation. For mentions and reconstructions of Rawls's concept of rights, see, for example, Charles Fried, review of *A Theory of Justice*, by John Rawls, *Harvard Law Review* 85, no. 8 (1972): 1697; Frank Michelman, "Constitutional Welfare Rights and *A Theory of Justice*," in *Reading Rawls: Critical Studies on Rawls's A Theory of Justice*, ed. Norman Daniels (New York: Basic Books, Inc., 1975), 346; and Alistair Macleod, "Rights, Moral and Legal," in *The Cambridge Rawls Lexicon*, ed. Jon Mandle and David A. Reidy (Cambridge: Cambridge University Press, 2015), 731–32. For a work entirely dedicated to the attempt of providing a systematic exposition of Rawls's concept of rights, though not through the framework of Rawls's priority of right over good, see Rex Martin, *Rawls and Rights* (Lawrence: University Press of Kansas, 1985).

as his doctrinal framework rather than from his implicit conception of rights.[159]

With this in mind, I will follow Sandel's interpretation of the Rawlsian idea of priority of right over good. As noted, Sandel interprets Rawls's idea that right is prior to the good in the sense that the principles of justice that specify our rights do not depend for their justification on any particular conception of good life. It is precisely this claim that captures the essence of Rawls's framework for his arguments on the law-morality intersection.

Before proceeding further, a brief terminological clarification is in order. When Rawls presents his idea of the priority of right over good, he clearly does not employ the concept of "right" in a juridical sense. Rather, he uses the term "right" according to his reconstructed version of the contractualist understanding of the term. That is, right is construed as an outcome of the system of those principles of practical reasoning that would be agreed upon by all persons participating in an appropriately constructed initial situation.[160] Hence, when employing this concept of right, Rawls does not envisage the juridical realm of the right (*ius*): rather, he seeks to denote the outcome of his construction of a fair procedure.

It is in Rawls's first major work, *A Theory of Justice*, in which he presents his conception of "justice as fairness," that he explains that right is prior to good in the sense that persons

159. An analysis of those elements of Rawls's theory pertinent to his concept of rights has yielded, according to Martin, very complex and ultimately uncertain conclusions. "Rawls's conception of rights is opaque. He does not attempt an analysis of the concept, and though he uses term 'rights' freely, he does so without explication. The context is usually unhelpful. Rawls's failure to deal with the analytic issues poses an obstacle to his program as a justification of rights" (Martin, *Rawls and Rights*, 26).

160. See Rawls, *A Theory of Justice*, 110–11; John Rawls, "Justice as Fairness," *The Philosophical Review* 67, no. 2 (1958): 178; and John Rawls, "Justice as Reciprocity," in *Collected Papers* (Cambridge, Mass.: Harvard University Press, 1999), 222–23.

implicitly agree, therefore, to conform their conception of the good to what the principles of justice require, or at least not to press claims which directly violate them.... The principles of right, and so of justice ... impose restrictions on what are reasonable conceptions of the good.... We can express this by saying that in justice as fairness the concept of right is prior to the concept of the good.[161]

According to Rawls, this idea of justice, applied to society, "provides a framework of rights."[162] That is, the fundamental idea of the priority of right over good imposes certain foundational operative criteria for the design of what Rawls refers to as the "basic structure of society," which in Rawls's view encompasses "society's main political, social, and economic institutions, and how they fit together into one unified system of social cooperation from one generation to the next."[163] Now, the basic structure of society is the locus in which the most fundamental institutional features of ordered social cooperation are constructed into a coherent system. The juridical domain of rights—or the "closely related"[164] rule of law—is itself constructed and modeled on the institutional framework of the "basic structure of society" according to the idea of the priority of right over good. As such, "A set of principles is required for choosing among the various social arrangements.... These principles are the principles of social justice: they provide a way of assigning rights and duties in the basic institutions of society."[165]

How, then, is the juridical domain constructed or "assigned" in the basic structures of society? Differences and contrasts re-

161. Rawls, *A Theory of Justice*, 31.

162. Rawls, *A Theory of Justice*, 31

163. Rawls, *Political Liberalism*, 11, 35, 201–2, 301.

164. "Now the rule of law is obviously closely related to liberty.... Liberty, as I have said, is a complex of rights and duties defined by institutions" (Rawls, *A Theory of Justice*, 235–36, 239).

165. Rawls, *A Theory of Justice*, 4.

garding their respective visions of the good notwithstanding, in Rawls's vision of a well-ordered society,[166] citizens may reach a reasonable overlapping consensus on the principles of right as "a final ordering among conflicting claims."[167] Citizens are, of course, left free to *privately* determine their conceptions of the "good,"[168] which in Rawls's view, may even "rely upon a full knowledge of the facts,"[169] but it is ultimately the citizens' simultaneous exercise of their capacity for a sense of justice (i.e., of that which is *right*) that sets the parameters for the public contextualization of their comprehensive doctrines of the good in a pluralistic society.[170] In other words, it is the right, not the good, that ultimately determines the arrangements in the political domain and the construction of legal institutions and juridical phenomena—laws and rights—within these arrangements.

Social unity and the allegiance of citizens to their common institutions are not founded on their all affirming the same conception of the good, but on their publicly accepting a political conception of justice to regulate the basic structure of society.... A just basic structure and its background institutions establish a framework within which permissible conceptions of the good can be advanced. Elsewhere I have called this relation between a conception of justice and conceptions of the good the priority of right (since the just falls under the right).[171]

This passage reveals several important points. First, the juridical domain is the object of justice in Rawls's theory, in a way that might appear, at first glance, to be akin to Thomas Aquinas's real-

166. Rawls, *Political Liberalism*, 35–40.

167. Rawls, *A Theory of Justice*, 447–48.

168. Rawls, *A Theory of Justice*, 448; Rawls, *Political Liberalism*, 30–35, 47–88.

169. Rawls, *A Theory of Justice*, 448–49.

170. See Rawls, *A Theory of Justice*, 563; Rawls, *Political Liberalism*, 19–20, 201–3.

171. John Rawls, "Justice As Fairness: Political, Not Metaphysical," *Philosophy and Public Affairs* 14, no. 3 (1985): 249–50.

istic juridical conception of law and rights. Rawls, however, clearly situates natural-law theory, which is foundational for a realistic conception of natural rights, within the scope of particular comprehensive doctrines of the good.[172] The *just* in Rawls's account is completely dependent on the procedure of positing an adequate system of prior principles inherent in his concept of *right*. As he says, the just falls under the right. This procedure and its principles "are independent and prior to the concept of goodness."[173]

In Rawls's version of the juridical domain, any concept of the good—even if it, as Rawls says, relies upon a full knowledge of the facts (!)—may ultimately be excluded from the basic structure of society (and consequently from the legal institutions that are modeled within that structure) if it does not fit within the limits of the idea of the priority of right. According to Rawls, a conception of the good will not fit within the limits of the right if it is unsuited to become a "political idea," in other words, if it is not, or could not be, shared by other free and equal citizens. The Rawlsian right must also dispense with those views of the good whose intelligibility or justification necessarily presupposes some comprehensive—religious, moral, or philosophical—doctrine.[174]

Although he developed his main ideas gradually and in stages, Rawls has at this point come to a clear understanding that his idea of the priority of right over good itself constitutes a moral value, a *sui generis* intrinsic political good.[175] He considers this idea to possess a moral value because, within his version of "Kantian constructivism,"[176] it locks the interplay between the

---

172. See Rawls, *Political Liberalism*, 97; John Rawls, "The Law of Peoples," in *The Law of Peoples: With "The Idea of Public Reason Revisited"* (Cambridge, Mass.: Harvard University Press, 1999), 103–5.

173. Rawls, "Justice As Fairness: Political, Not Metaphysical," 249.

174. See Rawls, "The Priority of Right and Ideas of the Good," 253.

175. See Rawls, "The Priority of Right and Ideas of the Good," 273.

176. For his political conception of justice, Rawls adopts a version of Kantian

right and the good within an adequate "answer to prior constraints springing from pure practical reason."[177] Such value is thereby grounded in precepts, since "rather than starting from a conception of the good given independently from the right, we start from a conception of the right—of the moral law—given by pure ... practical reason."[178] In addition, this idea establishes a political good because it embodies the social value of Rawls's political conception of justice: to "draw upon various ideas of the good"[179] toward the perspective of an overlapping consensus between citizens.[180] For these reasons, Rawls explicitly claims that his political conception of justice is not merely procedural but also substantive.[181]

Rawls thus endows his idea of the priority of right over good with a quality of political morality, which operates as a systematic feature that is prior to the construction of the juridical domain; it is a framework for establishing rights and the law. At the same time, the juridical domain is cut off *a priori* from any substantive, comprehensive account of the moral domain, should the latter prove inadequate for Rawls's vision of a political domain. In sum, the moral good, as such, is inherently unsuitable for the juridical domain. Even when it is filtered through the idea of the priority of right (in the sense of the outcome of a fair procedure),

---

constructivism: "This priority of the right over good is characteristic of Kantian constructivism." See John Rawls, "Kantian Constructivism in Moral Theory," *The Journal of Philosophy* 77, no. 9 (1980): 532.

177. John Rawls, *Lectures on the History of Moral Philosophy* (Cambridge, Mass.: Harvard University Press, 2000), 231.

178. Rawls, "Themes in Kant's Moral Philosophy," in *Collected Papers*, 509.

179. Rawls, "The Priority of Right and Ideas of the Good," 253.

180. "This deepens the idea that a political conception supported by an overlapping consensus is a moral conception affirmed on moral grounds" (Rawls, "The Priority of Right and Ideas of the Good," 274).

181. John Rawls, "The Idea of Public Reason Revisited," in Rawls, *The Law of Peoples*, 141.

substantive moral good never forms part of the juridical domain. The goodness of law and of rights is thus a result of a thorough constructivist procedure.

The Postwar Neo-Thomistic Accounts of the Juridical Status of Natural Law

The evidence of history confirms that every generation finds a new reason to restate natural law in light of its contemporary context. For a number of philosophers belonging to a generation of emigrants from continental Europe to the United States or United Kingdom, such as Jacques Maritain, Yves Simon, or Heinrich Rommen, "totalitarianism provided that occasion."[182] Invited as lecturers to prestigious universities abroad during the horrors of World War II and its immediate aftermath, these *émigré* intellectuals shared the common philosophical matrix of restating a natural-law doctrine as legal philosophy's antidote to the deep juridical metastasis of European totalitarian *régimes*. According to legal philosopher Alexander Passerin d'Entrèves (1902–1985), who wrote extensively on natural law during the same period as Maritain, Simon, and Rommen (though not from a neo-Thomistic point of view), the relationship between law and morality is "the crux of all natural-law theory."[183] D'Entrèves also claimed that "the notion of natural law partakes at the same time of a legal and of a moral character" and "provides a name for the point of intersection between law and morality."[184] The postwar

182. Russell Hittinger, introduction to *The Natural Law: A Study in Legal and Social History and Philosophy*, by Heinrich A. Rommen, trans. Thomas R. Hanley (Indianapolis, Ind.: Liberty Fund, 1998), xii.

183. Alexander P. D'Entrèves, *Natural Law: An Introduction to Legal Philosophy* (New Brunswick, N.J.: Transaction Publishers, 1994), 79.

184. D'Entrèves, *Natural Law*, 111.

neo-Thomists sought to indicate, at least tangentially, some elements for discerning the questions on the interrelation of the moral domain and the juridical status of natural law.

French philosopher Jacques Maritain (1882–1973) develops an original restatement of Thomistic natural law in both his postwar writings and in lectures given at Princeton University and the University of Chicago. The contextual backdrop of these lectures is the postwar enthusiasm for drafting international documents protecting human rights, a phenomenon that flourished following the fall of the totalitarian Axis regimes. Maritain was strongly convinced that the philosophical foundation of human rights, as spheres of juridical protection for certain nonnegotiable values, is natural law.[185] As a neo-Thomist faithful to his teacher, Maritain fully endorses Aquinas's understanding of the concept of natural law.[186] In Maritain's reading of Aquinas, the "ought" arising from natural law, in its "basic ontological element," is "coextensive with the whole field of … natural morality": it is fundamentally a moral law.[187] It is also an unwritten law, not contained in "abstract and theoretical" rational formulas, with regard to its promulgation in both its ontological (what it is) and epistemological (how it is known) elements.[188] Nonetheless, it is real law, and its promulgation as law is discovered, in what Maritain labels natu-

185. Jacques Maritain, *Man and the State* (Washington, D.C.: The Catholic University of America Press, 1998), 80, 84.

186. See Maritain, *Man and the State*, 84–95; Jacques Maritain, "Quelques remarques sur la loi naturelle," in *Jacques et Raïssa Maritain: Oeuvres Complètes*, vol. 10, ed. Jean-Marie Allion et al. (Fribourg: Éditions Universitaires Fribourg, 1985), 955–59; and Jacques Maritain, "La loi naturelle ou loi non écrite," in *Jacques et Raïssa Maritain: Oeuvres Complètes*, vol. 16, ed. Jean-Marie Allion et al. (Fribourg: Éditions Universitaires Fribourg, 1999), 689–728.

187. Maritain, *Man and the State*, 87, 89; Maritain, "La loi naturelle ou loi non écrite," 704–8.

188. Maritain, *Man and the State*, 90–91, 94; Maritain, "Quelques remarques sur la loi naturelle," 956–57; and Maritain, "La loi naturelle ou loi non écrite," 709–11.

ral law's "epistemological element," through existential, practical knowledge.[189]

Does Maritain posit a specifically juridical domain as somehow arising from this natural moral law? The answer seems to be a qualified "no."

With regard to ... the element of knowledge which natural law implies in order to have force of law, it can thus be said that natural law—that is, natural law *naturally known*—covers only the field of the ethical regulations of which men have become aware by virtue of knowledge *through inclination*, and which are the *basic principles* in moral life.[190]

For Maritain, it is beyond academic doubt that "the same natural law which lays down our most fundamental [moral] duties" is the very law "which assigns to us our fundamental rights."[191] Natural moral law is also that law by virtue of which "every just law" is morally binding,[192] thus firmly establishing a necessary connection between law and morality.

But Maritain's account of the law-morality intersection leaves

189. "That kind of knowledge is not clear knowledge through concepts and conceptual judgments; it is obscure, unsystematic, vital knowledge by connaturality or congeniality, in which the intellect, in order to bear judgment, consults and listens to the inner melody that the vibrating strings of abiding tendencies make present in the subject" (Maritain, *Man and the State*, 91–92). In these words, Maritain introduces an interpretation of the so-called "epistemological element" ("how it is known") of Thomistic natural law based on his elaboration of "knowledge through inclination" or "knowledge by connaturality." See Jacques Maritain, "On Knowledge through Connaturality," *The Review of Metaphysics* 4, no. 4 (1951): 473–81; Maritain, *Man and the State*, 91–94; Maritain, "Quelques remarques sur la loi naturelle," 955–59; and Maritain, "La loi naturelle ou loi non écrite," 708–17. For a critique of Maritain's "knowledge through connaturality" at the border between the epistemological and ontological elements, see Brock, *The Light That Binds*, 119; Stephen L. Brock, "Natural Inclination and the Intelligibility of the Good in Thomistic Natural Law," *Vera Lex* 6, no. 1–2 (2005): 58; and Stephen L. Brock, "Natural Law, Understanding of Principles and Universal Good," *Nova et Vetera* 9, no. 3 (2011): 674.

190. Maritain, *Man and the State*, 92–93.

191. Maritain, *Man and the State*, 95.

192. Maritain, *Man and the State*, 95.

natural law itself wholly in the domain of morality. As is the case with other authors presented in this section, Maritain sometimes seems to operate with elements that could indicate a juridical dimension predicable of natural law. However, when he claims that "there is no right unless a certain order ... is inviolably required by *what things are* ... an order by virtue of which certain things like life, work, freedom are due to the human person,"[193] Maritain presupposes that the order of natural law gives immediate origin only to the moral due. This is made particularly clear when he compares the natural law to the system of rules belonging to the so-called law of nations (*ius gentium*) and those belonging to the positive law of the state.

The law of nations and positive law are, in Maritain's view, an *extension* of natural law, since they rationally determine what natural law and its "knowledge through connaturality" leave underdetermined. Thus, the positive law contains necessary reference to the principles of natural law by means of artifactual legal regulation proper to the political community in question. The law of nations is, in Maritain's view, the set of unwritten (but easily positivized) legal principles that are (1) common to all the civilized world and (2) understood through the conceptual exercise of human reason considered not at the level of the individual but at the level of common humanity of civilized people.[194]

For example, the rational principle that "one must obey the laws of the political community" is a *ius gentium* norm established by way of inferences and conclusions from a prior set of norms related to the overlaps between the concept of the good and the social nature of man. It seems that for Maritain, the essential difference between natural law and *ius gentium* is both

193. Maritain, *Man and the State*, 96–97.
194. Maritain, *Man and the State*, 98–99.

ontological, to the extent that only natural law embraces the very first principles of morality, and epistemological. It is epistemological because the content that constitutes *ius gentium* norms may be considered to form part of natural law to the extent that they are known not through "rational deduction," inferences, or conclusions but through connatural or inclinational knowledge.[195] Regardless of their differences from the ontological and epistemological standpoints, it is safe to say that, according to Maritain, natural law and *ius gentium* significantly and necessarily overlap.

Natural law is distinguished from both *ius gentium* and positive law by its relation to the juridical domain. Both the *ius gentium* (even if not contained in a written code) and positive law formally constitute the juridical order.[196] In this respect, Maritain's comparison of the relationships between positive or natural *law* and positive or natural *right* helps clarify his position on the juridical status of natural law. He asserts that positive right (*droit positif*) and positive law are actually synonyms, "because the notion of right [*droit*] or of the juridical order stands for a code of laws ... which human persons are not only obligated to obey with their conscience, but may be coerced to obey through the coercive power of society":[197] "Thus, we have the order of legality or the juridical order—which presupposes the moral order, but adds something to it, that is, this very possibility of social coercion."[198]

Since the natural law pertains to the moral order, not to the juridical order, Maritain asks how could we even "talk of a natural *right* in these circumstances, and do we not find ourselves here before a simple contradiction of terms?"[199] He answers this

195. Maritain, *Man and the State*, 99–100.
196. Maritain, *Man and the State*, 98.
197. Maritain, "La loi naturelle ou loi non écrite," 729.
198. Maritain, "La loi naturelle ou loi non écrite," 729.
199. Maritain, "La loi naturelle ou loi non écrite," 730.

question by affirming that we can validly speak of natural right "not only in this sense that this or that precept of the natural law may be the object of a precept of the positive law."[200] Apart from positive law, we can speak of natural right in the domain of what he calls the "*virtual* juridical order."[201] Maritain understands this "virtual juridical order" as a "natural juridical order enveloped in natural law and in the natural order of morality, but merely in a virtual way." As a virtual juridical order, it is simultaneously "analogous" and "real."[202]

Where does this quality of the virtual juridicity of natural law originate? Maritain claims that every man carries within himself the "judicial authority of humanity," and consequently the "right to impose coercion which derives from this authority." He immediately adds that this judicial authority "transcends the domain of 'what is *mine*' and points to the author of the nature and of humanity."[203] The domain of natural right is juridical, though only in an analogous way, and is only virtually contained in the order of morality. In contrast to the *ius gentium* and to positive law, *droit naturel*, according to Maritain, is never a juridical order in the proper, actual, and formal sense of the term.[204] The "first formal juridical order which is necessarily derived from the natural order of morality" is the *ius gentium*.[205]

Maritain thus strongly supports the thesis that there is a necessary point of contact between law and morality regarding natural law. His vision of natural law, however, seems to be circumscribed to the moral domain and touches only virtually upon the

---

200. Maritain, "La loi naturelle ou loi non écrite," 730.
201. Maritain, "La loi naturelle ou loi non écrite," 731.
202. Maritain, "La loi naturelle ou loi non écrite," 731.
203. Maritain, "La loi naturelle ou loi non écrite," 730–31. Emphasis added.
204. Maritain, "La loi naturelle ou loi non écrite," 732–33.
205. Maritain, "La loi naturelle ou loi non écrite," 738.

juridical domain. As Maritain himself says, *droit naturel* is "barely even *droit*."[206]

Perhaps Maritain's theory that *droit naturel* pertains to the virtual juridical order, as well as his general understanding of the specific domain of the juridical, is underdeveloped.[207] It does contain certain elements, however, that could imply the existence of a juridical domain that arises from the natural law. Although he qualifies the juridical domain with a merely virtual juridicity, he still seems to imply that the natural law posits certain human goods as objects of a juridical order.

Maritain's colleagues in the postwar project of restating natural law as the necessary point of the law-morality intersection, offer little more than rudimentary elements of an argument on the juridical status of natural law. Maritain's friend and fellow wartime émigré to the United States, French philosopher Yves Simon (1903–1961), a professor at Notre Dame and the University of Chicago, dedicated much of his writing to the moral domain of natural law as the foundation of human rights.[208] At one point, Simon reflects on a possible connection between natural law and

206. Maritain, "La loi naturelle ou loi non écrite," 742.

207. This scarcity is visible, for example, in his identification of positive law and positive right as synonyms, and in his understanding of the specificity of the juridical domain as being reducible to the presence of social coercion. Also, his qualification of the juridical order of natural right as merely virtual is unclear and, given its importance for legal philosophy, merits further elaboration. Maritain probably could not have offered such elaboration, given the predominantly moral-philosophical context of his writings. "We have here a notion of a *virtual juridical order*, which always remains virtual and is never unfolded as a juridical order expressed in the positive law and in the judicial authority of human society, since we cannot envisage the idea of a tribunal which would be authorized to apply the natural law.... The *natural right* itself, insofar as it is natural *right*, remains *virtual*, enveloped in the *natural law*, and it is not actively manifested except in certain exceptional cases" (Maritain, "La loi naturelle ou loi non écrite," 732).

208. See Yves R. Simon, *The Tradition of Natural Law: A Philosopher's Reflection*, as well as his *Philosophy of Democratic Government* (Chicago: University of Chicago Press, 1964).

what he, like Aquinas, understands to be the "primary sense of the Latin *ius*," namely, "that which is right, the thing that is right, the objective right," later elaborating, "For instance, we make a contract by reason of which the amount of money I owe you on the first day of March is one hundred dollars. The payment of one hundred dollars on March 1st is the right, the thing that is right."[209]

This "objective sense of right," which, according to Simon, "both doctrinally and historically … may be treated as the primordial [one],"[210] was subsequently relegated to a secondary or even ephemeral meaning. In what he labels an "epoch-making event in the history of notions concerning the law," the subjective sense of "a claim, a faculty" was assigned to the concept of right as its primary meaning.[211] Simon seems to favor the former primary meaning of right, in the sense of *that which is right*. He outlines his thoughts on the juridical status of natural law within the question of whether there are things which are right by nature: "The right by nature … would be that which is right by reason of what the things are. In other words, [the existence of a law in the nature of things has an implicational value for the fact that] some things are right by nature."[212]

It is regrettable that Simon did not explore these reflections, originating in his course on "The Problem of Natural Law" at the University of Chicago in the winter quarter of 1958, more extensively in a course dedicated to issues of legal philosophy. Perhaps such exploration would have allowed the topic of natural law to be addressed with specific attention to its relationship with the juridical domain of the right, as Simon understands the term.

209. Simon, *The Tradition of Natural Law*, 118.
210. Simon, *The Tradition of Natural Law*, 119–20.
211. See Simon, *The Tradition of Natural Law*, 120.
212. Simon, *The Tradition of Natural Law*, 120.

Another legal scholar, Heinrich Rommen (1897–1967), who fled Germany in 1938 and eventually became a professor at Georgetown University in Washington, D.C., gives a more detailed, though not systematic, account of the possibility of predicating a juridical domain on natural law. For Rommen, natural law is a sort of framework law, that is, although it does not exactly provide "a concrete norm directly applicable to action here and now,"[213] it still constitutes an actual obligation, which is "by no means merely an ideal program *de lege ferenda*."[214] What, ultimately, is the status of this legal—*de lege lata*—obligation constituted by the natural law? Is it essentially moral, or does it somehow situate natural-law precepts within the juridical domain? Although "all right must stem from morality,"[215] Rommen claims that there seems to be a distinct domain in what he refers to as the "teleological character of things, goods and actions,"[216] wherein these "goods" are not "owed" solely according to morality. Rather, this distinct domain of natural law is somehow related to natural rights.

This *suum* [from the classical maxim that justice means "to each one what is his," *suum cuique*,] is what is generally or individually related to any specific person or to any organized group of persons.... The first and proximate principle of knowledge for this *suum* is the rational, social, free nature of man.... What is just and what is *suum* ought to be, because it follows from human nature, is conformed with it.... There is, therefore, a right born with us ... a sphere that is sacred according to natural law. And this is typically a juridical sphere.[217]

Prior to the state, then, there exist rights of the person. Yet these rights are not mere facts, to which the state thereupon attaches legal

213. Rommen, *The Natural Law*, 235.

214. Heinrich A. Rommen, *The State in Catholic Thought: A Treatise in Political Philosophy* (St. Louis, Mo.: B. Herder Book Co., 1950), 212.

215. Rommen, *The State in Catholic Thought*, 202.

216. Rommen, *The Natural Law*, 182.

217. Rommen, *The State in Catholic Thought*, 187.

effects.... Here it is really a question of natural right. For this reason, too, the *suum cuique* is not simply dependent upon material realization through the positive law. There exists a *suum*, a right, which comes into existence with us.[218]

In opposition to a totalitarian system that purports to follow legitimate legal procedures in order to revest the most perversely immoral conduct with the juridical validity of the positive laws of the state, Rommen clearly sees that the natural law must somehow be constituted in the specific domain of the juridical. This is why he claims that "there exists a perennial kernel in the concept of *suum* which precedes its concrete determination in positive law,"[219] and that this "perennial kernel" arises from natural law. Unlike Maritain and Simon, Rommen was a trained and practicing jurist, and thus may be considered more accurate in his intuitions in the sphere of legal philosophy. Unfortunately, he dedicated his academic interests to other aspects of jusnaturalist doctrine, never developing these intuitions and arguments into a more grandiose system.

The Prejuridical Status of Natural Law according to John Finnis

A distinguished Oxford professor of legal theory and philosophy of law, steeped in the Thomistic tradition of natural-law theory, John Finnis is surely one of the most significant contributors to the reestablishment of the dialogue between the natural-law tradition and leading contemporary legal theorists such as H. L. A. Hart, Ronald Dworkin, or Joseph Raz. It was Hart who, as editor

218. Rommen, *The Natural Law*, 205.
219. Rommen, *The State in Catholic Thought*, 189.

of the prestigious Clarendon Law Series of the Oxford University Press, commissioned—and titled—Finnis's 1980 seminal book *Natural Law and Natural Rights*.[220] The Oxford graduate seminars that hosted the debates between Finnis, Raz, and/or Dworkin, often with all three scholars together, are remembered by their former students as a "time when legal giants roamed among Oxford's spires."[221] In an intriguing blend of Thomistic natural-law theory with what he professes to be a "modern tradition that can be labeled 'analytical jurisprudence,'"[222] Finnis attempts to restate a natural-law argument for the contemporary public. At the same time, he certainly succeeds at diminishing polarizations between the two opposing camps in legal philosophy, namely, legal positivism and natural-law theory. His theory is often referred to as part of the larger philosophical project labeled as the "new natural-law theory,"[223] although he prefers the name "new classical natural-law theory."[224]

My present interest is not to provide a detailed presentation

220. For more details on this, see John Finnis, postscript to *Natural Law and Natural Rights*, 2nd ed. (Oxford: Oxford University Press, 2011), 414–15. See also Santiago Legarre, "HLA Hart and the Making of the New Natural Law Theory," *Jurisprudence* 8, no. 1 (2017): 82–98.

221. Neil M. Gorsuch, "Intention and the Allocation of Risk," in *Reason, Morality and Law: The Philosophy of John Finnis*, ed. John Keown and Robert P. George (Oxford: Oxford University Press, 2013), 413.

222. John Finnis, preface to *Natural Law and Natural Rights*, vi.

223. This term is meant to denote a main cluster of ideas shared also by other authors, like Robert P. George and Germain Grisez. Some of the authors usually associated with the "new natural-law" theory subscribe to this cluster to a lesser degree than others regarding particular issues of the natural-law theory, as is the case, for example, with Martin Rhonheimer. It seems that the term itself was coined by Russell Hittinger. See Russell Hittinger, *A Critique of the New Natural Law Theory* (Notre Dame, Ind.: University of Notre Dame Press, 1987), 5. The proposed common term was rejected on various occasions by proponents of the theory, perhaps most notably by Finnis himself in "Reflections and Responses," in Keown and George, *Reason, Morality and Law*, 468, n. 31.

224. See John Finnis, "Aquinas and Natural Law Jurisprudence," in *The Cambridge Companion to Natural Law Jurisprudence*, ed. George Duke and Robert P. George (Cambridge: Cambridge University Press, 2017), 17.

of Finnis's legal theory.[225] Neither do I intend to assess the claims of numerous critics who, over the course of the last half-century, have challenged Finnis's theory from a variety of perspectives, deeming it insufficiently "Thomistic"[226] or otherwise deficient in its account of legality[227] or nature[228] in Aquinas's natural law. I will address only those aspects of Finnis's theory that deal with the immediate focus of this study, namely, his arguments regarding the juridical status of natural law.

From the opening pages of his seminal work *Natural Law and Natural Rights*, Finnis makes it clear that he employs a somewhat novel terminology compared to the traditional approach. He cautions that instead of the term "natural law," he often makes use of the following formulations to denote the various interconnected aspects of the same term: "basic practical principles," "basic methodological requirements of practical reasonableness," and "general moral standards."[229] The essential feature of Finnis's pe-

225. For more details on Finnis's account of the ontology of law and rights and the various levels of overlap between these concepts and the concept of good, see Popović, *The Goodness of Rights and the Juridical Domain of the Good*, 95–156.

226. For example, see Michael Pakaluk, "Is the New Natural Law Thomistic?" *The National Catholic Bioethics Quarterly* 13, no. 1 (2013): 57–67; Hittinger, *A Critique of the New Natural Law Theory*, 27–30, 61–65; and Henry B. Veatch, *Human Rights: Fact or Fancy?* (Baton Rouge: Louisiana State University Press, 1985), 95–104.

227. For example, see Brock, *The Light That Binds*, 10, 100–6; Russell Hittinger, "Natural Law as 'Law,'" in *The First Grace*, 39–62.

228. Henry B. Veatch, "Natural Law and the 'Is'—'Ought' Question," *Catholic Lawyer* 26, no. 4 (1980–1981): 251–65; Ralph McInerny, "The Principles of Natural Law," *The American Journal of Jurisprudence* 25, no. 1 (1980): 1–15; Ralph McInerny, "The Primacy of Theoretical Knowledge: Some Remarks on John Finnis" in *Aquinas on Human Action: A Theory of Practice* (Washington, D.C.: The Catholic University of America Press, 1992), 184–92; Brock, "Natural Inclination and the Intelligibility of the Good in Thomistic Natural Law," 57–78; and Brock, "Natural Law, Understanding of Principles and Universal Good," 671–706.

229. Finnis, *Natural Law and Natural Rights*, 23. It is questionable whether this new vocabulary, which focuses on the principles of practical reason, amounts to a natural-law theory that would differ from the Thomistic tradition. Of course, Finnis is convinced that his vocabulary mostly represents a straightforward reception of Aquinas or a licit

culiar natural-law method can be summarized in his own words: "working out the (moral) 'natural law'"[230] from the basic practical principles, which, as "the evaluative substratum of all moral judgments,"[231] indicate the "basic forms of human flourishing as *goods* to be pursued and realized."[232]

From the whole of his writings, it is quite clear that Finnis understands natural law exclusively as a moral normative concept, and he never really addresses this concept in terms of its unmediated juridical aspects. The moral domain of natural law, in his view, provides juridical phenomena, such as positive law and legal rights, with value-based content or otherwise with a viewpoint that is inherently practically reasonable. But the natural law itself, in Finnis's system, always remains firmly within the moral realm.

---

interpretation of his thought. Other contemporary Thomists have, by contrast, noticed that in the often-cited textual locus of his *Summa Theologica* (I-II, q. 94, a. 2), in his *respondeo dicendum*, and in replies to objections, Aquinas predominantly uses the formulation "precepts of natural law" over "principles of practical reason." See Hittinger, "Authority to Render Judgment," 98. "Thomas evidently regards the proof for the existence of first principles of practical reason, by itself, as somewhat inadequate for a disclosure of something answering to the name *natural law*" (Brock, *The Light That Binds*, 38). Also, an admonitory note in a 2009 document of the International Theological Commission, directed at "some contemporary theories of natural law," warns against the theoretical exclusion of a broader metaphysical framework, especially of those aspects that "take into account the rationality immanent in nature." The document particularly highlights those exclusions that conceptually replace "the rationality of the natural law with a univocal ideal of rationality generated by practical reason alone." See International Theological Commission, *In Search of a Universal Ethic: A New Look at the Natural Law* (2009), 79, especially n. 75 (for more information on this document, see *infra* the concluding section of this chapter). It remains uncertain to what extent Finnis's natural-law theory falls under the scope of this admonitory note. Finnis has certainly openly criticized the ITC document's position on the status of the natural inclinations, which the document also refers to as *prerational natural dynamisms*. He believes that the document "heads in the wrong direction" by making these dynamisms, which are expressions of the "rationality immanent in nature," the guide to "the content of natural law's (or practical reason's) first or first moral principles." See Finnis, "Reflections and Responses," 477, n. 64.

230. Finnis, *Natural Law and Natural Rights*, 103.
231. Finnis, *Natural Law and Natural Rights*, 59.
232. Finnis, *Natural Law and Natural Rights*, 23.

In his analysis of the concept of *justice*, Finnis claims that the "requirement of justice" essentially consists in "concrete applications of the basic requirement of practical reasonableness that one is to favor and foster the common good of one's communities."[233] Thus, justice adds the aspect of other-directedness to the structure of natural moral law in a social context.

[The requirement of justice is] an ensemble of requirements of practical reasonableness that hold because one must seek to realize and respect human goods not merely in oneself and for one's own sake but also in common, in community.[234]

Moving then to the connection between this conception of justice and the notion of *rights*, Finnis attempts to reinstate the traditional Thomistic doctrine on the origin of the juridical domain, according to which "the object of the virtue of justice ... is *rights*."[235]

In short, the modern vocabulary and grammar of rights is a many-faceted instrument for reporting and asserting the requirements or other implications of a relationship of justice *from the point of view of the person(s) who benefit(s) from* that relationship. It provides a way of talking about 'what is just' from a special angle: the viewpoint of the "other(s)" to whom something ... is owed or due, and who would be wronged if denied that something.[236]

Rights, therefore, are essentially understood as specific moral or legal positions of the claim-holders with regard to their corresponding debtors on the basis of determinate requirements of justice. Finnis's line of argument related to the juridical aspect of

---

233. Finnis, *Natural Law and Natural Rights*, 164.

234. Finnis, *Natural Law and Natural Rights*, 161.

235. John Finnis, "Grounding Human Rights in Natural Law," *The American Journal of Jurisprudence* 60, no. 2 (2015): 214.

236. Finnis, *Natural Law and Natural Rights*, 205. Emphasis in original.

these positions and requirements concludes with his account of the link between rights and the concept of *law*.

These two main meanings of *ius*—right(s) and law(s)—are rationally connected. To say that someone has a right is to make a claim about what practical reasonableness requires of somebody (or everybody) else. But one's practical reasonableness is guided and shaped by principles and norms, in the first instance by the principles of natural reason, i.e., of natural law—*lex naturalis* or, synonymously, *ius naturale*—and then by any relevant and authoritative rules which have given to natural law some specific *determinatio* for a given community: positive law, i.e., *lex positiva* or, synonymously, *ius positivum*, usually *ius civile*.[237]

This argument testifies to Finnis's understanding of natural rights essentially as moral rights or, as he says in the above quote, "claims about what practical reasonableness"—natural moral law—"requires of somebody."[238] At the same time, it sheds light on how Finnis considers positive law and legal rights derived thereof as phenomena that are the exclusive carriers of juridicity, even if these same phenomena may be said to essentially constitute a proximate conclusion[239] or a *determinatio* of the precepts of practical reason (i.e., of natural moral law).

---

237. John Finnis, *Aquinas: Moral, Political and Legal Theory* (Oxford: Oxford University Press, 1998), 134–35.

238. Natural rights are, in a Finnisian perspective, essentially mere juridical extensions—specifications in the form of subjective claims—of the principles of practical reason. As such, they are not necessarily or inherently juridical, since Finnis seems to refer to rights as, interchangeably, "natural," "human," or "moral." See Finnis, *Natural Law and Natural Rights*, 198–99. "Thus law, natural or positive, is the basis for one's right(s) (*ratio iuris*), precisely because the proposition 'X has such-and-such a right' cannot rationally be other than a conclusion from, or a *determinatio* of, practical reason's principles" (Finnis, *Aquinas*, 135). For other instances of Finnis's treatment of the concept of natural rights as juridical extensions of principles of practical reason, see, for example, Finnis, *Natural Law and Natural Rights*, 205, 219, 221, 225; Finnis, *Aquinas*, 138–40.

239. "True, some parts of the legal system commonly do, and certainly should, consist of rules and principles closely corresponding to requirements of practical reason, which themselves are conclusions directly from the combination of a particular basic

Throughout this line of argument, Finnisian natural law—even when inbuilt in the arguments on rights, moral or legal, and on the law, natural or positive—always remains a moral law. We have already seen how Raz comments in one of his articles that Finnis's theory represents precisely the "variety of Thomist natural law views which regard the law as *good in its very nature*."[240] Raz probably means to say that in Finnis's theory, natural law somehow replicates the domain of moral good in the content of positive law and of subjective claim-rights. At the same time, the normative nucleus proximately related to "basic human goods"—the principles of practical reason or the natural law—remains entirely circumscribed to the domain of morality.[241]

Jeremy Waldron, in his intriguing contribution to a collection of essays on Finnis's legal philosophy, presents a strong critique of Finnis's understanding of natural law. Waldron writes that he was amazed to discover how Finnis's account of the point of contact between natural law and positive law cannot be categorized as

value (e.g., life) with one or more of those ... basic 'methodological' requirements of practical reasonableness. Discussion in courts and amongst lawyers and legislators will commonly, and reasonably, follow much the same course as a straightforward moral debate" (Finnis, *Natural Law and Natural Rights*, 282).

240. Raz, "About Morality and the Nature of Law," 167, n. 4. Emphasis added.

241. Other adherents to the key features of the "new classical natural-law theory" seem to follow Finnis in the argument on the essentially nonjuridical status of natural law. Thus, Robert P. George claims that positive law derives "from natural law; or ... translates natural principles of justice and political morality into rules and principles of positive law ... by a process akin to deduction from the moral proposition." See Robert P. George, "Natural Law and Positive Law," in *In Defense of Natural Law* (Oxford: Oxford University Press, 1999), 108. George sometimes seems to make an argument that could imply a connection between the natural law and the strictly juridical obligations in justice. For example, he affirms that "activities prohibited by moral laws" are wrong not only because they are "intrinsically immoral" but also because one has an "obligation in justice" to one's fellow citizens not to engage in those activities. See Robert P. George, "Moralistic Liberalism and Legal Moralism," in George, *In Defense of Natural Law*, 310. Unfortunately, he never develops an argument in which these "obligations in justice" would amount to something (e.g., the constitution of natural law in its *juridical* domain) other than Finnis's "requirements of justice" as, essentially, aspects of social morality.

pertaining to legal theory at all but rather as a "full-blown complex moral and ethical theory."[242] Waldron is aware that natural-law theory ordinarily seeks to somehow posit morality as "an immanent standard for defining and evaluating human law,"[243] but he's amazed to find that Finnis's account never really interrelates natural moral law with specifically juridical reasoning on a level that is prior to positive law.

I am going to suggest that Finnis has not really given us a theory of natural law at all—certainly not a theory of natural law considered as … something that is capable of fulfilling the governance functions of law in the absence of positive institutions.… One of the things that was intriguing but also disconcerting about Finnis's book [*Natural Law and Natural Rights*] was that his account of what he called "natural law" presented itself, in the first instance, in the form of a well worked-out moral and ethical theory.[244]

Aspects of Finnis's "'natural-law' account of positive law"— that is, of his nonpositivist framework of the "set of moral criteria for evaluating positive law"—amount to, in Waldron's opinion, "the best 'natural-law' account of positive law that we have."[245] In his observations on what he had expected Finnis's natural law to be like, Waldron admits to have conceived it to be, in a way, "separable from ethics and morality," though not "as a comprehensive separation."[246] Still, conceptualizing the juridical features of natural law in a hypothetical situation of the absence of positive law would certainly, according to Waldron, "not be the same as imagining the undifferentiated rule of objective morality"; rather,

---

242. Jeremy Waldron, "What Is Natural Law Like?" in Keown and George, *Reason, Morality and Law*, 78.

243. Waldron, "What Is Natural Law Like?" 78.

244. Waldron, "What Is Natural Law Like?" 74.

245. Waldron, "What Is Natural Law Like?" 74.

246. Waldron, "What Is Natural Law Like?" 75, 83.

"rule by natural law" should amount to a "positive presence of natural law among us."[247] In my estimation, Waldron is correct to note that Finnis ultimately fails to provide sufficient explanations of the juridical status of natural law itself.[248]

Finnis's Thomistic Critics and the Juridical Status of Natural Law

It would seem that Jeremy Waldron's amazement due to the lack of specific juridical argumentation in Finnis's presentation of natural law could be easily extended to at least some natural-law scholars who do not subscribe to the so-called new classical natural-law theory. In fact, we might be surprised to discover that some natural lawyers, otherwise fervent Thomistic critics of many aspects of Finnis's account of natural law, share his essentially nonjuridical reading of natural law.

Henry B. Veatch (1911–1999) arrives at remarkably similar conclusions as Simon regarding the need to understand the con-

---

247. Waldron, "What Is Natural Law Like?" 83, 87.

248. It remains uncertain whether Finnis, in his response to Waldron's essay, perceives the actual dimensions of Waldron's challenge. In this text, Finnis forwards the claim that Waldron's question of the possibility of a "positive presence of natural law in abstraction from positive law" in his theory still amounts to "absolute human rights which correspond to exceptionless duties." He then admits having taken for granted "that these duties are moral." See Finnis, "Reflections and Responses," 476, n. 62. In addition, Finnis claims that his account of natural law includes the feature of its enforceability. He immediately adds that the aspects of this enforceability do not amount to anything more than a purely moral domain. "Is not the objectivity and communicability of moral principles and norms, taken with their inherent deontic normativity for everyone in the human community, enough to entitle them to the term 'law?'" (478–79). Finnis's response is actually a restatement of arguments from his previous works. Take the following example: "The moral obligation to obey the law as such is ... reinforced by moral obligations that would exist in the same form (e.g., not to murder) or at least inchoately ... even if the law did not re-enact them ... or concretize them." See Finnis, *Natural Law and Natural Rights*, 318.

cept of natural rights according to a more objective approach. Natural-rights talk should, in Veatch's view, shift the emphasis from "what it is someone's natural right to do" from a predominantly subjective sense toward the sense that highlights "what is naturally right for someone to do."[249] Although he opts for a more objectivist approach to the concept of right, Veatch shares Finnis's view that natural rights are an instrument for expressing what is essentially a juridical extension of the moral obligations arising from natural law.[250]

Finnis's understanding of natural-law-based social morality as the foundation of law seems to coincide with the main vectors of Veatch's argument that the telic order of the attainment of man's natural end includes relational or social aspects of human nature. The whole human good thus necessarily also includes the fulfillment of the common good of all men.[251] It is precisely the link between the human person's telic perfection and the common good that gives rise to natural rights: each of us has the duty to attain proper perfection as a human person in a society.[252] Again, positive law is, in Veatch's view, "nothing but the assemblage of those how-to-do-it rules that a given society has worked out over time with a view to achieving its natural end as a human community, that is, the common good."[253] Nowhere does Veatch refer to

249. Henry B. Veatch, "Natural Law: Dead or Alive?" *Literature of Liberty* 1, no. 4 (1978): 13–14.

250. "Notice, however, that if every human being be under this natural obligation [to perfect himself by following a natural order toward his natural end] it follows that it is no more than right that such a person not be impeded or interfered with in his efforts to acquit himself of those duties.... With this we have that very foundation and justification that we have been seeking, so far as our so-called natural rights are concerned.... Accordingly, life, liberty and property being means in this sense, it is to such things that we can be said to have a natural moral right." See Henry B. Veatch, "On Taking Rights Still More Seriously: Comment," *Harvard Journal of Law and Public Policy* 8 (1985): 118–19.

251. Veatch, *Human Rights: Fact or Fancy?* 116, 121–22, 134–35, 150, 152.

252. Veatch, *Human Rights: Fact or Fancy?* 164–65.

253. Veatch, *Human Rights: Fact or Fancy?* 210.

the telic duties (i.e., to duties deriving from natural law) in a way that would be distinct from their sole moral domain.[254]

Veatch's argumentation seems particularly pertinent in the context of his devastating critique of Finnis's natural-law theory.[255] Given his concerns about the peculiarities of Finnis's approach, it is all the more curious that he speaks only in superlatives when referring to Finnis's essentially and exclusively moral foundation of natural rights. In his review of Finnis's *Natural Law and Natural Rights*, Veatch asks some questions that, at least on first sight, might seem similar to Waldron's.

What do all such ethical considerations regarding natural ends and goods ... have to do with law in the usual sense? ... Is not Finnis's book supposed to be about law in a proper sense, and not about any mere requirements of practical reasonableness as there may be in morals or ethics?[256]

His response, however, lauds those aspects in Finnis's theory where the natural law is conceived in its moral aspect:

Finnis is better at showing how law needs to be grounded in ethics, than he is at showing how the principles of ethics are discoverable right in the very fact of nature.... Finnis does manage to show, and show most successfully, how human law ... can only draw life and sustenance from ethics, and from a regard for the needs of man's very nature.... Law is but the extension of those ethical and moral obligations that are incumbent upon all individuals.... Indeed, it is in these reaches of his book that Finnis would seem to be really at his best, and his performance truly non pareil.[257]

254. For example, see Veatch, *Human Rights: Fact or Fancy?* 168, 172, 177.

255. For example, see Veatch, "Natural Law and the 'Is'—'Ought' Question," 251–65; Veatch, *Human Rights: Fact or Fancy?* 95–104.

256. Henry B. Veatch, review of *Natural Law and Natural Rights*, by John Finnis, *The American Journal of Jurisprudence* 26, no. 1 (1981): 251–52.

257. Veatch, review of *Natural Law and Natural Rights*, 250, 253.

Veatch is arguably one of the few critics of the new classical natural-law theory to systematically address the intersection between the natural law and natural rights. Other Thomistic critics of the theory deal mainly with the moral elements in the structure of the natural-law argument; they explore the broader issues of the connection of this argument to natural rights or positive law only incidentally. For this reason, when assessing their position on the question of juridicity of natural law, one can only investigate a limited subsection of their ideas. These authors do, however, highlight the necessity to expand consideration of the natural law beyond the moral domain to the question of its juridical status, even if they often do not take this insight to its ultimate doctrinal consequences.

Ralph McInerny (1929–2010) develops the connections between the natural moral law and the classical Thomistic concept of *ius* even further than Simon and Veatch. Among contemporary Anglophone scholars rooted in the tradition of Thomistic natural law, McInerny is certainly one of the most sympathetic to Michel Villey's project of recovering the classical doctrine of *ius*.[258]

McInerny is well aware that in the classical Thomistic framework, a discussion of *ius naturale* is not simply reducible to *lex naturalis*,[259] noting that within this framework, right (*ius*) was defined objectively, as those things (*res*) that form part of a relation or proportion in the sphere of justice.[260] The law is not iden-

---

258. In a review of the books by two of Villey's critics, namely, Brian Tierney and Annabel Brett, McInerny states that he retains "a perhaps visceral preference for the Michel Villey approach." See Ralph McInerny, "On Natural Rights and Natural Law," review of *The Idea of Natural Rights: Studies on Natural Rights, Natural Law and Church Law 1150–1625*, by Brian Tierney; *Liberty, Right, and Nature: Individual Rights in Later Scholastic Thought*, by Annabel S. Brett, *Modern Age* 41, no. 2 (1999): 178.

259. Ralph McInerny, "Natural Law and Natural Rights," in *Aquinas on Human Action: A Theory of Practice*, 212–13.

260. McInerny, "Natural Law and Natural Rights," 214.

tical or reducible to right but rather an "expression" of a rational directive "as to what needs to be done."[261] The natural law is conceptualized within this definition of law in general, precisely as a phenomenon distinct from right: "If human [positive] law is to guide human action, it must be governed by the first principles of practical reason.... Natural law provides such first principles."[262]

As the object of justice, on the other hand, right does not "exhaust the field of morality or of law."[263] Thus, responding to the question of "what is the relation between *ius naturale* and *lex naturalis*," McInerny readily affirms that in Aquinas's doctrine, natural law is somehow "an expression of natural right."[264] Under the aspect of its being a rational directive (*ratio*) of natural right, the status of natural law is accommodated within the sphere of juridical justice. Thus, the natural law is not separated from *ius*, and "we can relate *ius naturale* and *lex naturalis* without equating the two."[265]

If there is to be any conjunction of the natural law tradition and natural or human rights, the latter are going to have to be grounded in the same thing as the former.... It is because the human person, any human person, is what it is that we owe one another things in justice.[266]

Because McInerny develops his argument only as a tangential issue within his broader interest in connecting the classical tradition of *ius naturale* with the notion of human rights, it is not fully developed. Still, it is an argument that establishes certain essential

261. McInerny, "Natural Law and Natural Rights," 216.

262. Ralph McInerny, "The Basis and Purpose of Positive Law," in *Lex et Libertas: Freedom and Law According to St. Thomas Aquinas*, ed. Leo J. Elders and Klaus Hedwig (Vatican City: LEV, 1987), 141.

263. McInerny, "Natural Law and Natural Rights," 217.

264. McInerny, "Natural Law and Natural Rights," 216.

265. McInerny, "Natural Law and Natural Rights," 216.

266. McInerny, "Natural Law and Human Rights," 13.

elements of the claim that the juridical domain somehow pertains to natural law in a way that, as McInerny says, clearly does not exhaust the field of morality or of law.

In a similarly tangential fashion, Russell Hittinger's analyses occasionally bring into focus certain aspects of the juridical status of natural law. To be sure, his line of argumentation regarding this particular issue is not systematic, but his insights bear an interesting resemblance to the realistic juridical conception of law and rights to be presented in the subsequent chapters.

Hittinger observes that whereas contemporary philosophers of law ordinarily engage with the question of whether and how "positive law is to be placed in the order of morals," the premodern juridical tradition was more concerned with another perspective of this question, namely, "How are moral norms to be placed in the genus of law?"[267] Whereas contemporary natural lawyers formulate the law-morality problem in terms of the "morality of law," their premodern colleagues operated within the framework of the "legality of morals."[268] This premodern framework is no doubt highly congenial to the focus of my present analysis since it approaches the law-morality intersection at the level of inquiry into the juridical status of morality (i.e., of the natural law), but *legality* is not identical to *juridicity*. To inquire into the legal status of the natural moral law does not necessarily mean to observe the natural law according to its juridical status. Nonetheless, I think that Hittinger's shift of focus to the "legality of morals" already

267. Hittinger, "Natural Law as 'Law,'" 62.

268. Hittinger, "Natural Law as 'Law,'" 62. "Generally, the thinkers of late antiquity and the Middle Ages took it for granted that jurisprudence falls under the genus of morals. They thus set out to understand how moral reasoning is set within a cosmological order that has legal properties. Where jurisprudence, however, is by default a positivist account of the powers of the state it becomes all the more necessary to focus narrowly on how to render state law permeable to moral premises" (Hittinger, introduction to *The First Grace*, xvii).

implies the core viewpoint of this book, which is to consider jointly two discrete perspectives related to the juridical status of natural law: the goodness of law *and* the juridicity of the good.

We have already seen how both Finnis and Veatch locate natural law within the sphere of prejuridical legality. Hittinger, in contrast, sometimes seems to build his argument in terms of the natural moral law, which he then envisions as foundational to the juridical domain of rights and positive law.

For ordinary legal purposes, it would seem sufficient to recognize that positive laws ... make moral norms effective, or more fully effective, in the political community by way of determination (*determinatio*). These *determinationes* simply sanction at (positive) law what is morally binding by nature.... It is quite enough to understand how "law" in its ordinary sense, which is positive law, makes (moral) norms of practical reason determinate in the political community.[269]

Elsewhere in his works, however, Hittinger does, in fact, imply that certain elements of juridicity might be predicated on morality. The immediate doctrinal context for his inquiry into the juridical status of natural law is the very framework of the hierarchy of various orders of legality, wherein the natural law is superior to positive law. In a second moment, he proceeds to develop his argument on the fully legal character of natural law by appealing to its various concrete manifestations in the broader order of justice.

Contrary to Finnis's argument that natural law is only "analogically law,"[270] Hittinger claims that, for Aquinas, the "natural law is *real* law, because basic moral norms are actually made-to-

---

269. Hittinger, "Natural Law as 'Law,'" 51.

270. Finnis considers natural law to be "only analogically law," to the degree where he admits having "avoided the term" *natural law* in the chapter dedicated to the treatment of the concept of law in his *Natural Law and Natural Rights*. See Finnis, *Natural Law and Natural Rights*, 280.

be-known (promulgated) to the rational creature."[271] In Aquinas's doctrine, the legal dimension of morality (i.e., natural law) is crowned as the "higher order of law," in comparison to the order of positive human law.[272] In contemporary juridical mentality, marked by a profound disagreement on the necessary points of connection between law and morality, positive law has become the dominant analogue of the term *law*. Given the fact that Aquinas approaches legality from the standpoint of the *ratio* that moves all things to their due end,[273] there is no doubt that in his view, the primary analogue in the order of being is the eternal law, in which the legality of natural law essentially participates.[274] Since in Aquinas's view natural law is supreme over and above positive law in the order of legality, positive law bears the qualification of legality only insofar as it is a determination of the natural law, or a conclusion thereof.[275] Stephen L. Brock has made this point of Aquinas's doctrine even more obvious: "natural law displays a fuller share in the nature of law than does human positive law, not only insofar as it is seen as proceeding from the supreme law, but also in virtue of the very fact that it wins the mind's assent without need of any advertence to its authoritative institution."[276]

271. Hittinger, "Natural Law as 'Law,'" 52. Emphasis added.

272. See Hittinger, "Natural Law as 'Law,'" 294, n. 58.

273. See *ST* I-II, q. 93, a. 1.

274. See Hittinger, "Natural Law as 'Law,'" 60. Hittinger claims that, in Aquinas's thought, natural law is never defined in terms of what is first in the human mind or first in nature. In what is largely understood as the foundational textual locus for Aquinas's doctrine on natural law—*ST* I-II, q. 94, a. 2—Thomas truly does focus on what is first in the mind and first in nature. According to Hittinger, however, it is a mistake to start from this textual locus when seeking Aquinas's definition of natural law, "what it is" and "what makes it law." Aquinas provided the necessary definitions in questions 91 and 93 of this part of his *Summa Theologica*, in which he always defines natural law and identifies the source of its legality in reference to the eternal law. See Hittinger, "Natural Law and Catholic Moral Theology," 8–12.

275. See *ST* I-II, q. 95, a. 2.

276. See Brock, *The Light That Binds*, 104–5.

Hittinger's emphasis on the hierarchy of the orders of law, of course, does not yet complete the argument for a specifically juridical domain predicable of natural moral law. Certain textual references to the place of natural law within this hierarchy may imply, however, that he ultimately does recognize the need to assign the status of juridicity to some aspects of natural law. In his writings, Hittinger sometimes refers to what he calls the *natural norms of justice.*[277]

Given the conviction that there exist *rules* and *measures of justice* antecedent to the positive law of the state, it would seem to follow that whoever makes law is most immediately responsible for ensuring that statutes and policies are in harmony with the natural law.[278]

By natural norms of justice, Hittinger clearly does not intend what he elsewhere calls "principles of procedural fairness,"[279] or what Hart would in turn call "principles of natural justice." The natural norms of justice denote the precepts of natural moral law understood as the "basic principles of the order of justice."[280] Is the concept of justice for Hittinger, then, somehow foundational for determining the juridical status of natural moral law? His argument on the subject is not fully developed, since this topic has really never been the focus of his works, but he clearly makes a distinction between the natural moral law that underlies positive law, on the one hand, and, on the other, the obligations of justice—natural norms of justice—that arise from the structural points where natural moral law and positive law "overlap."[281] He

277. See, for example, Hittinger, "Natural Law and Catholic Moral Theology," 8; Hittinger, "Natural Law as 'Law,'" 51; and Russell Hittinger, "Natural Law in the Positive Laws," in *The First* Grace, 76–77.

278. Russell Hittinger, "Natural Rights, Under-Specified Rights and Bills of Rights," in *The First Grace*, 119. Emphasis added.

279. Hittinger, "Natural Law in the Positive Laws," 70–71.

280. Hittinger, "Natural Law as 'Law,'" 61.

281. See Hittinger, "Natural Law in the Positive Laws," 73.

seems only a step away from connecting this argument with his observation that natural moral law falls under the domain of *ius* arising from "the nature of the thing."[282] In this regard, Hittinger, like Simon, Finnis, and McInerny, is aware of the historical shifts in the meaning of right: "the word *ius* was first used to denote the 'just thing itself.'"[283] However, he clearly does not consider the locus of natural law in the order of justice and juridicity to amount to quandaries involving complex but ultimately inessential or purely historical aspects of Thomistic exegesis.

In a congenial cluster of arguments, Hittinger elsewhere affirms that because natural law is a "real law," it is thus an order "by which men are moved to common good,"[284] since being ordered to the common good is one of the elements of Aquinas's definition of law. Now, the orderedness of natural law to the common good can be realized according to two modes of justice, which Hittinger refers to as justice *as right* and justice *as right order*. The domain of justice as right, or juridical justice, certainly has its own structural place within the legal and social order of attaining the common good. Justice as right implies the meaning of justice from a different point of view than that of justice understood as a predominantly moral social virtue (or, as Hittinger calls it, justice as right order). Hence, the juridical domain (justice as right), even when predicated on the legality of natural law, does not exhaust the whole content of the common good.[285] I will return to

---

282. See Hittinger, "Natural Rights, Under-Specified Rights and Bills of Rights," 115–16. Hittinger cites Javier Hervada's book *Critical Introduction to Natural Right* as an inspiration for this understanding of the concept of justice (303, n. 1).

283. See Hittinger, "Natural Law in the Positive Laws," 63.

284. Hittinger, "Natural Law and Catholic Moral Theology," 11.

285. See Russell Hittinger, "The Coherence of the Four Basic Principles of Catholic Social Doctrine: An Interpretation," in *Pursuing the Common Good: How Solidarity and Subsidiarity Work Together*, ed. Margaret S. Archer and Pierpaolo Donati (Vatican City: Pontificia Academia Scientiarum Socialium, 2008), 114–16; Russell Hittinger, "*Quinquagesimo Ante*: Reflections on *Pacem in Terris* Fifty Years Later," in *The Global Quest for*

this important argument of Hittinger's in subsequent chapters. For the present purposes, suffice it to say that from the point of view of at least one of these two modes of justice, natural law conceptually belongs to a juridical dimension of *ius*.

One can only regret that Hittinger has been unable to dedicate more time to connecting these elements within a coherent and fully developed line of argumentation, but even his tangential views on the juridical status of natural law are sufficient to conclude that he is aware of a specific domain of the natural law, or as he says, natural norms of justice. He recognizes that this domain is superior to positive law in the order of legality, but at the same time, it is also somehow discretely connected through the concept of justice to the specifically juridical domain. As the subsequent chapters will make clear, Hittinger is, as with Simon and McInerny, only a step away from positing and developing a juridical domain within the structural overlap between the natural moral law and the origin of the specifically juridical due.

Stephen L. Brock comes even closer to establishing the natural law as the immediate origin of the juridical due in the Thomistic perspective of the virtue of justice. Brock builds his argument from the claim that the notion of natural right (*ius naturale*) is not the same as (or synonymous with) the concept of natural law (*lex naturalis*). According to Aquinas,[286] *ius* primarily denotes the things that are "right or well adjusted, things that are just," whereas law "properly speaking, is a certain conception (*ratio*) of what is right or just,"[287] or an "intelligible conception that es-

---

Tranquillitas Ordinis: Pacem In Terris, Fifty Years Later, ed. Mary A. Glendon, Russell Hittinger, and Marcelo S. Sorondo (Vatican City: Pontificia Academia Scientiarum Socialium, 2013), 48–49.

286. Brock here refers to *ST* II-II, q. 57, a. 1, ad 1 and 2. I will return to this passage from Aquinas's *Summa Theologica* in subsequent chapters.

287. See Brock, *The Light That Binds*, 85.

tablishes or measures or determines *ius*—a kind of formulation of it, a *ratio iuris*."[288] When this distinction is applied to the connection between natural law and natural rights, Brock claims that all the moral precepts of the natural law "pertain absolutely to *ius naturale*, natural *right*," and, as such, they "have juridical force independently of any merely positive institution."[289] He argues that the "sphere of the things that belong absolutely to natural law" are reconstituted as natural rights—namely, as things that are naturally right—when viewed from the specific perspective of the duties of the virtue of justice: "justice is the only virtue whose acts directly affect things belonging to others."[290] Hittinger's and Brock's arguments are so congenial to my presentation of the juridical realm of natural law that the subsequent chapters may be said to only continue their lines of analysis.

The ITC Document: "A New Look" at the Juridical Status of Natural Law?

The International Theological Commission (hereafter ITC), an advisory commission instituted in connection with the Holy See's Congregation for the Doctrine of the Faith, published a document in 2009 entitled *In Search of a Universal Ethic: A New Look at the Natural Law*. The document, drafted at the special request of Pope John Paul II and, subsequently, Pope Benedict XVI, is a modern-day Catholic reflection on the tradition and contemporary status of natural-law doctrine.[291]

288. See Brock, *The Light That Binds*, 88.
289. See Brock, *The Light That Binds*, 222.
290. See Brock, *The Light That Binds*, 222–25.
291. For an overview of the structure and drafting history of the document, see John Berkman and William C. Mattison III, introduction to *Searching for a Universal Ethic:*

Although the ITC document's initial question—"Are there objective moral values which can unite human beings and bring them peace and happiness?"[292]—may certainly imply many topics and contexts, one angle it adds is particularly pertinent for this present study: "How can [these objective moral values] be put into action in the lives of people and of communities?"[293] The ITC document provides an answer to this question in its fourth chapter, "Natural Law and the Human City" (§§ 83–100). The same chapter also contains doctrinal aspects reflective of the ITC's understanding of various issues at the law-morality intersection. Although the document offers a synthesis of natural-law tradition, including its connection to the juridical domain, it contains certain ideas that represent genuine developments of that tradition, the main one of which regards the juridical status of natural law, as such: "[There is an] essential distinction between natural law [*lex naturalis*] and the norm of natural justice [*ius naturale*]."[294]

Multidisciplinary, Ecumenical, and Interfaith Responses to the Catholic Natural Law Tradition, ed. John Berkman and William C. Mattison III (Grand Rapids, Mich.: William B. Eerdmans Publishing Company, 2014), 1–23. The book contains the official English translation of the document, which was made accessible in the year 2012 on the International Theological Commission's section within the official website of the Roman Curia and the Holy See, http://www.vatican.va/roman_curia/congregations/cfaith/cti_documents/rc_con_cfaith_doc_20090520_legge-naturale_en.html.

292. ITC, *In Search of a Universal Ethic*, 1.

293. ITC, *In Search of a Universal Ethic*, 1.

294. ITC, *In Search of a Universal Ethic*, 83. Throughout this section, the official English translation of the document translates *ius naturale* as *norm(s) of natural justice*. Joseph Bolin's unofficial English translation of the document opts for the use of the term *natural right*. In my opinion, both linguistic options are satisfactory, as they succeed in conveying the essential meaning of the Latin *ius naturale*. The terminology of the unofficial translation is perhaps more faithful to the ordinary understanding of the premodern concept of *ius*, translatable as *right*, and distinct from a reduction to the norm, *lex*. However, I prefer the official translation of the document, norms of natural justice, believing it more adequate in view of its immediate context in the document. The concept of *ius naturale* is expounded in the document from the perspective of a domain inherent in the concept of natural law. With that said, the translation of *ius naturale*

The term *norm of natural justice*, employed throughout the document to translate the Latin term *ius naturale*,[295] largely overlaps with Hittinger's natural norm of justice. True, it is also similar to Hart's principles of natural justice, but unlike Hart's or Fuller's procedural principles, the norms of natural justice denote the normative orderedness to certain substantive moral values.[296] More precisely, since the document refers to them under the rubric of *ius naturale*, they are natural precepts that possess a specific juridical status. When explaining the origins of the norms of natural justice under the heading "From Natural Law to the Norm of Natural Justice," *In Search of a Universal Ethic* affirms that "Natural law (*lex naturalis*) becomes the norm of natural justice (*ius naturale*) when one considers the *relations of justice among human beings*."[297] The document is persistent in delineating the explicit distinction between the moral domain of natural law and the juridical domain of the norms of natural justice: "We pass from the anthropological category of the natural law to the juridical and political category of the organization of the city."[298]

The norm of natural justice ... articulates the judgment of practical reason in its estimation of what is just. Such norm, as the juridical

---

as norms of natural justice is highly congenial to the main ideas of this book, since it terminologically highlights a juridical domain that is predicable of natural law. For the unofficial English translation, by Joseph Bolin, see http://www.pathsoflove.com/universal-ethics-natural-law.html.

295. *In Search of a Universal Ethic* does not consider the concept of natural right to be a synonym of norms of natural justice, as is evidenced by the textual occurrences of both terms throughout the document. Instead, the ITC advocates the claim that the structural connection between natural rights and natural law may legitimately be envisioned as essentially normative and inherently juridical.

296. The document mentions substantive moral values like human life, the integrity of one's person, religious liberty, freedom of thought, family, and participation in the life of the community. See ITC, *In Search of a Universal Ethic*, 92.

297. ITC, *In Search of a Universal Ethic*, 88. Emphasis added.

298. ITC, *In Search of a Universal Ethic*, 88.

expression of the natural law in the political order, thus appears as the measure of the just relation among the members of the community.[299]

The document stands firm on its position that the norms of natural justice are anchored in the anthropological orderedness of the natural moral law. As Tracey Rowland notes, "*In Search of a Universal Ethic* describes natural law as the anthropological category to which the natural right doctrine corresponds as a juridical … category."[300] At the same time, *ius naturale* is clearly delineated as belonging to the juridical domain, given its specific connection with justice.[301]

The norm of natural justice is the inherent standard of the right interaction among members of society. It is the rule and immanent measure of interpersonal and social human relations.[302]

[Right][303] is not arbitrary: the requirements of justice, which

299. ITC, *In Search of a Universal Ethic*, 90.

300. Tracey Rowland, "The Role of Natural Law and Natural Right in the Search for a Universal Ethic," in Berkman and Mattison, *Searching for a Universal Ethic*, 159.

301. Perhaps this decisive connection, deeply rooted in the Thomistic tradition, between *ius naturale* and justice partially influenced the translation of the Latin term as norm of natural justice. Since the official English translation was published in 2012, three years after the publication of the document itself, and after the appearance of the unofficial English translation (which contains the "natural right" terminological option), this official translation of *ius naturale* seems to be a deliberate and pondered decision.

302. ITC, *In Search of a Universal Ethic*, 88.

303. Here, the official English translation renders the original Italian and French (respectively, *diritto* and *droit*) as "this norm," in clear reference to the preceding discourse about the norms of natural justice. However, it seems that the document itself does not refer here to the specific juridical domain of the norms of natural justice, but more generally to *right* (*ius, diritto, droit*). Therefore, I offer a revision of the translation of this part of the text, in accordance both with the original Italian and French, and with the unofficial English translation, translating *diritto* and *droit* simply as *right*. This is far more consistent with the text itself, which strives to explain that right in general is shaped by the "requirements of justice which flow from the natural law" and "are prior to the formulation and enactment of the right." Right (*ius, diritto, droit*) is the juridical domain, distinct, though not separated from law: in the context of natural law, the right is shaped and formulated by the requirements of justice arising from the natural law. One can find the doctrinal equivalent to the norm of natural justice elsewhere in this passage, more precisely when the text mentions the "requirements of justice which flow from the natural law."

flow from natural law, are prior to the formulation and enactment of [right]. Nor is politics arbitrary: the norms of justice[304] do not result only from a contract established among men but arise from the very nature of the human being.[305]

The document does not explain why it considers the concept of justice as the decisive factor for the constitution of the juridical aspect inherent in natural moral law, but it does make continual reference to the fact that justice introduces a social element into the domain of morality, which is, in turn, an essential property of both social morality[306] and juridicity. When the social nature of the orderedness toward the common good is viewed according to relations of justice, the legal structure of this order (i.e., natural law) is constituted as the norm of natural justice: "The passage from person to society sheds light on the essential distinction between natural law and the norm of natural justice."[307]

Both subjective rights and positive law, to the extent that they denote certain things that are just (*res iusta*) according to human nature, are secondary juridical phenomena that emerge from the

304. Here the Italian and French original texts both mention, respectively, *le norme della giustizia* and *les normes de la justice*. The English translation of *ius naturale* as norm of natural justice thus actually corresponds to the intentions of the drafters of the document, who otherwise translate *ius naturale* with the habitual Italian or French expressions *diritto naturale* and *droit naturel*, while obviously understanding this term to denote, from the perspective of the connection with natural law, the norms of justice, as well.

305. ITC, *In Search of a Universal Ethic*, 89.

306. See, for example, the document's discussion of the concept of common good in ITC, *In Search of a Universal Ethic*, 85.

307. ITC, *In Search of a Universal Ethic*, 83. In the context of another argument, I have already quoted the document's statement that "natural law (*lex naturalis*) becomes the norm of natural justice (*ius naturale*) when one considers the relations of justice among human beings" (88). Compared to the overall concise, rather than scientifically exhaustive, character of the ITC documents, the text of *In Search of a Universal Ethics: A New Look at the Natural Law* is very dense, and each statement is potentially pertinent to multiple arguments within the same subject matter. This particular statement is thus, among others, very significant for the understanding of the role of the concept of justice in the origin of the juridical domain of natural law.

norms of natural justice. Through this aspect of natural law, these phenomena are also mediately rooted in the moral domain.

The document explicitly highlights the foundational role of the norms of natural justice for the concrete content of positive law.[308] Appealing to the tradition of natural law, the ITC affirms that "positive human law" is "just," is "truly a law," and is "binding in conscience" only to the extent that it is derived from the norms of natural justice.[309] The document does not clarify the meaning of (and the distinction between) these three properties of positive law in accordance with the norms of natural justice. Nonetheless, the claim that positive law is juridically binding on account of its participation in the juridicity of the norms of natural justice, is gathered from Aquinas's texts, which the document quotes as the direct source for this argument.[310]

Similarly, the ITC document affirms that "the norms of natural justice are expressed in a particular way in the subjective rights of the human person."[311]

The rights of the human person emerge therefore from this order of justice that must reign in relations among human beings. To acknowledge these natural rights of man means to acknowledge the objective order of human relations based on natural law.[312]

---

308. "The norm of natural justice anchors human law in the natural law" (ITC, *In Search of a Universal Ethic*, 89).

309. ITC, *In Search of a Universal Ethic*, 91.

310. In the text (*ST* I-II, q. 95, a. 2) invoked by the ITC document (*In Search of a Universal Ethic*, 91), Aquinas claims that "the force of law depends on the extent of its justice." Then he goes on to say that "in human affairs a thing is said to be just, from being right [*rectum*] according to the rule of right reason [and] the first rule of reason is the law of nature." Furthermore, regarding the question of whether human law binds in conscience, Aquinas responds that adequate "laws framed by men" can be positively described according to three *distinct* rubrics: *iustae sunt, obligant in foro conscientiae*, and *sunt leges legales* (*ST* I-II, q. 96, a. 4). A more elaborate treatment of Aquinas's arguments on just and unjust laws will be provided later in the book.

311. ITC, *In Search of a Universal Ethic*, 92.

312. ITC, *In Search of a Universal Ethic*, 92.

Considering that *In Search of a Universal Ethic* reintegrates the Thomistic notion of right as the object of justice, it is strange to find that the document elsewhere refers to natural rights as *subjective rights*. On the other hand, the ITC does not seem to intend a subjectivistic meaning of natural rights as essentially powers and faculties of the individual (i.e., subjective claim-rights). The paragraph dedicated to subjective rights begins with the argument that "the norms of natural justice are thus measures of human relationships [which] express what is naturally just, prior to any legal formulation." It continues by affirming that "these rights do not have their source in the fluctuating desires of individuals, but rather in the very structure of human beings and their humanizing relationships."[313] The ITC document thereby gives certain precedence to a more objective reading of the notion of rights as, fundamentally, "what is naturally just," although it does not discard a more subjectivist meaning of rights as "claims."[314]

Overall, the concise nature of *In Search of a Universal Ethic* makes it unsuitable for extensive academic discussion of the important topics to which it makes reference, some of which call for

313. ITC, *In Search of a Universal Ethic*, 92.

314. ITC, *In Search of a Universal Ethic*, 92. Roland Minnerath, a professor of social ethics and human rights and member of the ITC document's drafting team, ordinarily employs the term *subjective rights* in reference to the modern and contemporary notion of rights or human rights. Although he frequently employs the term in his writings, Minnerath expresses certain doctrinal reservations in its regard, given the potential individualistic and relativistic interpretations of the term. See Roland Minnerath, "La doctrine sociale de l'Eglise et les droits subjectifs de la personne," in *Catholic Social Doctrine and Human Rights*, ed. Roland Minnerath, Ombretta Fumagalli Carulli, and Vittorio Possenti (Vatican City: Pontificia Academia Scientiarum Socialium, 2010), 49–59. The similarities between Minnerath's texts and *In Search of a Universal Ethic* go beyond this. Minnerath also claims that the right (*droit*) is the "expression of an order of relations inscribed in human beings themselves" and "therefore, the measure of that which objectively appears as just." In addition, he affirms that "natural right [i.e., *droit naturel*] is that part of natural law which concerns the relations of justice between persons." As such, he concludes, the right is "a measure inherent" to the very nature of the relation of justice. See Roland Minnerath, *Pour une éthique sociale universelle: La proposition catholique* (Paris: Les Éditions du Cerf, 2004), 21, 24–25, 39.

a more extensive treatment, among them the insufficient distinction between the juridical domain (*ius*) and the juridical status of natural law implied in the concept of *ius naturale*.[315] In addition, the essential features of juridicity are insufficiently determined,[316] the conception of subjective rights proves ultimately underdeveloped, and the relation of subjective rights to the premodern notion of right could have been more accurately formulated. Nonetheless, in its few relatively short sections (n. 83, 88–92), the document does a remarkable job of restating the tradition and setting the course for future, more detailed academic efforts.

In a commentary on this section of the ITC document, Jean Porter supports the thesis that the "premodern natural-law tradition" commended in the document does not, in fact, advocate what was once the common understanding of so-called "natural-law jurisprudence."[317] Such jurisprudence, in Porter's assessment, usually adopts a position according to which natural law is conceived of as a sort of precise, pre-developed and ready-made "code," which then serves as an immediate source for positive law, or is, at least, readily accessible for the evaluation of enacted laws. As such, natural law would, in fact, have direct legal force, regardless of the institutionalized procedures associated with what is usually referred to as the autonomy of positive law.[318] Porter is convinced that, regardless of their defunct visions of the substantive

315. The specific domain of *ius* in the treatment of the concept of *ius naturale* is addressed predominantly through norm-based concepts. *Ius naturale* (norms of natural justice) is thus almost exclusively described as a certain standard (*misura* in Italian, or *mesure* in the French original) or rule (*regola* in Italian or *règle* in French), and ultimately as the "requirements of justice which flow from the natural law." See ITC, *In Search of a Universal Ethic*, 88–89.

316. It seems that the document envisions the juridical domain as arising solely from the transition from the focus on the individual to the focus on society.

317. Jean Porter, "Natural Law, Legal Authority, and the Independence of Law: New Prospects for a Jurisprudence of the Natural Law," in Berkman and Mattison, *Searching for a Universal Ethic*, 150–51, 154–55.

318. Porter, "Natural Law, Legal Authority, and the Independence of Law," 148–51.

content of natural law, Hart, Fuller, Raz, and Dworkin, among others, have nonetheless highlighted the importance of certain systemic and procedural features of the law-morality intersection. To disregard those features and directly "legislate morality," would mean "to bring together law and morality too closely."[319] She advocates the thesis that these systemic and procedural features of positive law should be doctrinally compatible with the traditional natural-law approach.[320] Her claim is pertinent to this present research, since it cautions of the need to adequately set the bar of the points of intersection between law and morality neither too high nor too low.

Leaving aside the important issue of how natural-law theory addresses the purely systemic and procedural features of the concept of law, I believe that an equally important question of natural-law jurisprudence is left unresolved at the end of this chapter. I am convinced that the answer to this unresolved question has always been an inbuilt feature of the realistic juridical conception of law and rights, throughout its historical manifestations. This answer has been rediscovered in the work of some twentieth-century legal historians and philosophers, but instead of working out their theories from the viewpoint of the degree to which moral evaluations are necessary for the identification and validity of law, their lines of research brought them to adopt an alternative approach and ask the following question: under what conditions may the juridical domain and juridical phenomena be predicated on the natural-law conception of the good?

319. Porter, "Natural Law, Legal Authority, and the Independence of Law," 149.
320. Porter, "Natural Law, Legal Authority, and the Independence of Law," 151–55.

2

The Realistic Conception of Right and Juridicity

This chapter seeks to demonstrate that what I will henceforth call a *realistic conception of right and juridicity* provides the best philosophical context for a clear theoretical grasp of the juridical domain of natural law. Until now, I have referred to this approach as a realistic juridical conception of law and rights, but both names are correct, since the tradition of juridical realism presented in this chapter addresses and elaborates the concepts of law and rights, both natural and positive. The analysis in this chapter is developed, however, on an even more general level than the one which addresses the nature of law and the concept of rights. As we will see, the realistic conception of right and juridicity explores the fundamental nature or constitution of the juridical phenomenon—what constitutes that which is juridically right—especially as distinct but not necessarily separate from that which is morally right. As the previous chapter demonstrates, moral principles can be understood to have a prepositive legal character or significance, but that does not fully explain whether and how they also belong to the juridical domain.

So, at this point, there is a series of questions that should be addressed regarding the basic constitution of the juridical domain. Is the conception of the juridical domain necessarily confined only to the realm of positive law and the legal rights derived thereof? Are prepositive natural rights really conceivable only as a moral phenomenon? Finally, does natural law possess only a moral status? An affirmative answer to all of these questions would amount to, strangely enough, a positivistic or norm-based position at the semantic level of the notion of juridicity (i.e., at the level of the meaning of the classical term *ius*) despite the fact that this position advocates the necessity of a natural-law framework for the constitution of the law-morality intersection.

Before presenting the central claims of the realistic conception of right and juridicity from the standpoints of their most prominent advocates in the last half-century—Michel Villey and Javier Hervada—it may be useful first to situate this juridical-philosophical account within the broader context of Thomistic realism. Despite the fact that the tradition of juridical realism cannot be reduced only to Thomas Aquinas's ideas, I am convinced that his relevant arguments represent the diachronic epicenter of the tradition. I will then establish the criteria for preventing a possible terminological confusion between Villey's and Hervada's realistic position on right and juridicity and American and Scandinavian *legal realisms*. The philosophical context of *Thomistic realism* is a doctrinal home to a variety of jurisprudential theories, some of which partly differ from those of Villey and Hervada. I will, therefore, present a schema for an internal stratification of juridical perspectives relatable to Thomistic realism. Then, having provided the terminological and doctrinal contours of juridical realism, I will argue that the term realistic conception of right and juridicity is the adequate label for the jurisprudential tradition that begins with Aristotle and runs from the Roman jurists and Thomas Aquinas to Villey and Hervada.

In the second part of this chapter, I will focus on Villey's and Hervada's essential claims in favor of a realistic conception of that which is juridically right. Since both authors root their understanding of the essence of juridical right in a constant appeal to what they call the classical or premodern texts, I will present their claims through their own rereading of Aristotle, the jurists of the Roman legal tradition, and Thomas Aquinas.

The third part of this chapter is dedicated to Hervada's and Villey's respective accounts of a realistic conception of juridicity. In their theory, juridicity denotes the sum of those properties that, when verified in relation to a given thing or good (particularly natural human goods but also things apportioned to determinate persons through positive law), contextualize this thing or good in the juridical domain precisely as rights. These properties will prove to be particularly important for a clear distinction between the juridical and moral domains.

Villey's and Hervada's Realistic Conception of Right and Juridicity

Juridical Realism as a Subcategory of Thomistic Realism

The best way to understand Villey's and Hervada's juridical realism is to approach their arguments for what they essentially are: a faithful rereading of classical premodern juridical-philosophical texts rather than an autonomous jurisprudential account. Both authors seek to make their accounts dependent on the principles of the realistic epistemological approach to reality in general. In order to fully understand the foundational elements of their juridical realism, therefore, it is necessary to trace their arguments back to metaphysical realism, paradigmatically outlined in the thought of Thomas Aquinas.

Given that within the context of juridical realism the realistic epistemological principles are applied to a more practical setting, I will present the basic characteristics of Thomistic realism only to the degree that they are pertinent for an adequate understanding of a realistic approach to the essence of the right. As an epistemological account, Thomistic realism is not exclusively relatable to a particular philosophical school. Rather, it is a "natural position of ordinary knowledge"[1] available to various schools of thought and, thus, to various jurisprudential traditions.

In the words of Stephen L. Brock, the basic postulate of Thomistic realism is that it "simply takes for granted that we can grasp real things, as they really are, and that we can thereby measure against them our own thoughts of them."[2] According to this epistemological "method," as Étienne Gilson calls it, the "real is posited as distinct from thought."[3] In contrast to the modern tendency to understand cognition as "bearing primarily on representations of things," which are "inherent in the cognitive power,"[4] Thomistic realism maintains that "our knowledge truly attains reality ... as it really is because our intellect grasps what is intelligible in reality."[5]

1. Juan J. Sanguineti, *Logic and Gnoseology*, trans. Myroslaw A. Cizdyn (Bangalore: Theological Publications in India, 1988), 172.

2. Stephen L. Brock, *The Philosophy of Saint Thomas Aquinas: A Sketch* (Eugene, Ore.: Cascade Books, 2015), 89.

3. Étienne Gilson, *Methodical Realism: A Handbook for Beginning Realists*, trans. Philip Trower (San Francisco: Ignatius Press, 2011), 21.

4. Brock, *The Philosophy of Saint Thomas Aquinas*, 90.

5. Étienne Gilson, *Thomist Realism and the Critique of Knowledge*, trans. Mark Wauck (San Francisco: Ignatius Press, 2012), 203.

The form is only that by which the thing from which it originates is known. The heart of the matter, I think, is the very notion that external things themselves can be the proper determinations of our cognition of them. The modern tendency is to suppose that they cannot. In the Thirteenth century it was not so hard to think that they can, because there was current a notion of something enabling them to do so, something in them that is intrinsically self-communicative: the very notion of the form. With the overthrow of Scholasticism, that notion fell into virtual oblivion. Today … hardly anyone conceives of cognition as a kind of union with things.[6]

Epistemological realism owes its name to what it envisions as the foundational cognitive element—reality itself, or *res*. Cognition starts with the "immediate experience of the thing-in-itself."[7] The being, which is this thing-in-itself, transcends the thought, since the real thing is not the conceptualized or thought-out thing. Reality, *res*, is thus ontologically independent from the thought of the subject.[8]

Thomistic realism is radically distinct from both materialistic realism and idealistic antirealism. Whereas materialistic realism is opposed in principle to the horizons of the transcendence of the spirit, idealistic antirealism holds that human thought, or thought itself, is the sole source of cognition.[9]

Hence, Thomistic realism denotes the method inherent in the "entire structure of knowledge of the Thomistic sort, from the lowest sciences right up to metaphysics."[10] In light of this claim,

---

6. Gilson, *Thomist Realism*, 203.

7. Gilson, *Methodical Realism*, 88, 94–95. "[The realist] uses his power of reflection, but keeping it within the limits of a reality given from without. Therefore, the starting point of his reflections has to be being, which in effect is for us the beginning of knowledge: *res sunt*" [98].

8. See Sanguineti, *Logic and Gnoseology*, 15, 172.

9. See Sanguineti, *Logic and Gnoseology*, 16.

10. Étienne Gilson, *Thomism: The Philosophy of Thomas Aquinas*, trans. Lawrence K. Shook and Armand Maurer (Toronto: Pontifical Institute of Medieval Studies, 2002), 271.

Thomistic juridical realism represents a subcategory of Aquinas's realism that has as its immediate object the phenomena of the juridical domain, starting from the essence of *ius*. Juridical realism thus necessarily claims that the specific reality (*res*) that is the object of the juridical science is also fundamentally attainable within a grasp of what is intelligible in reality. In juridical realism, as we will see in greater detail later in this chapter, the essence of the juridical domain, right itself, is not a thought, a mental construct, or a concept. Instead, the very *res*—the thing-in-itself in its multiple manifestations—is at the center of that which is juridically right. The juridical domain is therefore necessarily determined by the specific characteristics of the thing-in-itself. Given that what is juridically right cannot be conceived of in abstraction from the givenness of the thing in reality, the *res* brings its own ontological identity to the juridical domain.

The Distinction from the American and Scandinavian Legal Realisms

The reference to realism may appear somewhat confusing to a reader well-versed in legal philosophy, as the first half of the twentieth century saw the emergence of two trends in legal philosophy that subscribed to the theoretical position labeled as legal realism, namely, the Scandinavian and the American. I will limit the presentation of these trends' respective basic arguments to the extent necessary to clarify that these two legal realisms have almost nothing in common with the juridical realism of Villey and Hervada.

The Scandinavian realists, such as Axel Hägerström and Alf Ross, seek to "locate a legal system of norms" or legal "oughts" in a world that is so "naturalistically conceived by empirical sciences" as to be really "composed of nothing other than physical, chemical and biological facts."[11] In the words of Brian Leiter, they "wanted to find a way of understanding legal norms that was compatible with a semantic, metaphysical, and epistemological picture of the world in which there were no objectively existing moral values or norms."[12]

In the absence of objective normative patterns for moral values to order human conduct,[13] the Scandinavian realists' project of explaining the phenomenon of juridical obligation remains confined to a translation of positive law and judicial provisions in terms of the noncognitive attitudes (i.e., feelings or psychological states) of persons who accept these norms. The emotional or psychological conditions that generate the duty to obey the law have, for example, a following form: "I, the legislator or judge, feel very strongly that 'x' should perform the pattern of conduct 'y' and that this is the pattern of justice in such-and-such situation, therefore it is obligatory."[14]

American legal realism, represented in authors such as, for example, Jerome Frank, Karl Llewelyn, and Max Radin, has a somewhat different doctrinal focus. It is concentrated exclusively on the judicial application[15] of legal rules. Given that this

11. Brian Leiter, "Legal Realisms, Old and New," *Valparaiso University Law Review* 47, no. 4 (2013): 951–52.

12. Leiter, "Legal Realisms, Old and New," 952.

13. "[Scandinavian legal realists] shared the view that it is vital to destroy the distorting influences of metaphysics upon scientific thinking in general and legal thinking in particular in order to pave the way for the scientific understanding of the importance of law and legal science for the life of human beings within a state." See Jes Bjarup, "The Philosophy of Scandinavian Legal Realism," *Ratio Juris* 18, no. 1 (2005): 1.

14. Leiter, "Legal Realisms, Old and New," 952.

15. "The center of gravity of legal developments lies not in legislation, nor in juristic science, nor in society, but in the judicial decision itself." See J. B. Crozier, "Legal Realism and a Science of Law," *The American Journal of Jurisprudence* 29, no. 1 (1984): 159. Crozier has recognized this sentence, originally found in the texts of Eugen Ehrlich, as containing a synthesis of the basic thesis of American legal realism. See Eugen Ehrlich, foreword to *Fundamental Principles of the Sociology of Law*, trans. Walter L. Moll (New Brunswick, N.J.: Transaction Publishers, 2002), lix.

branch of legal philosophy has not yielded any coherent school of thought,[16] there are many different interpretations of its central features.

For the limited purpose of this analysis, it is sufficient to present two accounts of the central thesis of American legal realism. According to Ronald Dworkin, American realists argued that, in opposition to "the orthodox doctrine that judges merely apply existing rules," judges "actually decide cases according to their own political or moral tastes, and then choose an appropriate legal rule as a rationalization."[17] Brian Leiter similarly holds that the "core claim of realism is that judges reach decisions based on what they think would be fair on the facts of the case, rather than on the basis of the applicable rules of law." He immediately adds that this means the primary role of judges would be that of "responding to the underlying facts of the case, facts that are not made relevant by any legal rule."[18]

Clearly, there are notable differences between Scandinavian and American legal realisms. American legal realism lacks Scandinavian realism's explicit, elaborated background in semantics and philosophical epistemology. Nonetheless, it is said that in both, the implicit common ground is a version of juridical empiricism, either in the form of the appeal to positive natural science as the ground for all knowledge (Scandinavian realism) or in the framework of judicial personal estimations of the facts of the case (American realism).[19] Both types of realism hold that the objects of the juridical domain pertain to metalegal facts and do not nec-

---

16. Crozier, "Legal Realism and a Science of Law," 159.

17. Dworkin, *Taking Rights Seriously*, 3.

18. Brian Leiter, "Rethinking Legal Realism: Toward a Naturalized Jurisprudence," *Texas Law Review* 76, no. 2 (1997): 275.

19. See Brian Leiter, "American Legal Realism," in *The Blackwell Guide to the Philosophy of Law and Legal Theory*, ed. Martin P. Golding and William A. Edmundson (Malden: Blackwell Publishing, 2005), 50.

essarily entail any particular set of substantive moral values. The juridical phenomena related to those facts have the essential form of certain subjective individual, judicial, or legislative criteria superimposed on these facts, and neither of the two realisms could be associated with legal positivism or with a version of minimalist natural law.

It has been suggested that both forms of legal realism hold the view that the juridical domain is merely an extension of "functionalism" and "social engineering."[20] This means that they actually resist the classical binary system—versions of legal positivism versus natural-law theory—that is operative within the field of the debates on the correct framework for at the intersection of law and morality. In fact, it is almost as if these two forms of legal realism were conceived on the "other side of law and morality,"[21] for they focus on the law as essentially a practical enterprise in view of determinate social purposes. On their account, the legal solution, in order to be legitimate, must above all "work in practice."[22]

20. Heikki Pihlajamäki, "Against Metaphysics in Law: The Historical Background of American and Scandinavian Legal Realism Compared," *The American Journal of Comparative Law* 52, no. 2 (2004): 472.

21. I will return to this particular claim in the final chapter. For now, suffice it to say that although both legal realisms are generally considered to be superseded, some authors affirm that, at least in the American context, the legal culture, to a degree, still bears the mark of the exclamation "we are all realists now." See Leiter, "Rethinking Legal Realism," 267. Leiter holds that, currently, "realism is omnipresent in American law schools and legal culture, but almost entirely absent from serious legal philosophy" (274).

22. Pihlajamäki, "The Historical Background of American and Scandinavian Legal Realism Compared," 487. An opposite claim has also been made, namely, that Scandinavian legal realism, in fact, embraces an "extreme version of legal positivism." See Gregory S. Alexander, "Comparing the Two Legal Realisms—American and Scandinavian," *The American Journal of Comparative Law* 50, no. 1 (2002): 166. I am more inclined, however, to endorse the positions of authors who have first-hand experience of Scandinavian legal realism because they live and work as legal scholars in that particular context. In their view, this form of legal realism is strongly opposed to, or, at best, very ambiguous about, versions of legal positivism. See Bjarup, "The Philosophy of Scandinavian Legal Realism," 6–14; Pihlajamäki, "The Historical Background of American and Scandinavian Legal Realism Compared," 472.

The above-cited doctrinal elements point to the incompatibility between legal realism and Thomistic juridical realism. Interestingly, Jeremy Waldron tends to employ the term *moral realism* in the context of legal theory to denote the claim for the existence of an objective moral truth and its implications for "law, legality and adjudication."[23] This is a sign, at least, that the term *realism* need not be associated exclusively with legal realism in the context of the law-morality intersection.

The Internal Stratification of Thomistic Juridical Realism

Jean-Pierre Schouppe, the author of the only book entirely dedicated to the origins and the subsequent rediscovery of classical juridical realism, elaborates a framework of the internal stratification of juridical realism that will serve to contextualize the similarities and distinctions between the natural-law theorists mentioned in the first chapter, on the one hand, and the realistic conception of right and juridicity, on the other.

Schouppe likens the internal stratification of juridical realism to a three-level spiral stairway. Some authors reach only the first level of this stairway, while others also adhere to the postulates of the second and third levels. Although these levels are "complementary" and "interrelated,"[24] they are also stratified according to the transition from weaker to stronger versions of juridical realism.

The first level of juridical realism's spiral stairway is reached

23. Waldron acknowledges that the terms moral realism and legal realism may generate confusion, given the contrasting associative meanings and usages of the term realism, particularly in legal contexts. See Jeremy Waldron, *Law and Disagreement* (Oxford: Oxford University Press, 1999), 164.

24. Jean-Pierre Schouppe, "El realismo jurídico de Javier Hervada," in *Natura, Ius, Ratio: Estudios sobre la filosofía jurídica de Javier Hervada*, ed. Pedro Rivas (Lima: Ara Editores, 2005), 41.

by the adherence to the methodology of Thomistic realism. On this level, a legal theory cannot yet be qualified as juridical realism in any sense, since here it subscribes only to Thomistic openness to things-as-they-really-are, in contrast to any position that would deny the validity of this cognitive approach. Schouppe labels this type of theory as "realism in a philosophical sense," or "moderate philosophical realism."[25]

The second level is called "juridical realism in a broad sense," or "objectivism."[26] The authors who adhere to the postulates of Thomistic realism make an additional claim at this level: human moral and relational nature is imbued with objective normative content (i.e., the natural moral law). This natural law is the antecedent criterion for the legitimacy of the juridical domain, more precisely of subjective rights and positive law.[27] Schouppe remarks that the authors who remain on this second level usually subscribe to a vision wherein the *ius* is primarily defined as a subjective claim-right,[28] and they generally acknowledge that human relational reality somehow contains the "primary objective criteria" of justice.[29]

I would like to further this claim. The theories of the authors on the second level share a peculiar progression of arguments, which goes like this: if particular phenomena of the juridical domain—positive law and enactments of subjective rights—are in conformity with the natural moral law, then they legitimately constitute obligations of juridical justice. At this level, the juridical due—the obligation of juridical justice—is constituted only

---

25. Schouppe, "El realismo jurídico de Javier Hervada," 41–42.

26. Schouppe, "El realismo jurídico de Javier Hervada," 41–42. See also Jean-Pierre Schouppe, *Le réalisme juridique* (Bruxelles: E. Story-Scientia, 1987), 174–75.

27. See Schouppe, "El realismo jurídico de Javier Hervada," 41.

28. See Schouppe, *Le réalisme juridique*, 175.

29. Schouppe, "El realismo jurídico de Javier Hervada," 41; Schouppe, *Le réalisme juridique*, 176.

after the moral domain of natural law has already determined the content of positive law and subjective claim-rights through legislation or other means of positing the social sources of law. In the case of natural rights, according to this line of argument, the standard of legitimacy of claim-rights is inscribed exclusively in the moral status of the given aspect of human nature (i.e., in the moral *res*). The theories of Jacques Maritain, John Finnis, and Henry B. Veatch may be situated on this level given their understanding of the juridical domain as, essentially, a structural extension of prior, metajuridical, objective moral norms.

The third level, which Schouppe calls "juridical realism in the strict sense," gathers the theories of those authors who "climb" the first two levels of the spiral stairway, but these authors also endorse certain specific claims proper to the third level. The first claim is that the essential definition of *ius* is already provided by Aquinas and that it still constitutes the primary meaning of that which is juridically right. Aquinas defines *ius* as the just thing itself: a good or *res* precisely as owed in a relation of justice.[30] On this third level, therefore, the right is the object of the virtue of justice. The juridical due is established whenever a thing (*res*) is owed in justice to its titleholder.[31] This basic feature of juridical realism in the strict sense implies that certain things, including natural human goods delineated in the moral domain, are already juridical goods, on the basis of their being owed in justice to their titleholder. Besides certain aspects of arguments advanced by Hittinger, Brock, and, to some degree, Simon and Rommen, none of the authors from the first chapter have clearly articulated or endorsed this central feature of a realistic conception of right and juridicity. Villey and Hervada, however, as we are about to see,

---

30. *ST* II-II, q. 57, a. 1–2.

31. Schouppe, "El realismo jurídico de Javier Hervada," 41–42; Schouppe, *Le réalisme juridique*, 176.

have fully subscribed to all the claims of the juridical realism in the strict sense.

Villey's and Hervada's New Classical Juridical Realism

Villey and Hervada both affirm that their respective arguments are firmly rooted in the classical texts of Aristotle, the Roman jurists, and Thomas Aquinas. They highlight that even their doctrinal developments from these texts are made in clear reference to the framework of classical juridical realism.

Thus, Michel Villey's explicit embrace of Thomistic realism—wherein the right is "not situated in the subject but 'in the things themselves,' in what is real, in external reality"[32]—is always contextualized within his reading of the classical texts.

Now I invite you to a quick trip into the past, to the doctrines of Aristotle and of St. Thomas, doctrines that I call classical.... Personally, I repeat, I am very fond of these classical philosophies, as philosophies of law. It seems to me that Aristotle and St. Thomas Aquinas have analyzed juridical activity very well; they have understood its meaning and its values.... What answer does the philosophy that I call classical—the philosophy of Aristotle and St. Thomas—offer to our problem of the values that preside over law?... We need to rediscover the content that this notion [of 'justice'] had in classical philosophy.[33]

It is in Aristotle and then in St. Thomas, his interpreter—to whose principles the largest part of the classical Roman law and medieval scholarly law correspond—that we find the ancient classical conception ... of the right [*droit*].[34]

32. Michel Villey, *Philosophie du droit*, vol. 1, *Définitions et fins du droit*, 2nd ed. (Paris: Dalloz, 1978), 72–73.

33. Michel Villey, "Law in the Liberal Arts—Law and Values—A French View," *Catholic University Law Review* 14, no. 2 (1965): 164–65. For an explicit mention of classical realism as his own philosophical ideal, see Michel Villey, *La formation de la pensée juridique moderne* (Paris: Presses Universitaires de France, 2013), 618.

34. Michel Villey, "Droit subjectif II (Le droit de l'individu chez Hobbes)," in *Seize*

Javier Hervada seems to be equally aware of the fact that his legal philosophy is a faithful development of the approach already established in the classical texts. He frequently labels the main cluster of arguments within this classical approach as classical juridical realism (*realismo jurídico clásico*).

A realistic conception of right is the most classical conception that the juridical science has known.[35]

Classical juridical realism ... has received the name "realism" because it sees the right in the *res iusta* or the just thing. Aristotle, the Roman jurists, Thomas Aquinas, and the jurists in general—until the moment when subjective right had become the primary meaning [of *ius*]—have established the tradition of classical juridical realism, which has not ceased to exist among jurists and philosophers of law all the way through to our days.[36]

Under the label "classical juridical realism" we understand a certain way of comprehending the right and justice, which was essential for the European juridical tradition, from the Roman jurists, until ... the moment when the [primary] notion of right was usurped by the concept of subjective right.... This juridical-philosophical tradition was elaborated particularly by Aristotle and Thomas Aquinas. It is

---

Essais de philosophie du droit dont un sur la crise universitaire (Paris: Dalloz, 1969), 182. See also Villey's explicit mentions of classical natural right (*droit naturel classique*) in Michel Villey, "Abrégé du droit naturel classique," in *Leçons d'histoire de la philosophie du droit* (Paris: Dalloz, 2002), 110. Although this article has appeared in an English translation, I prefer the French original, due to the above-mentioned problematic issues of the nondifferentiated translation of the word *droit* in English as *law* in certain crucial passages, in which the author has clearly intended to highlight a contrast to the word *loi* (law). For the English translation of this article, see Villey, "Epitome of Classical Natural Law (Part I)," 74–97; Michel Villey, "Epitome of Classical Natural Law (Part II)," trans. Guillaume Voilley, *Griffith Law Review* 10, no. 1 (2001): 153–78. See also Michel Villey, "Droit Subjectif I (La genèse du droit subjectif chez Guillaume d'Occam)," in *Seize Essais de philosophie du droit*, 147–49; Villey, *La formation de la pensée juridique moderne*, 243.

35. Javier Hervada, avant-propos to *Le réalisme juridique*, vii.

36. Javier Hervada, "Apuntes para una exposición del realismo jurídico clásico," *Persona y Derecho* 18 (1988): 281. See also Javier Hervada, *Lecciones propedéuticas de filosofía del derecho* (Pamplona: EUNSA, 2008), 489, 501.

the philosophical system which seems to me to be the most adequate for the understanding and the explanation of the juridical phenomenon.[37]

Villey's and Hervada's new classical juridical realism does not, however, propose a purely historical rereading of a realistic conception of right and juridicity. Their arguments represent an important effort to unearth aspects of the tradition of Thomistic juridical realism that have perennial value for the correct understanding of juridical phenomena in general and that may be successfully contextualized in today's legal-philosophical debates.

The Realistic Conception of Right

Villey's and Hervada's Rereading of Aristotle

Virtually all Michel Villey's major works make reference to his rereading Aristotle's texts[38] pertinent to the Stagirite's understanding of the juridical domain. Together with Aquinas's relevant texts, Aristotle's arguments provide the backbone of Villey's realistic conception of right.

At the initial level of his rereading of Aristotle, Villey seeks to settle certain basic terminological issues. He observes how Aristotle, in book 5 of his *Nicomachean Ethics*, employs three terms that are crucial to his understanding of the main elements of the juridical domain. These terms are *dikaiosunê* (the virtue of justice, *iustitia*), *dikaios* (the just man, *iustus*) and *to dikaion* (a neutral noun in the Greek language, which, according to Villey,

37. Javier Hervada, "Le droit dans le réalisme juridique classique," in *Escritos de derecho natural*, 3rd ed. (Pamplona: EUNSA, 2013), 275.

38. For the English translation of *Nicomachean Ethics*, I will be using Aristotle, *Nicomachean Ethics*, 2nd ed., trans. Terence Irvin (Indianapolis, Ind.: Hackett Publishing Company, 1999), hereafter *Nic. Eth.*

may be translated as the just thing or right, *iustum* or *ius*).[39] This purely terminological analysis of Aristotle's texts already brings Villey to a series of conclusions. First, in Greek, a single term (*to dikaion*) serves to "designate the 'just' and the 'right.'"[40] Secondly, Villey concludes that Aristotle's conceptual understanding of the elements of the juridical domain includes an intentional structural link between the terms *that which is just* (*to dikaion*, which could be readily translatable as *right*) and *justice* (*dikaiosunê*). At the same time, *the just* (*to dikaion*) is clearly distinguished from the concept of *the just man* (*dikaios*).[41]

This terminological framework led Villey to conclude that Aristotle was the "first philosopher to argue for the right in the strict sense of the term" (i.e., to clearly delineate the distinctive elements of the juridical domain).[42] To be sure, *Nicomachean Ethics* was clearly not written with the concept of right as its primary focus.[43] Nonetheless, even Aristotle's tangential identification of the elements inherent in the concept of right[44] is sufficient for Villey's claim that "Aristotle had said everything on the subject, or at least that which is essential, in those few ingenious pages of the *Nicomachean Ethics* … where he analyzed the word *dikaion*."[45]

According to Villey, the key to correctly understanding the specifically juridical elements in Aristotle's theory of justice is to be found, above all, in his clear distinction between general

---

39. Villey, *La formation de la pensée juridique moderne*, 80, 84; Villey, *Philosophie du droit*, vol. 1, 57, 61, 69–73.

40. Villey, "Abrégé du droit naturel classique," 117.

41. Villey, *La formation de la pensée juridique moderne*, 84.

42. Michel Villey, *Le droit et les droits de l'homme* (Paris: Presses Universitaires de France, 1983), 38, 47.

43. Villey, *Philosophie du droit*, vol. 1, 56.

44. Michel Villey, *La nature et la loi: une philosophie du droit* (Paris: Les Éditions du CERF, 2014), 31.

45. Michel Villey, *Critique de la pensée juridique moderne (douze autres essais)* (Paris: Dalloz, 1976), 19.

and particular justice, as presented in book 5 of his *Nicomachean Ethics*:

In the Greek term *dikaiosunê*, [Aristotle] distinguishes two meanings. This distinction will prove to be of cardinal importance for the course of juridical science.... Aristotle distinguishes one type of justice, which he calls *general*, from the other, which he refers to as *particular*.[46]

Aristotle begins his argument on justice in *Nicomachean Ethics* with a presentation of general justice, which for Villey essentially consists of acting in conformity with universal standards of morality (i.e., the moral law). General justice, in fact, includes the virtue in its entirety and is thus a universal virtue.[47]

This type of justice, then, is complete virtue, not complete virtue without qualification, but complete virtue in relation to another.... And it is the complete exercise [of complete virtue] because the person who has justice is able to exercise virtue in relation to another, and not only in what concerns himself.[48]

In Villey's reading of Aristotle, general justice is justice in its moral sense: a virtue in the domain of social morality:[49] "In other words, it is possible to identify [general justice] with the observance of the whole of the moral law. This is where its other name comes from: 'legal justice.'... Justice, thus understood, is nearly a synonym for morality."[50]

This understanding of general or legal justice seems to have

46. Villey, *Le droit et les droits de l'homme*, 42.

47. Villey, *La formation de la pensée juridique moderne*, 80.

48. Aristotle, *Nic. Eth.* V.1, 1129b25; 1129b32.

49. "General justice is not to be identified with the whole moral dimension.... What the word justice evokes ... is especially an idea of order, or of the good relationship with others.... Thus, universal justice itself is a social virtue" (Villey, *Philosophie du droit*, vol. 1, 59–60). See also Villey, *La formation de la pensée juridique moderne*, 82.

50. Villey, *Le droit et les droits de l'homme*, 41. See also Villey, *Philosophie du droit*, vol. 1, 59, 75.

been the standard meaning of justice in pre-Aristotelian Greek philosophy.[51] Justice was understood as the virtue of a just man (*dikaios*) who sought to conform himself to the universal cosmic order and find his proper place therein.[52]

Since general justice is "defined by Aristotle as the observation of the moral norm" in interpersonal relations, Villey doubts that this mode of justice is suitable to capture the *differentia specifica* of the juridical domain: "Must we say that universal justice does not concern [the domain of] right at all?"[53]

On Villey's account, to make such a claim would be to ignore the "surely fundamental role that morality (i.e., the observance of the moral law) plays in the whole of the social order."[54] In Aristotle, as well as in all of Greek philosophy, moral (natural) laws were conceptualized according to their function of "preserving the stability" of the general harmonious order of the world.[55] However, in the pre-Aristotelian conception of justice as essentially general justice alone, the juridical domain would consist of the observance of moral laws. Villey maintains that the concept of right will be again reduced to denote the realm of the moral order, implied by the concept of general justice, in the mainstream mentality of modern legal philosophy.[56]

By contrast, according to Aristotle, laws ("whether natural or positive") are not equated with the right (*to dikaion*) although

---

51. "Right from the beginning of book V of the *Nicomachean Ethics*, [Aristotle] points out that by just conduct we rather frequently understand conduct 'conforming to the laws': the term 'just' makes us think of the term 'legal'" (Villey, "Abrégé du droit naturel classique," 123). For the application of the term legal justice to Aristotle's concept of general justice, see also Villey, *Critique de la pensée juridique moderne*, 19.

52. Villey, *Le droit et les droits de l'homme*, 42.

53. Villey, *Philosophie du droit*, vol. 1, 60, 75.

54. Villey, *Philosophie du droit*, vol. 1, 60.

55. Villey, *Le droit et les droits de l'homme*, 43–44.

56. See Villey, *Philosophie du droit*, vol. 1, 61.

"they are related to the [domain of] right."[57] The primary object of general justice is the subjective order of so-called "perfect justice."[58] At the level of perfect justice, persons seek the subjective good (i.e., to become subjectively just, *dikaios*) by giving to each one his due in the domain of social morality. In other words, a person becomes *dikaios* by observing the rules of moral conduct inherent in the overlapping domain of individual moral perfection and the perfection of various forms of social order.[59]

Villey affirms that it is not altogether misleading to understand the juridical domain as the general harmony of the world safeguarded by the acts in accordance with general justice. Nonetheless, the right (*ius*) and the object of general (or legal) justice are far from being identical. They are actually so diverse in their respective primary meanings that Villey is convinced that only a "formless, incomplete, undeterminable" right could correspond to general justice.[60]

Thus, according to Villey, the first author to point to the distinction—not only at the terminological level but also in scope and content—between (1) the sphere of that which is juridically right and (2) general justice, understood essentially as the domain of social morality, was Aristotle. Villey highlights that this new juridical level of Aristotelian justice (*to dikaion*) is not primarily concerned with the subjective sphere of "making the individual just."[61] It is possible for someone to perform "just things" in the distinct sphere of *to dikaion* and yet to perform them "unjustly"

---

57. Villey, *Philosophie du droit*, vol. 1, 61.

58. Michel Villey, "La philosophie grecque classique et le droit romain," in *Leçons d'histoire de la philosophie du droit*, 29.

59. See Villey, *Philosophie du droit*, vol. 1, 73–74; Villey, *Critique de la pensée juridique moderne*, 19; and Michel Villey, "Si la théorie générale du droit, pour Saint Thomas, est une théorie de la loi," *Archives de philosophie du droit* 17 (1972): 430.

60. See Villey, *Le droit et les droits de l'homme*, 43–45.

61. Villey, *Philosophie du droit*, vol. 1, 73.

according to general justice, that is "with ill [subjective] intention."[62] Aristotle labels this distinct sphere of *to dikaion* as the sphere of particular justice.

But we are looking for the type of justice, since we say there is one, that consists in a part of virtue.... It is evident, then, that there is another type of injustice, special injustice, apart from injustice as a whole.... For both have their area of competence in relation to another.... The unjust is divided into the lawless and the unfair, and the just into the lawful and the fair.... But the unfair is not the same as the lawless; it is related to it as part to the whole, since whatever is unfair is lawless, but not everything lawless is unfair.... Hence we must describe special as well as general justice.[63]

In Villey's interpretation of the foregoing text of Aristotle, there is a distinction, though not a complete separation, between particular (or special) justice and general justice. Particular justice is a part of general justice, of the universal order of morality. Both modes of justice remain distinct in their specific objects,[64] but particular justice aims to attribute to each his own share, proportion, or part,[65] but not primarily by seeking to establish or respect the complete social moral order according to general justice. In particular justice, the individual moral good and the common good are taken into consideration only to the extent that they fall within the scope of a certain particular object.[66] The primary object of particular justice is the "objective, external reality,"

62. For example, to "pay taxes only out of fear of the authorities." See Villey, "Abrégé du droit naturel classique," 126. "I can perform the *dikaion*—perform certain just acts—without being myself *dikaios*, namely, interiorly just" (Villey, *La formation de la pensée juridique moderne*, 84).

63. Aristotle, *Nic. Eth.* V.2, 1130a15; 1130a32–1130b2; and 1130b9–18.

64. Villey, *Le droit et les droits de l'homme*, 42–42; Villey, *Philosophie du droit*, vol. 1, 63.

65. Villey, *Critique de la pensée juridique moderne*, 19.

66. Villey, "Abrégé du droit naturel classique," 117.

which "consists in this *thing*, the good proportion between goods distributed among persons."[67] It is also the just relation in which "nobody takes 'more' or receives 'less' than that which is his part of 'external goods' attributed through division in a group."[68] *To dikaion*, as the specific object of Aristotelian particular justice, is primarily connected with the "effect, the external result, this equality in things and in relations."[69]

In fact, according to Villey, general justice is only the "derived and 'metaphorical' sense of justice."[70] The primary sense of justice is, precisely, particular justice.[71] Aristotle "seems to prefer" particular over general or legal justice, as is evident from his efforts to make *to dikaion* the primary focus of his analysis in *Nicomachean Ethics*.[72]

The vast majority of experts in the exegesis of Aristotle's texts, be they legal philosophers or not, concur with the French philosopher's argument on Aristotle's essential distinction of two types of justice.

Anton-Hermann Chroust and David L. Osborn, for example, claim that the term *just* is used by Aristotle with two separate meanings. In its first meaning, this term is related to the "virtue of righteousness" or "moral justice," wherein it denotes a conduct in conformity with an authoritative legal rule. In its second mean-

---

67. Villey, *Critique de la pensée juridique moderne*, 19.

68. Villey, *Le droit et les droits de l'homme*, 45.

69. Villey, *La formation de la pensée juridique moderne*, 84. "Particular justice alone manifests this peculiarity of envisioning an objective end, equality or harmony within the proportion of goods" [Villey, *Philosophie du droit*, vol. 1, 76].

70. Villey, *La formation de la pensée juridique moderne*, 82–83.

71. Villey, *La formation de la pensée juridique moderne*, 81, 83.

72. Villey, "Abrégé du droit naturel classique," 123–24. The author of the book on Aristotle's natural-law theory, Tony Burns, suggests that "it might be said that Aristotle's principal task throughout Book V [of *Nicomachean Ethics*] is to arrive at a definition of the concept of justice understood in its 'particular' sense." See Tony Burns, *Aristotle and Natural Law* (New York: Continuum International Publishing Group, 2011), 53.

ing, Aristotle employs the term *just* in the "narrower" sense of "proportionate" or "equitable" fairness, where it denotes an order directed toward achieving a standard of equality in external and commensurable things.[73] According to these authors, Aristotle developed a doctrine of two types of justice in which a person whose conduct is unjust because he acts contrary to certain moral principles is not necessarily unjust as far as proportionate or equitable fairness is concerned.[74] This proportionate or equitable fairness is related to "moral justice" in the "same way as a part is related to the whole."[75] In this sense, "every infraction of the principle of the 'justice in the narrower sense' (equality) constitutes an infraction of the principle of 'justice in the wider sense' (moral justice)."[76]

According to John Finnis, Aristotle wanted to introduce a technical distinction between two connotations of *dikaion*, namely, "just *qua* lawful (conforming to standard) and just *qua* equal (taking no more than one's share)."[77] Fred D. Miller, Jr. also highlights Aristotle's distinction of two forms of justice, "lawfulness" (universal justice) and "equality" (particular justice), wherein the term *to dikaion*, in denoting the just thing, "refers to a particular application of a virtue of justice."[78]

In sum, Aristotle's line of argumentation brings Villey to

73. See Anton-Hermann Chroust and David L. Osborn, "Aristotle's Conception of Justice," *Notre Dame Law Review* 17, no. 2 (1942): 129–30.

74. Chroust and Osborn, "Aristotle's Conception of Justice," 130.

75. Chroust and Osborn, "Aristotle's Conception of Justice," 131.

76. Chroust and Osborn, "Aristotle's Conception of Justice," 131.

77. Finnis, *Natural Law and Natural Rights*, 165. Without entering into detail on Finnis's incorporation of Aristotle's texts concerning justice into his own natural-law theory, I agree with Finnis that, today, we are equipped with the technical notion of *common good*, which Aristotle notably lacked for furthering his theory on general and particular justice. For another mention of Aristotle's clear distinction between general and particular justice, see Finnis, *Aquinas*, 130.

78. Fred D. Miller Jr., *Nature, Justice, and Rights in Aristotle's Politics* (Oxford: Oxford University Press, 1995), 68, 97.

the conclusion that the juridical domain of *to dikaion* should be identified with the object of particular justice. *To dikaion*, in his reading of Aristotle, *is* the right.[79] Furthermore, "With perfect precision, Aristotle perceived … the outline of a separation between the right and morality. The right is the objective just, the just relation externally established between two objects."[80]

In addition, according to Villey's reading of Aristotle, the realm of right as the object of particular justice, although distinct from the broader domain of general justice, is "specialized within morality";[81] it is "but a moment of morality."[82]

Javier Hervada closely follows most aspects of Villey's rereading of Aristotle. He concurs with Villey that Aristotle was the first known author in the history of legal philosophy to delineate the concept of right in the strict sense of the term within a broader realm of justice.[83] Hervada also notes that Aristotle accomplishes this clear conceptualization of the elements of the juridical domain already on a purely terminological level.

[Aristotle] clearly distinguishes justice—*dikaiosunê*—and the just—*to dikaion*—without confusing the two terms.… *To dikaion*, the just, is that which the Roman jurists have called *ius*, the right, when describing justice. The just [in Aristotle], thus, does not have a vague meaning, interchangeable with justice, but a precise meaning: what pertains to each, that which is his own.[84]

79. Villey, *Le droit et les droits de l'homme*, 45; Michel Villey, "Sur les essais d'application de la logique déontique au droit," *Archives de philosophie du droit* 17 (1972): 408–9; Villey, *Philosophie du droit*, vol. 1, 63–64; and Michel Villey, *Le droit Romain: Son actualité* (Paris: Presses Universitaires de France, 2012), 48.

80. Villey, "La philosophie grecque classique et le droit romain," 29.

81. Villey, *La formation de la pensée juridique moderne*, 84.

82. Villey, "Abrégé du droit naturel classique," 126.

83. Hervada, *Lecciones propedéuticas de filosofía del derecho*, 488–89; Javier Hervada, *Historia de la ciencia del derecho natural*, 3rd ed. (Pamplona: EUNSA, 1996), 53.

84. Hervada, *Lecciones propedéuticas de filosofía del derecho*, 102–3. See also Hervada, *Historia de la ciencia del derecho natural*, 17, n. 2, 60.

Like Villey, Hervada also acknowledges Aristotle's distinction between general and particular justice. Although for Hervada general justice consists in the virtue of observing laws, and thus may be called legal justice, Aristotle's concept of particular justice is that of "justice in a proper and strict sense."[85]

In clear contrast to Villey, however, Hervada does not situate the elements of the juridical domain exclusively within the range of Aristotle's conception of particular justice,[86] and he claims that the right is the object of justice, without any further qualification.[87] Hervada also recognizes that the juridical domain essentially inheres in Aristotle's concept of *to dikaion*: "The correct [translation of *to dikaion*] is the just or the right."[88]

Hervada agrees with Villey that Aristotle, in positing the notion of *to dikaion*, made a conscious theoretical move away from a concept of justice envisioned solely as a cosmic order or harmony. There is no doubt, in Hervada's opinion, that it was Aristotle's intention to push the notion of *to dikaion* toward a distinct domain of "that which is the right of each," of "the just thing," of "that or those things [or goods] that, since they are attributed to a subject, are owed to him."[89] As Hervada wrote, "This is the *dikaion*, that which the Romans have called *ius*, the right. As is obvious, the right is not primarily the law or a moral faculty, but a thing: that which must be received or given in justice. This is the core claim of juridical realism."[90]

85. Hervada, *Lecciones propedéuticas de filosofía del derecho*, 102.

86. I will return to this theoretical difference between the two authors later in this chapter after presenting Villey's and Hervada's respective understandings of the essence of right in Thomas Aquinas, since this same difference appears more clearly therein.

87. Hervada, *Historia de la ciencia del derecho natural*, 60, 62.

88. Hervada, *Lecciones propedéuticas de filosofía del derecho*, 103, n. 31. See also Hervada, *Historia de la ciencia del derecho natural*, 17, n. 2.

89. Hervada, *Historia de la ciencia del derecho natural*, 53, 60–61.

90. Hervada, *Historia de la ciencia del derecho natural*, 61.

Villey's and Hervada's Rereading of the Roman Jurists' Texts

Villey and Hervada share the opinion that Roman jurists' understanding of the essence of *ius* is firmly rooted in the continuity of their classical texts with the Aristotelian tradition.

As a legal historian specializing in Roman texts, Villey claims to have discovered the connection between the notion of *ius* in Roman law and Aristotle's doctrine on particular justice. In his view, the classical period of Roman law was influenced by an eclectic philosophical blend of various currents of Greek philosophy. With regard to the essence of *ius*, Roman legal philosophy was marked by the tension between two parallel concepts: Aristotle's concept of particular justice, on the one hand, and the stoic concept of right, essentially envisioned as an indistinct feature of morality, on the other. Eventually, Aristotle's influence prevailed,[91] and the obvious evidence for its ascendance, according to Villey, may be found in the Roman jurists' definition of justice as the virtue that has as its proper object the attribution to each person of that thing—the right—which pertains to him.[92] Moreover, in all instantiations of this definition, the meaning of Aristotle's *to dikaion* is contained in the notion of *ius*.

91. See Villey, *La formation de la pensée juridique moderne*, 101, 105–6; Michel Villey, "Les origines de la notion de droit subjectif," in *Leçons d'histoire de la philosophie du droit*, 235; and Villey, *Philosophie du droit*, vol. 1, 90–92.

92. Villey, *La formation de la pensée juridique moderne*, 104; Villey, "Les origines de la notion de droit subjectif," 232. See also the following citation from Ulpian: "Justice is a steady and enduring will to *render unto everyone his own right* [*ius suum cuique tribuendi*]. The basic principles of the right are: to live honorably, not to harm any other person, *to render to each his own* [*suum cuique tribuere*]" (*Dig.* 1.1.10). Emphasis added. For the English translation of the texts from *The Digest of Justinian*, I will use *The Digest of Justinian*, vol. 1, ed. Alan Watson (Philadelphia: University of Pennsylvania Press, 1999) and *The Digest of Justinian*, vol. 4, ed. Alan Watson (Philadelphia: University of Pennsylvania Press, 1998).

I hold that the Romans of the classical period translated *dikaion* with *ius*, and they did so for the purposes of juridical art, which was put into practice by Roman jurists. It is the art which Roman jurists have themselves defined as pertinent to the determination of the measure of a just division of "things," distributed between citizens in a social group or a city; *suum cuique tribuendi*, this is the function of the art of *ius*.[93]

It seems that for the Romans of the classical period the word *ius* served as a translation of the Greek word *dikaion*.[94]

Hence, under the influence of Aristotle, the Roman jurists understood *ius* to be a specific element—"the object or the final cause"—of justice.[95]

The question remains: which of the two types of justice proves decisive for the understanding of the *ius* as its specific object? In Villey's estimation, the Roman jurists adopted Aristotle's concept of particular justice as a reference point for their understanding of justice and, consequently, of the right as the object of that justice.[96] Commenting on the jurist Celsus's definition of the right as "the art of goodness and fairness [*ius est ars boni et aequi*],"[97] Villey affirms that Celsus determines the right as that which is just according to a "proportionate equality." He concludes that *ius* is "in service of the good" only within that specific range, characteristic of particular justice: *ars boni sub specie justitiae specialis*.[98]

In the foundation of classical Roman juridical science, it seems that [the word "fairness," Lat. *aequum*, from Celsus's definiton of *ius*] was

---

93. Villey, *Critique de la pensée juridique moderne*, 37.

94. Michel Villey, "Une définition du droit," in *Seize Essais de philosophie du droit*, 23.

95. Villey, *Le droit et les droits de l'homme*, 61, 64.

96. See Villey, *Philosophie du droit*, vol. 1, 93; Villey, *Le droit Romain*, 48.

97. The definition is reported by Ulpian and attributed to Celsus, in *Dig.* 1.1.1.

98. Villey, *Le droit et les droits de l'homme*, 62.

the primary choice for the translation of the Aristotelian idea of *proportional equality*, which was, in turn, constitutive of *dikaion*.[99]

Having settled the structural relationship between justice and the right, Villey moves on to analyze the concepts that depend on the primary meaning of *ius* understood as that which is juridically right, namely, the concepts of law and subjective right. He also explores the essential traits of *ius* in comparison with the moral domain.

Regarding the moral domain, Villey highlights how the Roman jurists, in opting for continuity with Aristotle's *to dikaion* as the object of particular justice rather than general justice, clearly understand *ius* as a domain essentially distinct from morality. In his view, this distinction constitutes the uniqueness of Roman juridical science in comparison to other antique civilizations, which organized their respective social orders around the lack of distinction between the right and morality.[100]

The reference to the conception of right as consisting of moral rules provided with legal coercion ... was only an occasional phenomenon in Roman law. In the whole of the Roman concept of right, the aim is not coercing people to achieve virtues (*honeste vivere*), but only to serve justice, that is, to determine the respective rights of each person (*suum cuique tribuere*).[101]

With regard to the relation between *ius* and the concept of law, Villey notes how these two terms, "whose frequent identification is a source of confusion," are carefully distinguished in Roman law[102] and cautions that the thematic division and nomenclature of certain parts of Roman law's *Digest* implies this distinction; in-

---

99. Villey, *Philosophie du droit*, vol. 1, 94.

100. Villey, *La formation de la pensée juridique moderne*, 104.

101. Michel Villey, "Morale et droit," in *Seize Essais de philosophie du droit*, 117–18.

102. Villey, *La nature et la loi*, 60; Villey, *Philosophie du droit*, vol. 1, 94.

deed, the first part of book 1 of the *Digest* is entitled *De iustitia et iure*, whereas the third part bears the name *De Legibus*.[103] Villey frequently returns to the principle of Roman law attributed to the jurist Paulus, according to which "*ius* may not be derived from a rule, but a rule must arise from the *ius* as it is [*non ex regula ius sumatur, sed ex iure quod est regula fiat*]."[104] In his reading, the juridical force of the legal rule is, in principle, reconstructed by starting not from the rule but from the just that is in the things themselves, paradigmatically so in the case of natural rights.[105]

Finally, Villey strongly advocates against projecting modern and contemporary conceptions of subjective rights onto the Roman jurists' notion of *ius*. The primary meaning of Roman *ius* is very different from the post-thirteenth-century conception of rights as subjective individual faculties, powers, liberties, or immunities understood as moral or legal superstructures above the concrete objects of the juridical domain.[106] Having spent his career analyzing the original source-texts of Roman law, Villey affirms that the word *ius* was always understood in those texts in the sense of that which is objectively just. The Roman jurists consistently defined *ius* as that precise "juridical status," that particular "place in the general order" which "justice attributes to each person."[107] By contrast, they never defined the primary meaning of right as "that benefit, that faculty, that power that we [in today's juridical mentality are inclined to] call right."[108] Even outside of the question of the primary meaning of *ius*, there is, as Villey

---

103. Villey, *La nature et la loi*, 60, 65; Villey, *Critique de la pensée juridique moderne*, 24.

104. *Dig.* 50.17.1.

105. Villey, *La formation de la pensée juridique moderne*, 104–5. See also Villey, *Le droit Romain*, 43–44, and Villey, "Une définition du droit," 27.

106. Michel Villey, "Les Institutes de Gaius et l'idée du droit subjectif," in *Leçons d'histoire de la philosophie du droit*, 169.

107. Villey, "Les origines de la notion de droit subjectif," 233.

108. Villey, "Les origines de la notion de droit subjectif," 233.

notes, an "extreme poverty of Roman vocabulary with regard to subjective rights."[109]

In Rome, that which is called *ius* is not the power of the creditor, the right corresponding to a debt, but the obligation itself, *vinculum iuris*, the objectively existent relationship between creditor and debtor.... I do not know of any instances or persons who can prove that *ius*, in the texts of classical jurisprudence, essentially assumes the sense of a power.[110]

In classical Rome, the right is, therefore, essentially defined as a *thing*:[111] a precise advantage, a particular value, a specific juridical status. Hence, it is the concrete juridical good owed to a person as his proper part in a relation of justice.[112] A classic example in support of this thesis is the frequent occurrence in the Roman jurists' texts of the so-called "right not to elevate one's immovables" (*ius altius non extollendi*). The titleholder of this right, according to the Roman source-texts, was the owner of the building that was not supposed to be elevated. This right, therefore, was not understood as attributed to the owners of neighboring buildings, who would, in a modern and contemporary subjectivist conception of rights talk, be the typical titleholders of the claim to negative servitude.[113]

Javier Hervada's focus on the original texts of the Roman jurists is notably narrower in comparison to Villey's. Nonetheless, he arrives at similar conclusions on the essence of *ius* in Roman law. Much like Villey, he is convinced that Aristotle's concept of

109. Villey, "Les Institutes de Gaius et l'idée du droit subjectif," 186.

110. Villey, "Droit Subjectif I (La genèse du droit subjectif chez Guillaume d'Occam)," 152. See also Villey, "Les Institutes de Gaius et l'idée du droit subjectif," 180–81.

111. Villey, *Philosophie du droit*, vol. 1, 94.

112. Villey, "Droit Subjectif I," 152–53; Villey, "Les Institutes de Gaius et l'idée du droit subjectif," 174; and Villey, "Abrégé du droit naturel classique," 160–61.

113. Villey, "Les Institutes de Gaius et l'idée du droit subjectif," 182; Villey, "Les origines de la notion de droit subjectif," 231; and Villey, *Le droit et les droits de l'homme*, 77.

to dikaion was accommodated in the Roman jurists' texts for the purposes of denoting the specifically juridical domain. That which belongs to each according to justice is precisely his right.[114]

They [i.e., the Roman jurists] referred to the thing which had to be given to each person as *ius* or *right*.... *Ius* was used by the Romans with various meanings in mind. The one that we point to in the text is the meaning that this word has according to the definition of justice: giving to each person his right, that which is his own.... This *ius* was *the just*, that which *justly* ... should have been attributed to each person.[115]

Villey's and Hervada's Rereading of Thomas Aquinas

It by no means diminishes the importance of Villey's and Hervada's research on Aristotle and the Roman jurists to say that their rereading of Thomas Aquinas represents the crowning achievement of their restatement of classical juridical realism. The overall importance which they attribute to Aquinas and the quantity of text they devote to interpreting his arguments suggest that they both consider him to be their primary classical source.

Villey acknowledges that Aquinas—"a great expert in Aristotle's philosophy" and "well informed in Roman law"[116]—was well-prepared to continue the development of the classical tradition. In Villey's view, Aquinas developed his understanding of the concept of right gradually throughout his life. He revealed his mature reflection on the juridical domain only "at the very end of his life and only at the time of writing of the *Secunda secundae* of his *Summa Theologica*."[117] According to Villey, Aquinas

114. Hervada, *Lecciones propedéuticas de filosofía del derecho*, 102, 104, 106.

115. Hervada, *Critical Introduction to Natural Right*, 1–2.

116. Villey, "Une définition du droit," 23.

117. Villey, *Critique de la pensée juridique moderne*, 40. Villey's opinion on the

contextualized his understanding of the concept of *ius* in clear continuity with the Roman jurists' *ius*, as well as with Aristotle's *to dikaion*. This choice was intentional, since Aquinas considered these sources to represent the finest juridical tradition.[118]

I will present Villey's analysis of Aquinas's texts on the concept of right on two structural levels. On the first level, where Aquinas's doctrine is observed from the point of view of the tradition, Villey attempts to establish the claim that Aquinas's treatment of *ius* is posited as the object of not just any kind of justice, but specifically of particular justice. On the second level, where the focus is on Aquinas's own concept of *ius*, Villey highlights Aquinas's primary meaning of this concept as the just thing itself (*ipsa res iusta*). He then shows how Aquinas's primary meaning of *ius* is distinguished from its subsidiary concepts, such as those of subjective rights and the legal norm.

Starting with the first level of analysis, Villey claims that Aquinas establishes the concept of right precisely as the object of

---

chronology of Aquinas's ideas is corroborated by the latter's famous biographer, Jean-Pierre Torrell. In Torrell's estimation, Aquinas wrote the *Secunda Pars* of his *Summa Theologica* in Paris "probably between January 1271 and Easter 1272," around the same time that he composed his *Commentary on Nicomachean Ethics*, that is, *Sententia Libri Ethicorum*. See Jean-Pierre Torrell, OP, *Saint Thomas Aquinas*, vol. 1, *The Person and His Work*, trans. Robert Royal (Washington, D.C.: The Catholic University of America Press, 1996), 146–47, 212, 227–28; Jean-Pierre Torrell, OP, *Aquinas's* Summa: *Background, Structure, and Reception*, trans. Benedict M. Guevin, OSB (Washington, D.C.: The Catholic University of America Press, 2005), 12. For other concurring opinions on the chronology of Aquinas's works, see J. C. Doig, *Aquinas's Philosophical Commentary on the Ethics: A Historical Perspective* (Dodrecht: Kluwer Academic Publishers, 2001), 195–229; Tobias Hoffmann, Jörn Müller, and Matthias Perkams, introduction to *Aquinas and the Nicomachean Ethics*, ed. Tobias Hoffmann, Jörn Müller, and Matthias Perkams (Cambridge: Cambridge University Press, 2013), 3, 6.

118. See, for example, Villey, *La formation de la pensée juridique moderne*, 162; Villey, *Critique de la pensée juridique moderne*, 40; Villey, "Si la théorie générale du droit, pour Saint Thomas, est une théorie de la loi," 431; Villey, "Abrégé du droit naturel classique," 116; Villey, "Une définition du droit," 23; Villey, "Droit Subjectif II (Le droit de l'individu chez Hobbes)," 183; and Villey, *Philosophie du droit*, vol. 1, 125.

particular justice, which is consistent with Villey's reading of the antecedent realistic tradition represented by Aristotle and the Roman jurists. Villey is convinced that Aquinas adopts and develops Aristotle's crucial distinction between general and particular justice, thereby delineating the border between the domain of social morality and the specifically juridical domain.

Villey's reading of Aquinas on the general/particular distinction corresponds to at least some of the elements of Aquinas's line of argument, for example, his affirmation that the right, *ius*, is the object of justice: "Justice has its own special proper object over and above the other virtues, and this object is called the just, which is the same as the right. Hence it is evident that the right is the object of justice."[119]

The whole of Aquinas's argument based on this text, however, does not provide a clear answer to the question on the type or mode of justice to which he would ascribe the domain of *ius*. In this regard, Villey's claim that Aquinas's notion of right can be predicated only on the domain pertaining to particular justice[120] has been challenged by Javier Hervada, as we will see later in this section.

In Villey's rereading of Aquinas regarding the relation between *ius* and morality, the borders between the moral and juridical domains are internal rather than external. *Ius* is, according to Villey, a domain within the broader sphere of morality; it is, as we have already seen, "a moment of morality."[121] The juridical right or good is not primarily concerned with the totality of human

---

119. *ST* II-II, q. 57, a. 1.

120. Villey, *La formation de la pensée juridique moderne*, 168. For a similar claim, see Villey, "Si la théorie générale du droit, pour Saint Thomas, est une théorie de la loi," 428, 430; Villey, "Sur les essais d'application de la logique déontique au droit," 408; M. Villey, "Abrégé du droit naturel classique," 126; and Villey, "Law in the Liberal Arts—Law and Values—A French View," 166.

121. Villey, "Abrégé du droit naturel classique," 126.

actions toward personal virtuousness,[122] or with the person's subjective "just intentions."[123] Viewed through the Villeyan conception of justice, Aquinas's treatise on right and justice in his *Summa Theologica* focuses principally on particular justice. General justice, in Villey's optic, is "not justice in the specific sense" but rather "a sum of morality, obedience to all kinds of moral laws."[124]

In fact, in the *Summa* of St. Thomas, just like in *Nicomachean Ethics*, the treatise on justice has as its object, above all, particular justice (II-II, q. 58 and following): this activity which has as its end not the general salvation or complete happiness of humanity, but specifically the right apportionment of material goods.[125]

But there is a place in the *Summa* where St. Thomas follows the example of book V of Aristotle's *Ethics*, and posits the right in the strict sense: II-II, q. 57 (*De Iure*) and the following questions. He does so on the occasion of an analysis of particular justice, the constant virtue of "taking neither more nor less" than the proper part of "external" things … apportioned in a social group.[126]

On the second level of analysis, Villey's reading of Aquinas's concept of right results in a doctrine that clearly embodies the basic principles of Thomistic realism. He notes that in the first article of question 57 of his treatise on justice in the *Summa Theologica*, Aquinas has envisioned the right primarily as "the just

---

122. Villey, *Philosophie du droit*, vol. 1, 127–28.

123. Villey, "Une définition du droit," 28.

124. Villey, *Philosophie du droit*, vol. 1, 123–24.

125. Villey, *Philosophie du droit*, vol. 1, 124. Other instances of this claim show that Villey had in mind a much broader idea of the object of particular justice than merely "material goods," as he claims in this text. This is evident from Villey's claim that "in the strictest sense, what St. Thomas, following Aristotle, calls particular justice is an effort to realize, in concrete circumstances, in the present, in the life of such-and-such a time and such-and-such a society, a fair distribution among citizens of goods, honors, responsibilities … a proportional distribution" (Villey, "Law in the Liberal Arts—Law and Values—A French View," 166).

126. Villey, *La nature et la loi*, 141.

thing itself" (*ipsa res iusta*), or "that which is just," in the broadest sense of the term.[127]

For St. Thomas (as for Ulpian, or for Aristotle), the right is that which is just … the just objective relation, the just proportion.… The term denotes, then, the *part* that one receives according to justice, because the object of justice is to attribute to each one his right: *suum ius cuique tribuendi*.… *Ius* denotes that thing … which constitutes the portion of this individual. The specificity of classical juridical language is to see a world of *things*, external goods, because it is solely in things and the distribution made in things, that the juridical relation is manifested *between* persons.[128]

In order to better understand the full reach of Villey's claims, it is necessary to push them to their logical consequences, slightly beyond his explicit line of argument. In his texts, the right is never a purely conceptual entity superimposed on real objects. *Ius* is, instead, always predicated on its concrete instantiations in reality: goods, personal status, advantages, benefits, obligations, competences, etc. According to this reading, Aquinas's term *res* denotes a certain real thing, or a concrete being in the metaphysical sense. This *res* receives the additional quality of being just (*iusta*) on account of its being a constituent part of a relation of justice, that is, insofar as it is owed in justice to another as its titleholder. Not only material things but also immaterial things, and even those things that are attributed to somebody according to nature—like, for example, life, good reputation or physical integrity, etc.—may constitute this real thing or being (*res*) that is owed in justice.

Perhaps the term *good*, in the sense of *juridical good*, would be much more adequate to denote that which is just or that which

127. Villey, "Si la théorie générale du droit, pour Saint Thomas, est une théorie de la loi," 428.

128. Villey, *La formation de la pensée juridique moderne*, 243–44.

is juridically right. The reference to the concept of good would certainly dispel the possible confusion of envisioning the term *res* as a conceptual tool for some sort of "reification" of all possible rights into material things or objects.[129] In addition, Aquinas's term *thing (res)* should be understood in its broadest possible sense, as a realistic reference to an already established concrete reality, in all the givenness of its ontological identity, as opposed to an idealistic separation of the concept of right from reality. The term *res*—or good, which is a universal convertible with being— is meant to denote any corporeal or incorporeal reality that may be the object of the interpersonal relation of justice. These terms are not intended as tools for conferring any kind of ontological status. If one says together with Aquinas that the right is essentially the thing itself, one necessarily presumes that the juridical domain has its foundations *in re*. Finally, the reference to rights as juridical goods seeks to highlight the aspect of *rei*-centric (or thing-based) goodness that is actualized in the realm of justice, that is, in the perspective of giving to each person those things that are his own.

Villey sometimes refers to the right as a concrete, just *thing*,[130] and on other occasions as a just, objective *relation*.[131] He often

129. As Massimo Del Pozzo rightly claims with regard to a realistic conception of *ius*, the thing in itself—in its ontological identity—does not essentially carry the domain of right; rather, "things are susceptible to constituting the right" in a relation of justice. See Del Pozzo, *L'evoluzione della nozione di diritto nel pensiero canonistico di Javier Hervada*, 56.

130. Villey, *La formation de la pensée juridique moderne*, 243-44; Villey, *Critique de la pensée juridique moderne*, 40, 42; Villey, "Si la théorie générale du droit, pour Saint Thomas, est une théorie de la loi," 428; Villey, "Droit Subjectif II (Le droit de l'individu chez Hobbes)," 190; and Villey, *Philosophie du droit*, vol. 1, 127.

131. "Right is a *supra, interpersonal* relation." See Villey, "Droit Subjectif I (La genèse du droit subjectif chez Guillaume d'Occam)," 148-49; Villey, "Si la théorie générale du droit, pour Saint Thomas, est une théorie de la loi," 428; and Villey, *La formation de la pensée juridique moderne*, 243.

uses both of these terms indiscriminately in the same textual loci. This possible inconsistency[132] should be properly contextualized in his overall intention to highlight various elements within a singular concept of right. The right is the just thing itself, but not in and of itself. Rather, it becomes juridicized (so to speak) only as the object of the relation of justice.[133] The primary meaning of *ius* as *ipsa res iusta* in the realistic conception of right becomes clearer when this meaning is confronted with the subsidiary concepts of subjective rights and legal norms.

With regard to legal norms, Villey often refers to Aquinas's effort to clear out any confusion that might lead to an identification between the *ius* and the law. According to Aquinas's most important text on this matter, he answers the objection that the law is "a kind of right," by affirming that "law is not the same as

132. Villey sometimes leaves the impression that he might even have a predominantly judicial understanding of the essence of *ius* as "the just solution," or "the good juridical solution." See Villey, "La méthode du droit naturel," in *Seize Essais de philosophie du droit*, 271.

133. Jean-Pierre Schouppe, in an ongoing academic debate on this particular matter, notes how Villey's interchangeable determinations of the essence of *ius*, sometimes as a *res* (a reality, or in a broad sense, a thing) and sometimes as an objective just relation, could imply that he envisions *ius* essentially as a relation. This would mean that Villey understands that the thing itself, *ipsa res iusta*, could be constituted as the focus of the concept of right only in a derivative, posterior sense, namely, only when the right, as essentially a relation, is seen from the perspective of the individual as his just share. For this side of the debate, see Schouppe, *Le réalisme juridique*, 136–37, and Jean-Pierre Schouppe, "Réflexions sur la conception du droit de M. Villey: une alternative à son rejet des droits de l'homme," *Persona y Derecho* 25 (1991): 153–54. On the other side of the debate on the metaphysical category of the concept of *ius*, Thierry Sol affirms that the very existence of a variety of determinations of the essence of *ius* bears witness to Villey's lack of interest in establishing a definite metaphysical category pertaining to this concept. Sol suggests that we should keep in mind the difficult and polemical academic context of Villey's texts. In Sol's reading, Villey was primarily interested in affirming the right as both a "just relation" *contra* subjectivism in general, and as a "just thing" *contra* the concept of right as essentially subjective rights. With this background in mind, the diversity of Villey's expressions regarding the essence of *ius* can be viewed as, indeed, convergent within a single coherent argumentative cluster. See Thierry Sol, "La notion de droit subjectif chez Villey et Hervada," *Ius Ecclesiae* 28, no. 2 (2016): 338–42.

the right [*ius*], but an expression [*ratio*] of the right [*iuris*]."[134] Together with Aquinas's systematization of the concept of law in two distinct sections of the *Summa Theologica* (the treatise on law in the *Prima secundae* (qq. 90–108) and the treatise on right and justice in the *Secunda secundae* (q. 57 and following), this claim forms the core of Villey's argument against the identification of *ius* with *lex* in Aquinas.

> In [Aquinas] the *ius* is distinct from the *lex*. The *lex* has the particular function of directing human conduct, at least it is from this perspective that he has primarily envisioned *lex* in the treatise on law. The right (the object of justice), which St. Thomas addresses in a completely different place in the *Summa*, is defined as "the just thing" or "that which is just."... In [II-II, question 57 and the following sections], where St. Thomas explicitly addresses the problem of the definition of right, he firmly distinguishes *ius* from *lex*. It is of little interest to me that in other places of the text, where this problem was not at issue, he may happen to yield to different and improper language of some of the authorities to whom he makes reference.[135]

> In the first article of question 57 [of the *Summa Theologiae*], the *ius* is not at all defined as a law, but as a thing, *res iusta*.... Is it not clear that *lex* and *ius* belong to two different registers?[136]

In Villey's estimation, Aquinas's denial that right and law are synonyms[137] may cut the ground from under "many neo-Thomists" who "mistakenly seek Thomas's doctrine on right in his treatise on law."[138]

---

134. *ST* II-II, q. 57, a. 1, ad 2. Emphasis added. I will return to this Aquinas's text and elaborate on it in the next chapter.

135. Villey, "Sur les essais d'application de la logique déontique au droit," 408.

136. Villey, "Si la théorie générale du droit, pour Saint Thomas, est une théorie de la loi," 428.

137. Villey, *Critique de la pensée juridique moderne*, 42.

138. Villey, *Philosophie du droit*, vol. 1, 126. See also Villey, "Droits et règles," 222, and Michel Villey, "Saint Thomas et l'immobilisme," in *Seize Essais de philosophie du droit*, 96n.

Finally, although an extensive analysis of the relationship between Aquinas's *ius* and the concept of subjective right—which was already identified as Villey's primary academic interest[139]—is beyond the scope of this study, one vital point should be noted. Villey persistently claims that nothing permits the conclusion that the word *ius* was ever seen to denote subjective right in any primary or essential way prior to the fourteenth century. Indeed, all the lists of the essential meanings of the term *ius* in both glossators and Aquinas seem to ignore the sense of subjective right.[140] Rather, according to Villey, the individual faculties and powers inherent in the structure of subjective rights were considered to pertain precisely to the prejuridical realm of human conduct that the juridical domain seeks to delimit and order.[141] Hence, in Villey's reading of Aquinas, nothing could be further from the concept of *ius* than predicating individual power or faculty of its essential meaning.[142]

Javier Hervada agrees with Villey that Aquinas's theory of the juridical domain is in continuity with both the Roman jurists ("whose definition of justice is cited in the introduction of his treatise on justice") and Aristotle ("whom Aquinas closely follows throughout this treatise [on justice]").[143] Aquinas's *ius* is identical to Aristotle's *to dikaion* or the just.[144] He reads Aquinas with more precision than Villey, however, with regard to the relation between right and justice. Much like Villey, Hervada is in full ac-

---

139. See, for example, Villey, "Droit Subjectif I (La genèse du droit subjectif chez Guillaume d'Occam)," 140–78; Villey, "Les Institutes de Gaius et l'idée du droit subjectif," 167–88; and Villey, "Les origines de la notion de droit subjectif," 221–50.

140. Villey, "Droit Subjectif I (La genèse du droit subjectif chez Guillaume d'Occam)," 157–58.

141. Villey, "Droit Subjectif I (La genèse du droit subjectif chez Guillaume d'Occam)," 149.

142. Villey, "Droit Subjectif I (La genèse du droit subjectif chez Guillaume d'Occam)," 153–54.

143. Hervada, *Lecciones propedéuticas de filosofía del derecho*, 109.

144. Hervada, *Lecciones propedéuticas de filosofía del derecho*, 110, n. 62.

cord with Aquinas's position on the right as the object of justice (in *ST* II-II, q. 57, a. 1), but he insists on the thesis that right has a certain priority over justice.[145] Indeed, he affirms that Aquinas's theory contemplates justice precisely from the standpoint of the specifically juridical domain since justice is understood to be the virtue of fulfilling the right,[146] that is, of giving to each his own right (*ST* II-II, q. 58, a. 1). The existence of right generates the virtue of justice, not vice versa.[147]

This is a crucial point in order to understand what justice is in the sense that we ascribe to it here. If the act of justice consists of giving to each person that which is his own, in giving to each person his right (*ius suum cuique tribuere*), it is evident that justice may only be exercised where two subjects have things that are their own. Justice does not attribute things, but follows the fact that they are already attributed.... In order to properly understand justice, we must bear in mind the following fundamental principle: justice follows the right. There cannot be an act of justice where there is not a title to a thing, where the thing is not—by virtue of a title—something owed, a right. Justice is the virtue of fulfilling and respecting the right, not the virtue of creating it.[148]

Hervada also agrees with Villey regarding Aquinas's understanding of *ius* as primarily and essentially the *ipsa res iusta*, the

145. We have already seen certain occasions on which Villey refers to the concept of justice as, in a sense, antecedent to and foundational of the juridical domain. For example, justice is referred to as "attributing" things to persons as their *rei*-centric rights. See Villey, "Les origines de la notion de droit subjectif," 233.

146. Hervada, *Lecciones propedéuticas de filosofía del derecho*, 110.

147. Javier Hervada, "La definición clásica de la justicia," in *Vetera et nova. Cuestiones de Derecho Canónico y affines (1958–2004)* (Pamplona: Navarra Gráfica Ediciones, 2005), 633.

148. Hervada, *Critical Introduction to Natural Right*, 8–9. Hervada admits to having found the inspiration for the argument on the priority of right over justice in Josef Pieper's discussion of justice. See Hervada, *Critical Introduction to Natural Right*, 8, n. 4. For Pieper's argument on the priority of right over justice, see Josef Pieper, *Four Cardinal Virtues: Prudence, Justice, Fortitude, Temperance*, trans. Richard and Clara Winston, Lawrence E. Lynch, and Daniel F. Coogan (New York: Harcourt, Brace & World Inc., 1965), 45–46.

just thing, and not the legal norm or the right in the subjective sense.[149] These latter phenomena may be considered analogues of the *ius*. Although they certainly have their structural place in a realistic conception of *ius*, they do not manifest its essence.

We have already seen how Villey sometimes refers to the right as either the thing or the just relation. Hervada is careful to, in all instances, refer to the right as the just thing. The right is the concrete *res* that is owed in justice to its titleholder.[150] *Ius* is, for example, the land, the conduct regulated by positive law, the payment of a price, the house, the goods inherited, and so on.[151]

There is, however, one important element of the juridical domain on which Villey and Hervada significantly differ. I have already alluded to this difference in presenting their respective readings of Aristotle and the Roman jurists. While both authors substantially agree that the right is the object of justice, they differ in their qualification of the precise mode or type of justice, general or particular, that has the right as its object. Hervada, of course, does not question the evident distinction in Aquinas's texts between the general or legal justice, on the one hand, and the particular justice, on the other. General justice is, in his view, "ordered to the common good" and, as such, "pertains to the dimension of the law." By contrast, particular justice "orders men with regard to things connected to another individual person." Thus, the objects of particular justice are the "external things and actions."[152]

---

149. Hervada, *Lecciones propedéuticas de filosofía del derecho*, 181.

150. "The right [*derecho*] is that thing which, given its attribution to a subject, who is its titleholder, is owed to him in virtue of a debt, in the strict sense of the term" (Hervada, *Lecciones propedéuticas de filosofía del derecho*, 198).

151. Hervada, *Lecciones propedéuticas de filosofía del derecho*, 198–99. See also Hervada, *Critical Introduction to Natural Right*, 19–20; Hervada, "Apuntes para una exposición del realismo jurídico clásico," 284; Hervada, *What Is Law?* 46; and Hervada, "Le droit dans le réalisme juridique classique," 275.

152. Hervada, *Lecciones propedéuticas de filosofía del derecho*, 110.

If legal justice regulates the person's relationship with the community (which is why it orders toward the common good), particular justice regulates relationships with respect to the individual person, either between the community and the individual (distributive justice), or between individual persons themselves (commutative justice).[153]

Since Hervada clearly understands both general and particular justice to be essentially social virtues marked by the quality of other-directedness,[154] the *differentia specifica* that distinguishes the two modes of justice in his theory must be identified elsewhere. As seen previously, Villey is firm in his conviction that the right is the object of particular justice alone. In his view, general or legal justice, insofar as it is ordered to the fulfillment of the moral law, necessarily falls under the rubric of the moral domain, precisely as distinct from the juridical. When recalling Villey's arguments on the matter,[155] Hervada remarks that "there is a certain inaccuracy [in Villey] with regard to general or legal justice."[156] Unlike Villey, Hervada is convinced that the juridical domain may be predicated also on general or legal justice.

General justice relates to the ordering of conduct toward the common good, and this, indeed, pertains to the office of the jurist, because the relationship of the person with the political community has a juridical dimension. It is not exclusively moral; the juridical realm is also present in this relationship.[157]

Insofar as moral or positive laws order persons toward the common good, Hervada is convinced that legal justice not only

---

153. Hervada, *Lecciones propedéuticas de filosofía del derecho*, 110.

154. "Complete justice is the general virtue or the sum of virtues ... insofar as it is referred to the other person, that is, not to one's own good, but to the others' good." See Hervada, "La definición clásica de la justicia," 636.

155. Hervada, *Lecciones propedéuticas de filosofía del derecho*, 159–60.

156. Hervada, *Lecciones propedéuticas de filosofía del derecho*, 160.

157. Hervada, *Lecciones propedéuticas de filosofía del derecho*, 160.

can be circumscribed to the sole moral domain but must also necessarily include the specific juridical due of persons toward the community. The juridical due of the person—which is the *suum* or the right of the community—is precisely his contribution to the common good through the fulfillment of legal norms with regard to the community.[158] The sphere of apportionable equality, which Villey reserves to particular justice, is, in Hervada's view, applicable to legal justice with regard to the fulfillment of legal norms.[159]

Hervada predicts at least one possible critique of his own argument, namely, the question: how is this understanding of general justice as essentially the fulfillment of legal norms not *positivism* or *legalism*? He responds to this question with the claim that the fulfillment of legal norms pertains not only to the moral aspect of the relationship between an individual person and the community but also to the juridical aspect. Among our obligations to society, he says, there are both moral obligations (e.g., solidarity) and obligations that pertain to justice. The latter "represent the just thing which we owe to society" as each one's individual "quota of participation in the attainment of the common good."[160] Thus, the common good of the community, in his view, also has a juridical domain that generates the juridical due of the individual person toward the community.[161]

158. Hervada, *Lecciones propedéuticas de filosofía del derecho*, 161. See also Hervada, "Apuntes para una exposición del realismo jurídico clásico," 298, and Hervada, *Critical Introduction to Natural Right*, 37–38.

159. Hervada, *Lecciones propedéuticas de filosofía del derecho*, 212.

160. Hervada, *What Is Law?* 89–90. In a book of conversations with Javier Escrivá Ivars on various aspects of his juridical theory, Hervada affirms that "a part of general justice pertains to [the office of] jurists.... There is, hence, a legal just, which is not [the whole of] general justice, but consists in the faithful observance of the laws—of juridical norms." See Javier Escrivá Ivars, *Relectura de la obra científica de Javier Hervada: Preguntas, diálogos y comentarios entre el autor y Javier Hervada*, vol. 2, *Derecho natural y filosofía del derecho* (Pamplona: Servicio de Publicaciones de la Universidad de Navarra, 2009), 657.

161. Hervada, *Lecciones propedéuticas de filosofía del derecho*, 212–13. Can we consider the society and the individual person as equals and thereby qualify their relation as a

This line of argumentation brings Hervada to the conclusion that a distinction of justice according to the twofold framework, as general or legal and particular justice, does not entail in and of itself any immediate consequence for the juridical domain. Rather, this distinction is, he says, simply irrelevant for the delimitation of the juridical domain. He proposes instead that only a consideration of justice as a unitary concept, namely, as the virtue of giving to each what is his *suum*, is pertinent to the specific analysis of legal philosophy.[162]

This unitary concept of justice may be reasonably distinguished, at least for the purposes of legal philosophy, according to the threefold distinction between legal, distributive, and commutative justice.[163] However, this threefold distinction does not entail any sort of multiplication of the juridical domain along the frontiers of the three types of justice; it merely expresses different kinds of juridical relations between individuals themselves or between the individual and society.

The three types of that which is just represent three modalities of the relations of justice or juridical relations in virtue of distinct criteria of equality. Hence, they do not interest us as possible types or classes of justice, but as various modes of what is just, of the right.[164]

---

juridical relation in the strict sense? Hervada answers this question by saying that community's social ontology entails a specifically juridical sense in which we can envision equality in this relation. "Society is not ontologically superior to the person; it is a union of persons in relation to common ends.... Being a community of persons, society cannot constitute itself as an entity ontologically superior to its constitutive elements, which are [individual] persons. It has the same value as they do, not more. Its juridical subjectivity is a projection of the juridical subjectivity of the persons that compose it. This is why [society] as a subject of right is equal to the person in what pertains to juridical relations between an [individual] member and society" (214).

162. Hervada, *Lecciones propedéuticas de filosofía del derecho*, 161–62.

163. Hervada, *Lecciones propedéuticas de filosofía del derecho*, 162. See also Hervada, *Critical Introduction to Natural Right*, 30, and Hervada, "Apuntes para una exposición del realismo jurídico clásico," 296.

164. Hervada, *Lecciones propedéuticas de filosofía del derecho*, 162.

Clearly, Villey and Hervada have divergent understandings of justice with regard to the delimitation of the juridical and moral domains. This issue is of great importance for the scope of this book, namely, for establishing whether a juridical domain may be predicated on natural law, which is traditionally considered to be a normative structure pertaining to the sphere of morality. Is there some way to reconcile Villey's and Hervada's arguments on the relation between justice and the juridical domain? The authors who have commented on this specific issue have usually opted for either Villey's[165] or Hervada's[166] view rather than attempt to settle this apparent divergence on some more general level of argument. In my attempt to settle it, I will first have to return to Aquinas's original texts. After presenting a brief survey of the pertinent comments on those Aquinas's texts, one should have a clearer idea on how to establish the connection between right and justice, on the one hand, and how to delimit the right from morality, on the other.

165. On occasion, Jean-Pierre Schouppe explicitly embraces Villey's decision to understand the right as the object of particular justice. See Schouppe, *Le réalisme juridique*, 20–21, 39, 45, 56–57. On other occasions, interestingly enough, he also affirms, in accordance with Hervada, that there is a juridical *suum* of the community with regard to the individual person, determined by the law in favor of the common good, which corresponds to the community's legal right (*droit légal*). See Schouppe, *Le réalisme juridique*, 40, 43. Schouppe also repeatedly mentions a juridical due, according to general or legal justice, established in the opposite direction. He argues for the existence of the right of the individual person to his or her own share in the common good, within the relationship between the individual and the community. See Schouppe, *Le réalisme juridique*, 37–38, 40, 42.

166. Massimo Del Pozzo subscribes to Hervada's understanding that legal justice also inherently possesses a juridical dimension. "In fact, general justice also includes the virtues insofar as they refer to the good of another or of the community, and as such possesses a juridical dimension, which largely corresponds to the fulfillment of laws.... Legal justice is, therefore, in contrast with [Villey's] thesis, a part of justice pertinent to the art of the jurist" (Del Pozzo, *L'evoluzione della nozione di diritto nel pensiero canonistico di Javier Hervada*, 165, n. 431).

From Villey and Hervada to Aquinas's Original Texts

Thomas Aquinas presents his understanding of the distinction between general or legal and particular justice in two of his works: the *Commentary on Aristotle's Nicomachean Ethics* and the *Secunda secundae* of his *Summa Theologica*. We have already seen that most authors situate the drafting of these works in practically the same time frame, during the so-called mature period of his academic career.

In his *Commentary on Aristotle's Nicomachean Ethics*,[167] Aquinas claims that justice—prior to its distinction as general or particular—is always principally concerned with "what a man does externally,"[168] and he is prepared to consider the question of how justice pertains to man's internal dispositions "only as a by-product."[169] The property of outwardness (*res exteriores*), therefore, may be predicated on the concept of justice regardless of its subsequent divisions.

Next, Aquinas frequently claims that general or legal justice has the quality of other-directedness since it is always considered "in relation to another and not to [oneself] only."[170] Hence, in his view, both qualities (outwardness and other-directedness) are predicable of general or legal justice, as well as of particular justice.

In addition, nowhere in his *Commentary on Aristotle's Nicomachean Ethics* does he read or interpret Aristotle's doctrine on particular justice to be anything other than a part of general justice.[171]

---

167. For the English translation of the texts from Aquinas's *Commentary on Aristotle's Nicomachean Ethics*, I will be using Thomas Aquinas, *Commentary on Aristotle's Nicomachean Ethics*, trans. C. I. Litzinger, OP (Notre Dame, Ind.: Dumb Ox Books, 1993), hereafter *Sent. Eth.*

168. *Sent. Eth.* V, lec. 1.

169. *Sent. Eth.* V, lec. 1.

170. *Sent. Eth.* V, lec. 2.

171. See, for example, *Sent. Eth.* V, lec. 3.

There is more than one justice, viz. legal justice and justice aiming at equality, and … over and above legal justice, as a general virtue, there is particular justice.… Now, the unjust thing consisting in a desire for inequality and the illegally unjust thing are not altogether the same, but one is related to the other as a part to the whole so that every unjust thing consisting in a desire for inequality is an illegally unjust thing, but not the reverse.[172]

Furthermore, Aquinas comments that these two modes of justice in Aristotle's doctrine "agree in definition according to the same genus inasmuch as both are concerned about what relates to another." Their *differentia specifica* is due to the fact that "legal justice is taken into account in relation to what is the common good, whereas particular justice is ordered to another as pertaining to a private person."[173] Are there other elements that should be added to the distinction between the two modes of justice? In his commentary on Aristotle, Aquinas adds only the claim that legal justice encompasses "all moral matters in general in whatsoever way a man may be said to be good or virtuous about a thing."[174] In sum, whatever the *differentia specifica* between particular and general or legal justice in his *Commentary on Aristotle's Nicomachean Ethics*, Aquinas highlights the premise that particular justice must always be seen as one part of general justice.

In the *Secunda secundae* of his *Summa Theologica*, Aquinas addresses the distinction between general and particular justice in more detail than in his *Commentary on Aristotle's Nicomachean Ethics*.[175] He identifies the right (*ius*) as the specific object of more than one type of justice.

---

172. *Sent. Eth.* V, lec. 3.

173. *Sent. Eth.* V, lec. 3.

174. *Sent. Eth.* V, lec. 3.

175. Dominic Farrell notes that Aquinas is freer to "develop his own approach" and that the "argument of the *Summa* is more elegant and original" with respect to his

Aquinas affirms that justice, prior to any internal division, "denotes a kind of equality."[176] Furthermore, justice is characterized by the properties of other-directedness (*alteritas*)[177] and outwardness, since it is inherently indifferent to the internal dimension of "the way in which [a certain act] is done by the agent."[178] Regarding other-directedness, Aquinas affirms that justice directs man in his relations with other men in two ways, "first as regards his relation with individuals, secondly as regards his relations with others in general, insofar as a man who serves a community, serves all who are included in a community."[179] He concludes this argument with the claim that "accordingly justice in its proper acceptation can be directed to another in both these senses," for "all who are included in a community, stand in relation to that community as parts to a whole," so that "whatever is the good of the part can be directed to the good of the whole."[180] In this cluster of arguments, Aquinas clearly implies that particular justice is that part of general justice that is, in its own particular way, ultimately directed to the community and somehow ordered toward the common good, beyond just the good of the individual.

While a part, as such, belongs to the whole, so that whatever is the good of a part can be directed to the good of the whole. It follows therefore that the good of any virtue, whether such virtue direct man

---

discussion of justice in the *Commentary on Aristotle's Nicomachean Ethics*. See Dominic Farrell, "Wanting the Common Good: Aquinas on General Justice," *The Review of Metaphysics* 71, no. 3 (2018): 525.

    176. *ST* II-II, q. 57, a. 1; II-II, q. 57, a. 2; II-II, q. 58, a. 2; II-II, q. 58, a. 11; and II-II, q. 80.

    177. *ST* II-II, q. 57, a. 1; II-II, q. 57, a. 2; II-II, q. 58, a. 2; II-II, q. 58, a. 3, ad 3; II-II, q. 58, a. 4; II-II, q. 58, a. 5, ad 3; II-II, q. 58, a. 8; II-II, q. 58, a. 9, ad 3; II-II, q. 58, a. 11; and II-II, q. 58, a. 12.

    178. *ST* II-II, q. 57, a. 1; II-II, q. 58, a. 3, ad 3; II-II, q. 58, a. 8; and II-II, q. 58, a. 11.

    179. *ST* II-II, q. 58, a. 5.

    180. *ST* II-II, q. 58, a. 5.

in relation to himself, or in relation to certain other individual persons, is referrable to the common good.[181]

In an article specifically dedicated to particular justice, Aquinas claims that "besides legal justice which directs man immediately to the common good," there is also a mode of justice, particular justice, which "directs man in his relation to other individuals" with regard to particular goods.[182] He argues that legal justice directs man to the good of the individual only mediately, since the individual good is to the common good as the part is to the whole. Therefore, we need the mode of particular justice to direct man toward the individual good immediately.[183]

In the *sed contra* of the article dedicated to the "special matter" of particular justice, Aquinas calls to memory the fact that the "Philosopher" (Aristotle) envisions "particular justice to be especially about those things which belong to social life."[184] We have already seen, however, that Aquinas does not consider the *differentia specifica* of particular justice to be its social quality or other-directedness, which is also predicable of general or legal justice. In fact, he affirms that "since justice is directed to others, it is not about the entire matter of moral virtue, but only about external actions and things, *under a certain special aspect of the object*, insofar as one man is related to another through them."[185]

The quality of outwardness is similarly predicated on justice without further differentiation according to its general or particular mode. Aquinas distinguishes from within "the matter of moral virtue" (i.e., the domain of morality) first the "internal passions of

181. *ST* II-II, q. 58, a. 5.
182. *ST* II-II, q. 58, a. 7.
183. *ST* II-II, q. 58, a. 7, ad 1 and 2.
184. *ST* II-II, q. 58, a. 8.
185. *ST* II-II, q. 58, a. 8. Emphasis added.

the soul" and then "external actions or things." Justice, he explains, is "only about external actions and things."[186] In addition, the "internal passions which are a part of moral matter are not in themselves directed to another man." Rather, only "their effects, i.e., external actions are capable of being directed to another man."[187]

Aquinas concludes his analysis of the properties and modes of justice by saying that the specific object of justice does not essentially include "internal passions," since these are not directed to another man. He does perceive, however, that, with regard to legal justice, it may be difficult to clearly distinguish the internal passions from the outward domain.

Legal justice, which is directed to the common good, is more capable of extending to the internal passions whereby man is disposed in some way or other in himself, than particular justice, which is directed to the good of another individual, although legal justice extends chiefly to other virtues in the point of their external operations."[188]

Thus far, Aquinas's line of argument appears inconclusive with regard to the initial question on the structural link between the *differentia specifica* among the two modes of justice and the delimitation of the juridical domain. One can speculate, of course, that he did not perceive this issue as a problem at all, at least not in the form in which I am analyzing it here.

I would like, however, to return briefly to Aquinas's argument that "since justice is directed to others, it is not about the entire matter of moral virtue, but only about external actions and things, *under a certain special aspect of the object*, insofar as one man is related to another through them."[189] As noted, this argu-

---

186. *ST* II-II, q. 58, a. 8.
187. *ST* II-II, q. 58, a. 8, ad 3.
188. *ST* II-II, q. 58, a. 9, ad 3.
189. *ST* II-II, q. 58, a. 8. Emphasis added.

ment is taken from the textual locus where Aquinas answers the question of whether particular justice has a special matter. Hence, the immediate context of the article is the difference between general and particular justice regarding their respective objects. Aquinas here mentions the following properties of justice: other-directedness, outwardness, and a certain special aspect of the object of justice. These properties should be sufficient, he says, for a clear distinction between justice and the entire matter of moral virtue.

In my opinion, when these arguments on general and particular justice are read in light of the question where Aquinas discusses the right (II-II, q. 57, a. 1), it becomes possible to delineate his reference to a special aspect of the object of justice as directly related to the juridical sense of justice, and not to any broader moral sense of *iustitia*. To be sure, Aquinas does not explicitly elaborate on all the stages of this theoretical move, so I will have to develop his arguments toward what I consider to be their logical conclusions.

Aquinas seems to imply that the properties of outwardness and other-directedness, which pertain to both modes of justice, are insufficient for establishing the distinctiveness of the juridical domain. Both properties may also be predicated on social morality. On the other hand, I have so far analyzed Aquinas's texts on the "justice-right" relation from within the dialectical perspective between general and particular justice, inherited from the Villey-Hervada debate, and I would like to keep open the possibility that the juridical domain may somehow pertain to both modes of justice in a way that neither Villey nor Hervada have predicted.

A look at the elements in Aquinas's texts might shed some light on the characteristics of what he refers to as the certain special aspect of the object of juridical justice. We know from earlier discussion that right is defined precisely as the object of justice.[190] It is useful to note here that Aquinas consistently and carefully distinguishes the scope of justice that has right as its object (i.e., juridical justice) from other moral virtues that mobilize the internal dispositions of persons[191] and from what he calls divine justice;[192] he refers to these latter realms as "justice" only by way of extension, analogy, or metaphorical discourse.

What could constitute the special aspect of right as the object of juridical justice, other than the properties of outwardness and other-directedness? In the first place, a characteristic of the object of the virtue of justice is its being ordered toward the good. Legal justice, according to Aquinas, "stands foremost among all moral virtues" since the common good, which is its immediate object, "transcends the individual good."[193] On the other hand, particular justice is primarily ordered, as we have seen, to "matters relating to particular goods" in a person's "relations to other individuals."[194] Thus, the second mode of justice is ordered "to the private individual, who is compared to the community as a part to the whole."[195] The orderedness of particular justice toward the particular goods of another individual, therefore, constitutes a part of its orderedness toward the common good, according to the specific aspect of its particular object.[196] Hence, since particular justice is a part of general justice, both modes of justice, beyond their qualities of other-directedness and outwardness, are ordered toward the common good, each according to its own specific ob-

190. *ST* II-II, q. 57, a. 1.

191. *ST* I-II, q. 59, a. 5; I-II, q. 60, a. 2–3; II-II, q. 58, a. 2, II-II, q. 58, a. 5–6; and II-II, q. 58, a. 9, ad 2–3.

192. *ST* I-II, q. 113, a. 1; II-II, q. 57, a. 1, ad 3; and II-II, q. 58, a. 2, ad 1.

193. *ST* II-II, q. 58, a. 12.

194. *ST* II-II, q. 58, a. 7.

195. *ST* II-II, q. 61, a. 1.

196. *ST* II-II, q. 58, a. 12; II-II, q. 61, a. 1.

ject. General justice is ordered to the common good immediately, whereas particular justice is ordered to the common good under the aspect of the particular good of another individual.[197] Both modes of justice, each in its own way, represent the orderedness to the good. Thus, the perspective of right as the object of juridical justice denotes a special type of orderedness to the good.

In the second place, Aquinas affirms that the essential function of justice is to establish equality in our relations with others. In general justice, equality is established toward the community, whereas in particular justice, it is established toward other individuals as parts of the community.[198] Aquinas adds that "a person establishes the equality of justice by doing good, i.e., by rendering to another his due."[199] In another textual locus, he affirms that "the matter of justice is an external operation insofar as either it or the thing we use by it is made proportionate [*proportionatur*] to some other person to whom it is related by justice," since "each man's own is that which is due to him according to [*proportionis aequalitatem*]."[200]

I would like to add another element to the aforementioned argument that the juridical realm of right denotes a special type of orderedness to the good. The new version of the argument goes

197. Dominic Farrell expresses a similar understanding of Aquinas's difference between general and particular justice. "General and particular justice, however, differ from one another as follows. Through general justice, we tend immediately toward the common good, but not immediately toward the good that belongs to the other *qua* single person.... Hence, the object of legal justice is that which is due to others in general (*ius commune*), whereas that of particular justice is what is due to a private person (*ius privatum*).... This does not mean that general justice makes us concerned about an impersonal common good but unconcerned about the good of the single person. Rather, general justice orders us toward the good of other people taken singly, but always in terms of their relation to the common good (*mediate*), and never directly (*immediate*)" (Farrell, "Wanting the Common Good: Aquinas on General Justice," 531).

198. *ST* II-II, q. 79, a. 1. See also *ST* II-II, q. 57, a. 1; II-II, q. 57, a. 2; and II-II, q. 58, a. 2.

199. *ST* II-II, q. 79, a. 1.

200. *ST* II-II, q. 58, a. 11.

like this: the special aspect of right as the object of juridical justice refers to that type of orderedness to the good that is essentially determined by the specific kind of equality between persons within the relation of justice.

What is this specific kind of equality in the context of justice? Simply said, some things are made proportionate in a relation of justice in such a way that in order to establish the equality between the persons in that relation, the internal dispositions of these persons are almost always irrelevant. This is consonant with Aquinas's argument that a thing is said to have the "rectitude of justice … without taking into account the way in which it is done by the agent."[201] Hervada will refer to this set of arguments under the rubric of subjective *amorality*[202] of that which is juridically right.

The primary focus of juridical justice, its distinct form of good, is that the equality of the things that are made proportionate has been reached in its outward and other-directed aspects. In other words, justice is the operative principle of respecting, as Aquinas puts it, the difference between *suum* and *non suum*—the limits of *mine* as opposed to *yours*.[203] The right can be respected even in abstraction from the internal dispositions of persons within the relationship of justice. For example, from the perspective of the juridical domain, a person is not primarily interested in whether others have morally perfective subjective dispositions regarding his life, property, or inheritance. Rather, he is primarily interested that others do not interfere with his life, property, or inheritance.

The fact that the constitution of *ius* as the object of justice is detached from "the way in which [the act of justice] is done by the

201. *ST* II-II, q. 57, a. 1.
202. Hervada, *Lecciones propedéuticas de filosofía del derecho*, 227.
203. *ST* I-II, q. 66, a. 4, ad 1.

agent"[204] reveals certain properties of the thing itself that is constituted as the right. *Ius*, as the thing that is the object of justice, must be made proportionate or *apportionable*, so to speak, to its holder in a way that transcends the internal aspect in which the act of justice is done by the agent. This means that the thing that is constituted as *ius* has to be capable of being attributed to that person as a *res* that can also constitute a debt in juridical justice. A thing cannot be owed, according to juridical justice, if the equality in question depends on the way in which the act of justice is done by the agent (i.e., on the internal dispositions of the subject). In this sense, not all things may be made proportionate or apportionable as something that is *mine* or *ours* as opposed to *yours* in the relation of justice.[205] I believe that it is precisely in the light of these considerations that Aquinas's texts should be read in order to fully understand the special aspect of right as the object of juridical justice.

In conclusion, it seems that for Aquinas, the line delimiting the juridical domain does not necessarily correspond to the distinction between general and particular justice. Instead, based on the premise that particular justice must be viewed as a part of general justice, both modes of justice should be perceived as pertinent to the juridical domain. This is the case whenever their specific objects—the common good of societies or the particular goods of another person—are, in their outward and other-directed aspects, made proportionate to determinate persons as their *suum* and at the same time constituted as other persons' *non suum*.

---

204. *ST* II-II, q. 57, a. 1.

205. Think of all those aspects of relationships (e.g., familial relations) among persons that may only be participated in, without the possibility of determining the things, acts, or states of affairs that are owed as *mine* or *yours* in justice. I will return to this argument later in the text.

From Aquinas to Villey and Hervada via the Subsequent Thomistic Tradition

In light of these texts of Aquinas, Villey's conclusion that the juridical domain should be exclusively identified with particular justice seems too extreme. He fails to take into sufficient account the fact that the properties of other-directedness and outwardness pertain as well to general or legal justice, not only to particular justice. In addition, he never really considers the possibility that an aspect of the common good may pertain to the juridical domain.

On the other hand, Hervada's argument—that general or legal justice possesses a juridical dimension only because legal norms entail the specifically juridical due of their fulfillment—should be developed in greater detail. As seen before, aside from occasional observations on this point,[206] Aquinas does not understand legal justice in Hervada's terms.

Ultimately, both Villey and Hervada fail to pay sufficient attention to how Aquinas views both modes of justice as a united reality, wherein particular justice is a part of general justice.

After the exegesis of Aquinas's texts on the distinction between the two modes of justice and its connection to the juridical domain, it is now time to consult the subsequent interpretative tradition of these texts. I will narrow down this tradition to only those arguments that shed some light on how exactly the common good or particular goods are made proportionate to persons as their *suum* in the juridical sense.

We have already seen how Hervada claims that there is a juridical *suum* of the community with regard to the individual person, determined by the law in favor of the common good. We

---

206. See, for example, *ST* II-II, q. 58, a. 6; II-II, q. 79, a. 1; and II-II, q. 79, a. 3.

have also seen how other authors, such as Schouppe, mention the existence of a juridical due according to general or legal justice going in the opposite direction, namely, as the right of the individual person to his own share in the common good. Both arguments can be traced back to one traditional line of interpretation of Aquinas's texts, which is that the juridical domain may be predicated on the orderedness toward the fulfillment of the common good in general or legal justice. This interpretation fails to take into sufficient account, however, the fact that the common good may not in all its instances and aspects be readily apportionable for the constitution of the right and the correlative juridical due.

Josef Pieper, whom Hervada often quotes as an authority,[207] seems to understand the concept of the common good as the "social product, the total product of community life." Accordingly, Pieper holds that the common good may be readily apportioned and constituted as a set of rights,[208] but he also seems to add to the concept of common good a meaning that resists precise commensuration. He perceives that certain aspects of the common good are not readily apportionable for the juridical dimension. Rather, they are only participative.[209]

Another famous commentator of Aquinas's texts on justice, Jean Delos, is the direct source of Schouppe's understanding of the juridical domain as pertaining to the orderedness of general justice toward the common good.[210] Delos advocates the "right to the common good" as "immanent to the members of the com-

---

207. See, for example, Hervada, *Critical Introduction to Natural Right*, 5, 8, and Hervada, *What Is Law?* 174. For the influence Pieper had on Hervada, see Del Pozzo, *L'evoluzione della nozione di diritto nel pensiero canonistico di Javier Hervada*, 143–44.

208. Pieper, *Four Cardinal Virtues*, 96.

209. Pieper, *Four Cardinal Virtues*, 98–100.

210. See, for example, the quotations of Delos and Pieper in Schouppe, *Le réalisme juridique*, 36–45.

munity":[211] "The common good is, thus, fulfilled in individuals; it is for them and, thus, confers upon them a right to their just part of the common good; everyone may, in certain ways, claim the common good as 'mine.'"[212]

Hence, according to one interpretation of Aquinas's texts, particular and general justice are both relatable to the juridical domain, because their respective ends—the individual and common good—are commensurable, divisible, and apportionable.

A different interpretation is represented by Villey's argument that the juridical domain may be predicable only of particular justice, to the exclusion of general or legal justice, which is instead wholly identified with the moral domain.

It seems that both traditions converge in the argument that particular justice, which has as its immediate object the particular goods of other individuals, is undoubtedly relatable to the juridical domain. They differ with regard to the claim that this mode of justice exhaustively represents the juridical domain. The fulcrum of the debate is Hervada's claim, and Villey's denial, that the limits of juridicity are much broader than the object of particular justice, and that they also include an aspect of general or legal justice.

There is a third interpretation regarding this issue in the Thomistic tradition, which is that we may identify certain reliable criteria for the discernment of the commensurability of the common good and establish the exact way in which the common good could be said to be apportionable. The same interpretation also acknowledges those aspects of the common good that may not be apportioned for their constitution as rights.

Thus, Jean Porter echoes Aquinas in maintaining the neces-

---

211. Jean Delos, "Notes et appendices," in Thomas Aquinas, *Somme Théologique. La Justice: Tome Premier (II-II, Questions 57–62)* (Paris: Desclée & Cie, 1948), 205.

212. Delos, "Notes et appendices," 205, 243.

sary "part-whole" structural link between particular and general justice. She insists we cannot envision the relation between general and particular justice wherein each mode of justice is operative in isolation from the other with regard to their objects. To do so would be wrong because, although general justice "plays an architectonic role" with respect to particular justice as its part, "general and particular justice work together in such a way as to direct the agent rightly toward the human good."[213] Hence, justice as a virtue is always operative as a whole in personal agency. Their unity arises from the fact that the acts of particular justice, which concern the person's relationships to other individuals, "are directed toward the common good by legal justice."[214] With regard to the juridical domain, Porter holds that even "Aquinas's analysis of the right as the object of justice is integrally linked to what we would describe as his fundamental theory of morality."[215]

John Finnis also regards the necessary structural link between general and particular justice as a crucial element for a correct understanding of both modes of justice. He maintains that instances of particular justice should essentially be regarded as the specified forms of general justice.[216] However we might delimit the juridical domain with regard to species of justice, a unitary view on justice always has the consequence that "one cannot respect or promote common good without respecting and promoting rights."[217] In short, "Respect for rights is the specific form which respect for the common good and for the 'bond of human society' must take."[218]

---

213. Jean Porter, *Justice as a Virtue: A Thomistic Perspective* (Grand Rapids, Mich.: William B. Eerdmans Publishing Company, 2016), 116, 169.

214. Jean Porter, "The Virtue of Justice (IIa-IIae, qq. 58–122)," in *The Ethics of Aquinas,* ed. Stephen J. Pope (Washington, D.C.: Georgetown University Press, 2002), 273.

215. Porter, *Justice as a Virtue: A Thomistic Perspective,* 116.

216. Finnis, *Aquinas,* 133.

217. Finnis, *Aquinas,* 133.

218. Finnis, *Aquinas,* 133.

Finnis maintains that the unitary view of justice that has right as its object blurs the distinction between general and particular justice according to their respective objects. The common good of society as a whole includes the particular goods of individuals because "in respecting and promoting the rights of each of the 'parts' (members) of a group, one is acting for the good of that group ... and of 'other people in general.'"[219]

Finnis insists that the determination of the requirements of justice, as well as the distinction between particular and general justice, must focus on the consideration of the term "common good,"[220] which he highlights "is the object of all justice ... [and] is not to be confused with the common stock, or the common enterprises, that are among the means of realizing the common good."[221] While these means of realizing the common good are *divisible* in Finnis's view, the common good itself "logically *cannot be distributed.*"[222] Therefore, he argues that there are certain aspects of the common good that are not divisible or commensurable and apportionable, but other aspects that are.

Russell Hittinger offers a compelling argument in this regard. In his studies on the social ontology of group-persons or communities, Hittinger makes a distinction between common good in the strict sense and common *goods* (or common utilities). Common goods (in plural), like Finnis's concept of the "common stock," can be understood as divisible—material or structural—preconditions for the fulfillment of the common good in the strict sense.[223]

---

219. Finnis, *Aquinas*, 217.

220. Finnis, *Natural Law and Natural Rights*, 166.

221. Finnis, *Natural Law and Natural Rights*, 168.

222. Finnis, *Natural Law and Natural Rights*, 194. Emphasis added.

223. See Russell Hittinger, "Polity in Catholic Social Doctrine: Some Recent Perplexities," in *Religion and Civil Society: The Changing Faces of Religion and Secularity*, ed. Mary A. Glendon and Rafael Alvira (New York: Georg Olms Verlag, 2014), 42–43.

The common *good* (in singular)[224] is, in a sense, twofold. In its strict sense, it denotes the desired form of order of communal action, or the common good of shared action. He calls this the *intrinsic* common good. The common good also includes the end (or ends) sought through the entrance and membership of a societal union. Hittinger calls this aspect of the common good the *extrinsic* common good.[225] He claims that "the salient mark of a *bonum commune* is that it cannot, just as such, be distributed or divided in exchange, but only participated by its members."[226] The common good of a society "cannot be distributed or cashed-out" because the common good really "never exists as a private

224. With regard to the question of how we should envision the concept of *the* common good and its instantiations in various forms of communities, Stephen L. Brock has highlighted: "Although we speak of 'the' common good, there are in fact many common goods, the common ends of many communities. 'Common good' is predicated on each. So each of them is in a sense a 'particular' common good, that is, a particular instance thereof.... There is not always a relation of subordination among these; for instances, among sovereign nations. But there is sometimes subordination, with the lower common good being merely 'particular' relative to the higher." See Stephen L. Brock, "The Primacy of the Common Good and the Foundations of Natural Law in St. Thomas," in *Ressourcement Thomism. Sacred Doctrine, the Sacraments, and the Moral Life: Essays in Honor of Romanus Cessario, O.P.*, ed. Reinard Hütter and Matthew Levering (Washington, D.C.: The Catholic University of America Press, 2010), 237, n. 14.

225. Russell Hittinger, "Love, Sustainability, and Solidarity: Philosophical and Theological Roots," in *Free Markets with Solidarity and Sustainability: Facing the Challenge*, ed. Martin Schlag and Juan A. Mercado (Washington, D.C.: The Catholic University of America Press, 2016), 23. A similar account of the internal differentiation of layers within the concept of common good is given by Dominic Farrell. "Furthermore, given the nature of communities and unified wholes, the common good consists of a twofold ordering or disposition of their members. On the one hand, it consists of the intrinsic ordering of the community: ordering the members among themselves in such a way that a working, unified whole is brought about. In the case of human communities, this amounts to all those conditions that are considered, whatever one's standpoint, as necessary for the conservation of the community and the attainment of its ends.... On the other hand, the common good lies ultimately in the end of community and its attainment. Indeed, the common good *qua* order intrinsic to the community derives from and is directed toward the common good *qua* end" (Farrell, "Wanting the Common Good: Aquinas on General Justice," 522–23).

226. Russell Hittinger, "Divisible Goods and Common Good: Reflections on Caritas in Veritate," *Faith & Economics* 58, no. 2 (2011): 39–40.

good, and therefore when someone exits a marriage or a polity he cannot take away his private share."[227] A societal union—the common order itself—is not divisible,[228] and "like any true friendship, there is only one way to have it—to participate in it by action."[229]

Thus, for example, a family, marriage, university, church, or political community cannot readily be broken down into rights or distinctions between *suum* and *non suum*. There is an order of shared action in these and similar communities that—since it mobilizes internal dispositions of their members with regard to ways in which the communal action is lived-out by them—resists reduction to Aquinas's subjectively amoral coordinates of the juridical domain. To paraphrase Hittinger, the common good of a society cannot be "cashed-out" in rights.

Not everything in such societies, however, is unapportionable. There are certain aspects of the common good that are indeed divisible and attributable to determinate subjects and thus suitable for constituting rights. For example, Hittinger affirms that parents' natural right as primary educators of their children is not only relatable to particular justice and its particular goods but also is necessarily a part of general or legal (or social)[230] justice, which has as its object the common good of the family.[231] This

227. Hittinger, "The Coherence of the Four Basic Principles of Catholic Social Doctrine," 84.

228. Hittinger, "The Coherence of the Four Basic Principles of Catholic Social Doctrine," 115.

229. Hittinger, "Love, Sustainability, and Solidarity," 24.

230. For the argument that Thomistic general or legal justice has subsequently been developed under the name of *social justice*, see Russell Hittinger, "Social Pluralism and Subsidiarity in Catholic Social Doctrine," *Annales Theologici* 16, no. 2 (2002): 393–94; Hittinger, "Divisible Goods and Common Good," 37; and Hittinger, "The Coherence of the Four Basic Principles of Catholic Social Doctrine," 111–19. See also Jeremiah Newman, *Foundations of Justice: A Historico-Critical Study in Thomism* (Cork: Cork University Press, 1954).

231. For this argument, see Hittinger, "The Coherence of the Four Basic Principles of Catholic Social Doctrine," 115–16.

right represents an apportionable aspect of the common good of the family, a *suum* that is distinguished from other persons' *non suum*. It can be apportioned to specific persons as *mine*, or *ours*, as opposed to *yours*, both within the family and with regard to third persons. For example, the role of primary educators of determinate children is, in principle, a *non suum* of anyone other than the parents themselves, including the political community.

General justice is, according to Hittinger, the virtue that seeks to harmonize individual persons and relevant group-persons with the aspects of the common good *sub specie societatis*, in the perspective of society. General justice includes, as its part, particular justice, which seeks to harmonize individual persons and group-persons in view of particular goods *sub specie alteritatis*, in the perspective of the other individual person.[232] In both perspectives, particular good as well as aspects of the common good or the common good itself may be constituted as a *res* owed to another *sub specie iusti* (i.e., in the perspective of juridical justice).

We have seen before that certain authors, such as Hervada, Schouppe, and Delos, argue that, from the standpoint of general or legal justice, the individual is juridically obligated to contribute his necessary part or share of the common good. In light of the above arguments, this claim stands only with regard to those aspects of the common good that are suitable for constituting that which is juridically right.

In this way, the distinction between the specifically juridical domain and the domain of social morality can and should be envisioned as relatively autonomous from the distinction between general and particular justice.[233]

---

232. Hittinger, "The Coherence of the Four Basic Principles of Catholic Social Doctrine," 114–15.

233. For a detailed argument on the specifically juridical domain of the common

The Realistic Conception of Juridicity

While the doctrinal focus of the previous section was the primary meaning of right (*ius*) in juridical realism, my investigation will now shift toward the concept of *juridicity* as I address the following question from Hervada: "What does juridicity, or the nature of right, consist of and what do we intend to say by affirming that a thing is juridical?"[234]

Although the concept of juridicity overlaps with that of the right, it is important to understand where the two concepts differ. Juridicity is, according to Hervada, the "quality of being juridical,"[235] or "the essence of the juridical."[236] Whereas the right essentially denotes the just thing itself, juridicity encompasses the formal constitutive properties that render a given thing suitable for being introduced into the specifically juridical domain.

In the previous section, I made reference to some of the properties of juridicity, such as outwardness (*res exteriores*) and other-directedness (*alteritas*). This section will present Villey's and Hervada's respective accounts of the properties of juridicity so as to gain a clear understanding of the specific distinction of the juridical domain from the sphere of morality. Given that Hervada, as a jurist, is arguably more focused on strictly juridical issues than Villey, the historian, I will invert the chronological order of their texts and begin by presenting Hervada's line of argumentation.

---

good of group-persons, such as the political community, the family, and the Catholic Church, see Popović, *The Goodness of Rights and the Juridical Domain of the Good*, 211–91.

234. Hervada, *Lecciones propedéuticas de filosofía del derecho*, 230.

235. Hervada, *Critical Introduction to Natural Right*, 23.

236. Hervada, "Apuntes para una exposición del realismo jurídico clásico," 295.

Hervada on Juridicity

In his answer to the question of what the formal constitutive property of the juridical domain consists of, Hervada adopts a perspective that may be labeled as *realistic juridical epistemology*. Observing the specific qualities of the juridical phenomenon, he takes as his point of departure the things themselves rather than the legal norm or the moral powers and faculties implied in the concept of subjective right.

In order to expound precisely upon the art of the just, ... it is necessary to explain with clarity what the point of departure is. That is, it is necessary to explain from which social fact, or from which dimension of the life of the persons in society, we are explaining the virtue of justice and the art of the jurist.... That point of departure is none other than an easily verifiable social fact: *things are attributed to different subjects*, in other words, *things are apportioned*.... By being attributed to a subject, by being apportioned, things enter within the domain of a person, or of a collectivity: they are *his* or *theirs*.[237]

The attribution of things to persons—the simple fact that "things are allotted"[238]—is thus the starting point for the constitution of the juridical phenomenon.[239] To opt for the things

237. Hervada, *Critical Introduction to Natural Right*, 7.

238. Hervada, *What Is Law?* 16.

239. Hervada, *Lecciones propedéuticas de filosofía del derecho*, 80–81, 85, and 139. The "attribution of things," as the starting point for the cognition of the juridical phenomenon, makes particularly evident Hervada's realistic philosophical position. "The concept of right ... is a universal concept elaborated by reason *a posteriori*, taking the experience as its starting point.... It is not a pure *a priori* idea without content, or without any content other than pure reason. In order to elaborate on the concept of right, our mind takes as its starting point a particular experience, i.e., the knowledge of existent rights.... The concept of right proceeds from experience as its starting point—from existent rights—by way of abstraction, and through this concept, elaborated in such an experiential fashion, it is found to be equally actualized in each juridical phenomenon. We can, therefore, note that the philosophy of law does not have the function to study and elaborate 'pure' ideas or *a priori* formal concepts, but that its object of analysis is the reality, juridical

themselves as the primary point of reference for the identification of the juridical domain, rather than the legal norm, is to take a stand with regard to the "right-morality" distinction. Hervada affirms that "when the right is taken as a 'law' we are not dealing with the allotment of things but with the ordering of conduct."[240] By contrast, the starting point of the juridical domain is the state of affairs in which things are attributed.

The office of the jurist does not originate out of the necessity to order and direct social life toward the common good. Its origin derives from a different necessity: things, goods are apportioned and each must have that which is his own.... The right, then, originates in the context of the apportionment of things, of goods.[241]

Hervada affirms that even if the juridical and moral domains "coincide in a specific matter," the perspectives from which human action is "observed by the jurist and by the moralist do not coincide." From this, he concludes that "the juridical aspect and the moral aspect of an action are distinct."[242] He seems to suggest that with regard to aspects of human action, the juridical domain is related to the moral domain as a part to the whole: "Is the right a part of morality? Without a doubt it is."[243]

It is clear, then, that Hervada does not envision the juridical-epistemological fact that certain things are attributed to persons as subsisting in a morally neutral domain. The right as the object of justice falls within the broader order of the attainment of the moral good. For example, regardless of the differing perspectives

---

experience, from which it then abstracts certain concepts. These concepts, even though they are products of reason, have their foundations *in re*, that is, they express the 'universal' as fulfilled in the existentially 'particular'" (166–67).

240. Hervada, *What Is Law?* 19.

241. Hervada, "Le droit dans le réalisme juridique classique," 276.

242. Hervada, *What Is Law?* 94.

243. Hervada, *What Is Law?* 131.

of the juridical and moral domains, life as a natural right is in ontological continuity with the basic human good of life in the broader domain wherein this good is established as an aspect of the whole human moral good. Although the domain of that which is juridically right is in principle subjectively amoral (in the sense that justice does not primarily mobilize the internal moral dispositions of the subject), justice (or injustice) on the juridical level is not morally neutral.

This "part-whole" relationship of the juridical and moral domains, however, must also be understood under the aspect of their essential distinction. The right is not a "smaller" part of morality, or its mere extension. It is, rather, a specific domain that is constituted within the broader perspective of morality through the verification of the properties of juridicity.

According to Hervada, the state of affairs related to the moment of attribution of things has several correlative structural features. First, in order to say that things are attributed—indeed, apportioned—to determinate individuals or group-persons, those things must be capable of entering into the sphere of dominion of that particular subject of attribution. If they are insufficiently determinable, things are not attributable to any particular subject.[244]

The aspect of social life to which the art of the right corresponds emerges from [the fact that] if there are things which belong to one person or another, if they are their things (those of each one), if rights and what is just pertain to determinate subjects, it is clear that this is because not everything belongs to everyone—or, said in another way, [this is because] things are allotted.... If things are allotted, everything is not everyone's.... The non-attribution of everything to everyone is a social necessity which results in the fact that things are allotted.[245]

---

244. See Hervada, *Critical Introduction to Natural Right*, 8.
245. Hervada, *What Is Law?* 16–18.

In order that things might be attributed to determinate subjects, there must be a prior clear distinction of the subjects themselves ("everything is not *everyone's*"). As was noted earlier, however, the fact that the very things in question are apportionable is also an important and autonomous standard for the constitution of the juridical domain. The aptitude of the thing to be attributed as a *suum* of determinate subjects—its determinacy, commensurability, and divisibility, precisely as subsequently owed by other persons—is the necessary condition of its constitution as a right. It is not possible to exercise the virtue of juridical justice where things are unattributable due to the indeterminacy of the subject or of the nature of the thing itself. Hervada often highlights the importance of the *measure* of right as the intrinsic and extrinsic specification of the thing constituted as right with regard to its quantity, quality, value, modalities of belonging to its titleholder, juridical powers the titleholder may exercise over it, and so forth.[246]

Another correlative structural feature of the moment of attribution of things may be found in the fact that the attribution is realized by virtue of the specific act that creates the right, namely, the *title*:[247] "The title is that in which the right has its origin, that is, that in which—the source—the dominion of the subject over a thing originates. In other words, the title is that which attributes the thing to the subject, that by virtue of which the thing is his own."[248]

According to Hervada, the title of natural right is human nature, or, more precisely, as we will see in the next chapter, the juridical domain of the relevant set of precepts of natural law. Other

<hr>

246. See Hervada, *Critical Introduction to Natural Right*, 27–28; Hervada, *Lecciones propedéuticas de filosofía del derecho*, 206–7; Hervada, *What Is Law?* 53–54; and Hervada, "Apuntes para una exposición del realismo jurídico clásico," 291.

247. Hervada, *Critical Introduction to Natural Right*, 9–11, 26–27.

248. Hervada, *Critical Introduction to Natural Right*, 26. See also Hervada, *What Is Law?*, 52–53; Hervada, "Apuntes para una exposición del realismo jurídico clásico," 291; and Hervada, *Lecciones propedéuticas de filosofía del derecho*, 204–5.

titles of the right—which may be termed "positive titles" because they arise from "the agreement" or "human will"[249]—arise in many concrete instances, such as through a positive legal norm, custom, contract, will, and so on.[250]

The last correlative structural feature of the moment of attribution of things is the fact that the attributed thing becomes the *suum* of the titleholder.[251] That the thing becomes one's own (*suitas*) is, according to Hervada, the foundational feature of the realistic concept of right.[252]

Even as Hervada considers the attribution of a thing to a person to be a foundational moment, however, he deems it insufficient for the formal constitution of the juridical domain. Rather, the state of affairs denoted by the *suitas* of the thing must be conjugated to a subsequent property, which Hervada refers to as the *relation of debt*. Much like the fact of attribution, the property of the relation of debt includes a series of structural features, each of which adds an essential element to its constitution.

The thing that is attributed to someone by virtue of some title ... receives the name of *ius*, or right, by virtue of a quality that places it in the juridical sphere: this thing is *owed* in the strict sense, that is, it constitutes a debt.... The thing becomes juridical, becomes *ius*, or right, by virtue of its quality of being *owed*.[253]

The attribution of a thing to a subject does not yet contain a reference to the relational aspect or other-directedness that is essential for the virtue of justice. The state of affairs that is foun-

<hr>

249. Hervada, *Critical Introduction to Natural Right*, 51.

250. For examples of positive titles, see Hervada, *Critical Introduction to Natural Right*, 26, and Hervada, *Lecciones propedéuticas de filosofía del derecho*, 205.

251. Hervada, *Critical Introduction to Natural Right*, 7–8.

252. Hervada, *Lecciones propedéuticas de filosofía del derecho*, 202, 231–32; Hervada, *Critical Introduction to Natural Right*, 19–20.

253. Hervada, *Critical Introduction to Natural Right*, 22–23.

dational for the relation of debt, and for the formal constitution of the juridical domain, is the fact that things are or may be in the power sphere of another person. That "the things of each person, while remaining his, may pass to the sphere of power of another person" is the essential premise for justice as the "act of giving to each that which is his own."[254]

The apportionment [of things] does not itself constitute the juridical phenomenon.... This is because the thing apportioned is not constituted as the right by the sole fact that it is attributed. The juridical phenomenon finds its origin in the fact that the things which belong to each person may be interfered with, that is, in the fact that they are or may be under the power of other subjects distinct from their titleholder.[255]

The state of affairs connected to the factual overlap of juridical spheres between the *suum* and *non suum* generates what we may call the *obligatoriness of right*. It is generally connected with the property of juridicity that we have already encountered in the previous section, namely, other-directedness (*alteritas*). Since the right is the object of justice, and justice is essentially a virtue of social relations, juridicity always necessitates other-directedness, or intersubjectivity: "[Justice] always demands two subjects: the first, to whom the thing belongs and the second, who, by having it (or by being able to damage it) returns it to him, gives it to him (or respects it)."[256]

According to Hervada, two additional features of the property of obligatoriness of right are related to the thing itself that is attributed and owed in justice: outwardness and equality. I have

---

254. Hervada, *Critical Introduction to Natural Right*, 12–13. See also Hervada, "Apuntes para una exposición del realismo jurídico clásico," 285, and Hervada, *Lecciones propedéuticas de filosofía del derecho*, 85–86.

255. Hervada, "Le droit dans le réalisme juridique classique," 277.

256. Hervada, *Critical Introduction to Natural Right*, 13.

already outlined the property of outwardness (*res exteriores*) as it is described in Aquinas's texts. Accordingly, I will present here only those insights Hervada offers as developments from Aquinas's doctrine on that property.

Hervada holds that for a relation of debt to exist, it is necessary that the thing that is attributed to a subject be susceptible to interference. This is possible when the *res* in question is, so to speak, "outside" of the subject, if it "springs from the intimate sphere of the subject."[257] The thing in question does not necessarily have to be grasped by the senses: it is sufficient that it is determinable in its exterior manifestation and thereby capable of being grasped or interfered with directly or indirectly.[258]

In what sense is an incorporeal thing an external thing? It is external to the extent that it possesses a projection which is external to the person—being outward in its means or its effects—by virtue of which it enters into the social context of communication and personal interrelation. This is why, although the property of outwardness always entails a certain material dimension, it more properly means that the thing has a social projection … in itself or in some of its dimensions.[259]

Things that are socially incommunicable, even if they may potentially be attributed to a subject, do not constitute the right but rather, as Hervada says, a "nonjuridical domain of the person."[260] In sum, the moment of attribution of the thing requires that it be

257. Hervada, *What Is Law?* 48.

258. See Hervada, *Critical Introduction to Natural Right*, 20. "For example, when we speak of the right to religious freedom, it is clear that we are not speaking of the act of faith, as if this act itself could be usurped by others. In a mediate way, however, this act could be interfered with; it can be interfered with in its manifestations, and a person may be the object of coercion. In certain regards, religion is actively or passively externalized, the former through its manifestations, the latter through possible coercion. Religious belief may be the object of justice to the extent that it is externalized, even if in itself it is an intellectual act, which as such cannot be grasped by the senses" (20).

259. Hervada, *Lecciones propedéuticas de filosofía del derecho*, 224–25.

260. Hervada, *Lecciones propedéuticas de filosofía del derecho*, 225–26.

apportionable for the constitution of the juridical domain, with the consequence of leaving all those unapportionable or indivisible things outside of this domain. In a similar way, the moment of obligatoriness of right requires that the thing be outward, with the consequence of leaving socially incommunicable things outside of the juridical domain.

With regard to equality, the thing that forms part of the juridical domain may be attributed and then owed, equally to everyone, if it is based on that in which all men are equal, like human nature. Apart from such a case, equality is a property fixed not to the person but exclusively to each person's right.[261] This means that the establishment of equality essentially consists of giving to each person that which is his own right, not necessarily of giving everybody the same things. The juridical domain is thus characterized by the so-called equality of proportion (or apportionment), wherein the term *proportion* denotes the very thing that is attributed (or apportioned) to a creditor and is owed by others (i.e., debtors):[262] equal treatment in that which is equal and proportional treatment in that which is different.[263]

In this sense, justice is not envisioned as a free-floating, *a priori* concept corresponding to an idea of equality posited in abstraction from other elements of the givenness of reality.[264] On the contrary, in Hervada's view, justice with regard to the right is an *a posteriori* concept.

---

261. Hervada, *Critical Introduction to Natural Right*, 18–19, 24–26; Hervada, *What Is Law?* 30.

262. Hervada, *Lecciones propedéuticas de filosofía del derecho*, 143.

263. Hervada, *What Is Law?* 31. See also Hervada, "Apuntes para una exposición del realismo jurídico clásico," 297–98.

264. The idea of procedural justice in Rawls's theory would be an example of this conception of justice. Hervada affirms that "the more or less vague pleas to justice and to that which is just, when it is a matter of things over which one does not yet have a title—legal or natural—are appeals to justice in an analogical sense or a misleading use of this word" (Hervada, *Critical Introduction to Natural Right*, 9).

Justice does not attribute things, but follows the fact that they are already attributed.... In order to properly understand justice, we must bear in mind the following fundamental principle: justice follows the right. There cannot be an act of justice where there is not a title to something, where the thing is not—by virtue of a title—something owed, a right.[265]

The elements of Hervada's realistic conception of juridicity, together with his account on the essence of right as the just thing itself, should now suffice for a full understanding of his definition of right: "Right is that thing which, having been attributed to a subject who is its titleholder, is owed to him in virtue of a debt in the strict sense."[266]

Villey and the Properties of Juridicity

Villey's account of the properties of juridicity is far less complex than his line of argument regarding the realistic conception of right. For this reason, I will address his somewhat fragmented arguments on the properties of juridicity against the backdrop of Hervada's more systematic approach. This approach will reveal certain points that both authors share in their understanding of the formal constitutive factors of the juridical domain, and in this way, Villey's unsystematic arguments will be accommodated within the context provided by Hervada's well-elaborated system.

The first significant intersection of the two authors' respective positions on juridicity may be found in their choice of the start-

---

265. Hervada, *Critical Introduction to Natural Right*, 11–12. "The 'should be given' does not lie primarily in justice—which is a disposition of the subject, is an act—but in the just thing—in 'his own'—with respect to what is owed" (19). "If a positivist speaks of justice, he first changes the definition of justice; it is no longer giving to each his own" (21).

266. Hervada, *Lecciones propedéuticas de filosofía del derecho*, 198. See also Hervada, "Le droit dans le réalisme juridique classique," 277.

ing point for the cognition of the juridical phenomenon. We have seen that with Hervada, this starting point is denoted by the state of affairs according to which things are attributed to determinate subjects. Villey opts instead for a rather congenial starting point for his own structural context of juridicity. He labels this cognitive starting point the *observation of reality* (*consideratio rei*). In his view, the juridical domain has its origin in "the observation of the social reality," because the right is precisely the "correct proportion of things allotted" to persons as members of various social groups:[267] "Right should be 'extracted' from the observation of the whole of nature, or with more precision, from the nature of things … the things of the social universe, of social institutions."[268]

Throughout his works, Villey repeatedly invokes the thesis that we can recognize certain elements of juridicity through observing natural social groups.[269] He employs this type of juridical epistemology to draw a clear contrast with the positivistic dogma that takes the legal rule as the doctrinal starting point.

The *modus operandi* of the jurist must not consist of deduction, which takes a given rule as its point of departure, but of a precisely contrary operation—we should seek the rule by taking the observation of nature as our point of departure.[270]

In Villey's vocabulary, the expression *observation of nature* denotes the cognition of the nature of things precisely as the

267. Villey, *Le droit et les droits de l'homme*, 54.

268. Michel Villey, "La nature des choses," in *Seize Essais de philosophie du droit*, 50.

269. Villey, "La nature des choses," 52, 54. See also Villey, "Droit Subjectif I (La genèse du droit subjectif chez Guillaume d'Occam)," 148. "The jurist discovers the right through observation of the order included in the natural social body and it is from there that he can extract relations, proportions and objective conclusions" (Villey, *La formation de la pensée juridique moderne*, 243). "When we seek to … determine the precise objective relations which constitute the right we should turn to this other source of cognition, the observation of nature" (Villey, "Abrégé du droit naturel classique," 141).

270. Villey, *La formation de la pensée juridique moderne*, 593.

fundamental source of the right. For example, we can begin to understand basic family rights through the observation of the social-relational ontology wherein a set of things is attributed to the family as a group-person or to its members. In Villey's juridical epistemology, much like the method of the Roman jurists that was a constant inspiration to Villey, positive legal norm is always consulted but never considered the exclusive source of that which is juridically right.

Two things should be mentioned with regard to Villey's insistence on the observation of nature as the fundamental source of the right. First, Villey has been severely criticized on this argument for attempting—invalidly, according to his critics—to cross the bridge between fact (*is*) and value (*ought*) when extracting the juridical *ought* from the observation of nature.[271] On at least one occasion, he addressed this critique by claiming he was merely advancing what was, in his understanding, the central claim of the doctrine of natural rights: one can find the *ius* in connection with the things-as-they-are-in-themselves. As he claims, the only way to discover natural right—which is distinct from natural law, contrary to his critics' frequent interchangeable usage of the two

271. Among the first of such critics is John Finnis who in a 1972 exchange of arguments claims that this position of Villey and of his intellectual disciples "leaves the reader puzzled" in front of an argument that amounts to what is known as "naturalistic fallacy." See John Finnis, "Un ouvrage récent sur Bentham," *Archives de philosophie du droit* 17 (1972): 425. Although Finnis's critique of Villey is very brief, one might say that the whole body of Finnis's work represents, indeed, a critique of a position that he believes to find in Villey. A more recent and detailed restatement of this critique, in direct reference to Villey's thesis, may be found in Stamatios Tzitzis, "Controverses autour de l'idée de natures des choses et de droit naturel," in Niort and Vannier, *Michel Villey et le droit naturel en question*, 29–46. Rabbi-Baldi Cabanillas also cautions of the risk that some formulations in Villey's texts, in a post-Humean mentality, might be understood to reveal his lack of sensitivity to the nuances of avoiding the naturalistic fallacy. See Renato Rabbi-Baldi Cabanillas, "Michel Villey et la question des droits de l'homme: Une critique à partir de ses écrits et de ses sources intellectuelles," in *Michel Villey: Le juste partage*, ed. Chantal Delsol and Stéphane Bauzon (Paris: Dalloz, 2007), 172.

concepts—is to observe the nature of things (*consideratio rei*).[272]

Secondly, Villey's starting point is the domain of that which is juridically right rather than the phenomenon of law (whether understood as moral or positive). It is possible that the critics of Villey's argument on the observation of nature could be, at least in part, formulating their arguments on a level distinct from that on which Villey develops his thesis. In his realistic juridical epistemology, the domain of right predicable of the nature of things within the relation of justice has a certain cognitive priority with respect to the domain of legal norms, natural or positive, but not to the detriment of this latter domain. This peculiarity of his approach should not go unnoticed in any critique of his position on the *consideratio rei*.

In sum, Villey's discourse on the observation of the nature of things may be situated on the same level of analysis as Hervada's starting point for juridical epistemology, notwithstanding certain differences.[273]

A second significant intersection of the two authors' lines of argument regarding juridicity is their reference to the same properties of juridicity. Villey's treatment of these properties reveals once again a lower level of elaboration with respect to Hervada. Nonetheless, their remarkable similarities are worth noting and

272. Villey, "Si la théorie générale du droit, pour Saint Thomas, est une théorie de la loi," 429–30.

273. "We can easily notice that this schema of the Roman jurists corresponds to a description of the social reality through an observation of what occurred—and continues to occur—in real life.... Each person has a number of things that belong to him. The real possession and usage of these partly depend, however, also on other people.... It is a common fact from experience that because of the various arrangements of human relations things are not always in the possession ... of their owner, i.e., to whom they belong as the subject of their attribution. But at the same time, however, things should be returned to the hands of their owner, to the hands of the subject to whom they belong ... since this necessity (this duty or debt) is the immediate consequence of the fact that things are somebody's, are *his*" (Hervada, *Critical Introduction to Natural Right*, 2).

bespeak their subscription to the same juridical-philosophical matrix.

Throughout his texts, Villey explicitly references outwardness and other-directedness as the crucial properties pointing to the constitution of the juridical domain.[274] Much like Hervada, Villey argues that things that are apportioned between persons must be measurable,[275] delimited,[276] at least determinable,[277] and irreducible to morality.[278]

Finally, another significant intersection between Villey's and Hervada's realistic accounts of juridicity is the "part-whole" framework of the connection between the juridical and moral domains. Although Hervada is, arguably, more explicit than Villey with regard to this argument, Villey's position regarding this issue is clear enough. In his view, the right is "specified within morality,"[279] as its "moment," its "distinct phase and instrument,"[280] or its "well-determined sector."[281]

---

274. See, for example, Villey, *Philosophie du droit*, vol. 1, 66–67, 73; Villey, "Abrégé du droit naturel classique," 122; Villey, "Si la théorie générale du droit, pour Saint Thomas, est une théorie de la loi", 428, 431; Villey, *Le droit et les droits de l'homme*, 42, 45, 48; and Villey, *Critique de la pensée juridique moderne*, 19.

275. Villey, *Philosophie du droit*, vol. 1, 67.

276. Villey, "Abrégé du droit naturel classique," 160.

277. Villey, *Le droit et les droits de l'homme*, 100.

278. Villey, *Critique de la pensée juridique moderne*, 40, 42.

279. Villey, *La formation de la pensée juridique moderne*, 84.

280. Villey, "Abrégé du droit naturel classique," 126.

281. Villey, "Abrégé du droit naturel classique," 127.

3

The Juridical Status of Natural Law

Villey, Hervada, and Aquinas Revisited

In the first chapter of this work, I presented a kaleidoscope of what are usually considered to be the most relevant approaches to the law-morality intersection in the last fifty years. Although these approaches may be divided into different, often opposing, camps—legal positivism, interpretivism, juridical constructivism, minimalist natural law, Thomistic natural law—the debate between the camps' proponents seems to be locked in a framework of arguments that can be roughly formulated as follows:

- On the one hand, if there is a moral dimension pertinent to the juridical domain, it has no necessary structural link whatsoever, be it moral or juridical, with the full-scale Thomistic theory of natural law. This theoretical stance is represented by Raz's positivism and by minimalist natural-law theories, such as those that are developed in a crossover with legal positivism (Hart), interpretivism (Dworkin), and juridical constructivism (Rawls).

- On the other hand, the authors who adopt a full-scale Thomistic theory of natural law as the decisive feature of the law-morality intersection never really predicate an inherently juridical domain of natural law; rather, they predicate a predominantly moral one, and most contemporary restatements of Thomistic natural law theory are developed within this framework.

Under both aspects, the juridical domain of substantive morality, whether in its minimalist natural-law instantiations or in a full-scale Thomistic theory of natural law, remains mostly unintelligible.

In the previous chapter, I highlighted the realistic conception of right and juridicity as the approach that proposes a clear understanding of the properties of juridicity regarding the primary meaning of the concept of right, namely, the just thing itself.

A synthesis of the main conclusions of the preceding two chapters is in order, and it basically revolves around the following question: What if the *res*, which is constituted as right (*ius*), is actually a thing or good indicated by the precepts of natural law? In this chapter, I will present the answers to that question, as given within the contemporary restatement of Thomistic juridical realism by Villey and Hervada. True, neither one has written something similar to a treatise specifically dedicated to this question, nor have they elaborated a fully developed outline of a juridical domain of natural law. Still, both authors have laid down in their texts certain indispensable elements that indicate with sufficient clarity the existence of a juridical domain of natural law within their respective realistic conceptions. By doing so, they have, in fact, uncovered the elements that were already present in Aquinas's analysis of the relationship between *ius* and *lex*. Since Villey's and Hervada's arguments represent a unique attempt to postulate a juridical domain of natural law from the perspective of classical juridical realism, it is well worth the effort to closely follow the course of their exposition.

Villey's Reading of the Juridical Status of Natural Law

In a 1972 exchange of arguments between Villey and John Finnis—the only written record of their direct scholarly conversation—Finnis forcefully criticizes Villey's realistic conception of right and juridicity. A significant part of his critique is rooted in the argument that nothing resembling a "major opposition" between the terms *right* and *law* is to be found in Aquinas.[1] Later, in *Natural Law and Natural Rights*, Finnis summarizes the historical process in which Aquinas's primary meaning of *ius*—"the just thing itself" or "that which is just"—was gradually transformed to a subjectivist conception of right. In Finnis's view, when *ius* begins to essentially denote a subjective right, it is relocated from the "just thing itself" to "the beneficiary of the just relationship."[2] In subsequent works, Finnis adopts the understanding that Aquinas did, in fact, operate with a subjective meaning of *ius* in a way that resembles the modern usage of the term right: claim, power, liberty, immunity.[3] The main problem that Finnis

---

1. Finnis, "Un ouvrage récent sur Bentham," 424. See Finnis, *Natural Law and Natural Rights*, 207–8.

2. See Finnis, *Natural Law and Natural Rights*, 207.

3. "It is a sheer mistake to claim, as some have, that [Aquinas] lacked or repudiated

seems to perceive regarding this subjectivist shift of perspective is that in the modern juridical mentality, the concept of right could be seen as altogether detached from law, especially natural law.[4] Provided that the moral structure of natural law, and especially its continuity with positive law, is secured on theoretical and practical levels, Finnis never really perceives any serious problem in the fact that the argumentative *corpus* behind the classical realistic and *rei*-centric concept of *ius* as *ipsa res iusta* is completely absent from the contemporary perspective. The problem that remains, however, is that if the entirety of the Thomistic conception of that which is juridically right (*ius*) is transposed to the modern concept of subjective rights, moral or legal, the immediate juridical status of natural law becomes unintelligible. At the same time, the normative status of natural law is then essentially understood to be bifurcated in its moral domain or, alternatively, in the reception of its content in positive law.

In his brief response to Finnis's critique, Villey outlines his own understanding of the juridical status of natural law. The main elements of this response merit to be quoted in full, before commenting on them.

---

the concept of rights in the modern sense, in which a right is 'subjective' in the sense of belonging to someone (the subject of the right). When he defines justice as the steady willingness to give to others *what is theirs*, Aquinas immediately goes on to treat that phrase as synonymous with *their right* (*ius suum*); hence he treats a right/rights (*ius/iura*) as subjective" See John Finnis, "A Grand Tour of Legal Theory," in *Collected Essays*, vol. 4, *Philosophy of Law*, 116. See also Finnis, *Aquinas*, 132–38; John Finnis, "Aquinas on Ius and Hart on Rights: A Response to Tierney," *The Review of Politics* 64, no. 3 (2002): 407–10; Finnis, "Grounding Human Rights in Natural Law," 213–20; and Finnis, "Aquinas and Natural Law Jurisprudence," 29. Finnis's claim was refuted by Brian Tierney, "Natural Law and Natural Rights: Old Problems and Recent Approaches," *The Review of Politics* 64, no. 3 (2002): 389–406. For more details on the debate between Villey, Tierney, and Finnis, see Petar Popović, "The Concept of 'Right' and the Focal Point of Juridicity in Debate Between Villey, Tierney, Finnis and Hervada," *Persona y Derecho* 78, no. 1 (2018): 65–103.

4. Finnis, *Natural Law and Natural Rights*, 207–8; John Finnis, "'Natural Law,'" in *Collected Essays*, vol. 1, *Reason in Action* (Oxford: Oxford University Press, 2011), 206–7.

Our author [i.e., John Finnis], therefore, always faithful to his legalistic point of departure, wants to postulate that the right is necessarily derived from the law (which is one way of reducing the right to law)…. The term "law" [may be] understood according to another meaning: since it is certain that if we understand this word to denote the divine plan governing the cosmic order, including the order of societies, then natural right will be the effect of this type of unwritten law, without, however, any possibility that we, in some way, deduce it from this law.[5]

Thus, the first basic element that Villey highlights in this text is his conception of natural law as the normative structure inherent in what he refers to as the divine cosmic order that defines the measure of natural rights. This element may be considered together with Villey's doctrine, as presented in the previous chapter, regarding the observation of the nature of things as the starting point for the cognition of the juridical domain. In this way, each of Villey's claims presented over the course of this section may be said to instantiate a contextualization of his arguments on the juridical domain of natural law within the broader juridical epistemology founded upon the observation of the nature of things.

On the other hand, there are solutions according to positive law which are derived from written rules—in this sense St. Thomas observes that the *constitutio scripta* may be one of the "reasons" for the right—*aliqualis ratio iuris* (*ST* II-II, q. 57, a. 1).[6]

From this text, it follows that the second element relevant to the discussion on the juridical dimension of natural law is Villey's frequent appeal to Aquinas's doctrine on the juridical status of the

---

5. Villey, "Si la théorie générale du droit, pour Saint Thomas, est une théorie de la loi," 429.

6. Villey, "Si la théorie générale du droit, pour Saint Thomas, est une théorie de la loi," 429.

concept of law. In the *Secunda secundae* of his *Summa Theologica*, Aquinas is concerned with how to adequately interrelate the concept of law with the specific domain of right (*ius*) as the object of the virtue of justice. His basic position regarding the juridical status of the law in general is that, "strictly speaking," it is "not the same as the right," but is rather an "expression of right" ("*aliqualis ratio iuris*")—or, better yet, an underlying or foundational normative framework (*ratio*) of right.[7] Aquinas's brief reference to law in this text appears in his response to the second of the three objections, according to which the right is not the object of justice since, among other elements, "law is a kind of right." His response is truly illuminating, because, in premising his position that *lex* is *aliqualis ratio iuris*, he presents a comparison that illustrates what he intends by the term *ratio*:

Just as there pre-exists in the mind of the craftsman an expression [*ratio*] of the things to be made externally by his craft, which expression [*ratio*] is called the rule of his craft, so too there pre-exists in the mind an expression [*ratio*] of the particular just work which the reason determines, and which is a kind of rule of prudence.[8]

Aquinas's example indicates that the act of justice—of giving to each his own right—is an external manifestation that has been

---

7. *ST* II-II, q. 57, a. 1, ad 2. The official English translation of the Fathers of the English Dominican Province translates the expression *aliqualis ratio iuris* as "an expression of the right." When referring to this translation in the text, I will also add the original word *ratio* in order to maintain the original meaning of Aquinas's *dictum*, which is, perhaps, not entirely reducible to the word "expression." Hervada seems to translate Aquinas's concept of law, from the aspect of its being a *ratio iuris*, essentially as the rational "rule of the right." See Hervada, *Critical Introduction to Natural Right*, 89–94; Hervada, *Lecciones propedéuticas de filosofía del derecho*, 315, 362. Finnis translates the term *ratio iuris* as "foundation of or informing idea behind right(s)." See John Finnis, "Practical Reason's Foundations," in *Collected Essays*, vol. 1, *Reason in Action*, 21. We have already seen Brock's translation of the same term: "a certain intelligible conception that establishes or measures or determines *ius*—a kind of formulation of it" (Brock, *The Light That Binds*, 85, 88).

8. *ST* II-II, q. 57, a. 1, ad 2.

previously delimited according to a normative content, a rule that determines the relevant terms of this act of justice. The terms of the act of justice preexist "in the mind" as an underlying framework, a *ratio*, that has a normative structure.

Aquinas then argues that "if this rule be expressed in writing it is called a law."[9] He seems thereby to invoke the example of the written norm of positive law only in an exemplary fashion, however, since by using the word *lex*, he intentionally references the types of law already discussed in the *Prima secundae*: the eternal law, natural law, positive law, Old Law, and New Law. In that part of the *Summa*, Aquinas speaks generally of law and various orders of law without specifying, at least for the purpose of his doctrine of the right, the status of natural law in the juridical domain. What is common to his discourses on law from both relevant parts of the *Summa*, however, is not the important question of whether and how law should be positivized in the sense of its being written or otherwise formulated as human law. As is evident from the definition of law he gives in the *Prima secundae*—"an ordinance of reason for the common good, made by him who has the care of community, and promulgated"[10]—the common element is that from both the moral perspective and the juridical perspective, the law is essentially a *ratio* that structures a certain normative order.

Beyond Aquinas's treatment of the juridical aspect of law, including natural law, another important argument of the *Secunda secundae* for the present purposes is his concept of natural right (*ius naturale*). Aquinas elaborates this concept when arguing that things (*res*) may be attributed and consequently owed in justice (*iusta*), in virtue of the nature itself (*ex ipsa natura rei*).[11]

9. *ST* II-II, q. 57, a. 1, ad 2.
10. *ST* I-II, q. 90, a. 4.
11. *ST* II-II, q. 57, a. 2.

The "right" or the "just" is a work that is adjusted [*adequatum*] to another person according to some kind of equality. Now a thing can be adjusted to a man in two ways: first by its very nature [*ex ipsa natura rei*] ... and this is called "natural right." In another way a thing is adjusted or commensurate to another person by agreement, or by common consent.... This can be done in two ways: first by private agreement ... secondly, by public agreement, as when the whole community agrees that something should be deemed as though it were adjusted and commensurate to another person, or when this is decreed by the prince who is placed over the people, and acts in its stead, and this is called "positive right."[12]

At this stage of his debate with Finnis, Villey invokes this text from Aquinas's *Summa* to explain the particular interrelation between positive law and positive right. Aquinas's account of the written law as a *ratio* of right, however, may be interpreted to denote the most basic level of interrelation between law and right on a general level or, on a more specific level, between natural law and natural rights. Villey incorporates this interpretation in his complex argument for the continuity between *lex naturalis* and *ius naturale*.

This [type of derivation of right from law] does not take place with regard to natural right ... and the natural right cannot be a "conclusion" from the principles of "natural law," but rather a "determination" which is derived from its own sources.... But if we understand the term "law" in the sense of the rule of conduct, as St. Thomas envisions it in the treatise on law (*ST* I-II) and which is the essential meaning of the natural law—a rational moral rule ... then the relation of dependence between law and right is inexistent.... It is clear that the moral law, which dictates the conduct of the individual does not have the function of measuring that proportion which the judge seeks to

12. *ST* II-II, q. 57, a. 2.

re-establish between individuals. *Determinationes* of the right must be sought in a source distinct from the moral law.... St. Thomas uses the concept of *determinatio* to delineate both the relation and the distinction between the law in general and the right.[13]

In my reading, when highlighting the discontinuity between natural moral law and natural rights, Villey advocates a necessary distinction between the sphere of moral law and the relatively autonomous juridical domain in which to identify the right as the just thing itself. He does not argue for the inexistence of an overlap between the natural law and natural rights but rather affirms that the moral domain of natural law—the rule of individual conduct—is structurally insufficient to explain its causal dependence with regard to the juridical domain. The moral domain of natural law, taken by itself, does not possess all the necessary properties for measuring the proportion of the right. In Villey's reading of Aquinas, *determination* is the specific procedure that is somehow operative on a discrete level within the constitution of the natural moral law as the source of the right.[14] This cluster of arguments

13. Villey, "Si la théorie générale du droit, pour Saint Thomas, est une théorie de la loi," 429–30.

14. In a question dedicated to the analysis of whether every human law is derived from the natural law, Aquinas claims that "something may be derived from the natural law" also by way of "determinations of certain generalities," for example, "the law of nature has it that the evil-doer should be punished; but that he be punished in this or that way, is a determination of the law of nature." Aquinas concludes that "those things which are derived" by way of determination "are contained in the human law." See *ST* I-II, q. 95, a. 2. Aquinas's argument regarding *determinatio* of the natural law is paradigmatically considered to denote exclusively a mode of derivation of positive law from natural law. For example, see Finnis, *Natural Law and Natural Rights*, 281–90. Villey, however, maintains that Aquinas's line of reasoning may be understood to mean that the things that are derived from natural law by way of *determinatio* are, indeed, contained in human law, but they are primarily considered to refer to rights in the perspective of justice. In fact, as Villey notes, Aquinas quite consistently uses the term *determinatio* also to contextualize or directly denote the ways in which certain precepts, natural or positive, are viewed through the optic of justice (Aquinas, at times, refers to *determinationes iustitiae*).

constitutes Villey's third basic element for an adequate understanding of the juridical domain of natural law.

Of course, St. Thomas acknowledges that there may be certain overlaps between the two realities [law and right], which he calls *communicationes*. In his analysis of the Jewish *Torah* (*ST* I-II, q. 94, a. 4; q. 104; q. 108, a. 3), he shows that some juridical content is found to be obscurely included in the precepts that are called "judicial" (*judicialia*) of the Old Law.[15]

The fourth basic element is the existence of a certain structural overlap between the law and right—that is, between the natural moral law and the specifically juridical domain. Villey affirms that this overlap may even possess the structure of a precept, and here he references Aquinas's doctrine on the so-called "judicial precepts of the Old Law" as those precepts which determine what is juridically right. Over the course of this chapter, I will analyze the nature of the specific determinations of the right that are attributed to a precept of the natural moral law in order to provide this precept with a specifically juridical status.

See *ST* I-II, q. 95, a. 2; q. 99, a. 4; and q. 104, a. 1. For Villey's position on this subject, see Villey, "Si la théorie générale du droit, pour Saint Thomas, est une théorie de la loi," 430.

15. Villey, "Si la théorie générale du droit, pour Saint Thomas, est une théorie de la loi," 430. Aquinas advances the argument that the judicial precepts have something in common (*communicant in aliquo*) with the moral precepts, to the extent that the former "are derived from reason," and, as such, "applied to individual cases in a determinate way" (*ST* I-II, q. 99, a. 4, ad 2). Thus, judicial precepts specify the principles of natural law in four different kinds of order, according to Aquinas: the order that concerns the office of the sovereign; the order of interactions between citizens, such as "buying and selling, judgements and penalties"; the order related to warfare and the status of foreigners; and the order of the domestic household (*ST* I-II, q. 104, a. 4). Now, there is an overlap between, for example, the precept of natural law that is the *ratio* of the natural right that consists in the equal value in return when something determinate is given to another person (*ST* II-II, q. 57, a. 2), on the one hand, and, on the other hand, the judicial precept contained in the following Aquinas text: "As regards animals granted in loan, the Law enacted that if, through the neglect of the person to whom they were lent, they perished or deteriorated ... he was bound to make restitution" (*ST* I-II, q. 105, a. 2, ad 4).

Returning, however, to the first of Villey's elements—the natural law's normative structure inherent in the natural order of things that defines the measure of natural rights—he frequently cautions his readers that the concept of law, above all, natural law, may be understood as a composite concept that bespeaks a twofold structure of essential meanings. The failure to differentiate this twofold structure may, indeed, lead to the confusion of the essence of the concept of law, and ultimately to a confusion between the moral and juridical domains.[16]

The first meaning of the concept of natural law refers to its moral domain. Natural moral law is a rule of moral conduct. It is also a rule that regulates the internal dispositions of the subject[17] and is contextualized within the orderedness of the entire moral domain.[18] In Villey's interpretation of the standard meaning of natural moral law, it primarily consists of the order of human fulfillment or happiness corresponding to the natural inclinations of human nature,[19] considered predominantly under the aspect of an individualized or atomized abstraction of the human essence.[20]

The moral status of natural law, according to Villey, does not primarily bring into focus "just shares or proportions"[21] (the apportionment of things to persons as their rights). Natural moral law simply does not have the primary function of assigning what is juridically *mine* or *yours*,[22] nor does it determine with clarity the limits or proportions between the juridical spheres of each

16. Villey, *La formation de la pensée juridique moderne*, 593.

17. Michel Villey, "Les lieux communs des juristes contemporains et le 'De Cive,'" *Revue européenne des sciences sociales* 20, no. 61 (1982): 314–15.

18. Villey, *Philosophie du droit*, vol. 1, 127.

19. Villey, "Droit Subjectif II (Le droit de l'individu chez Hobbes)," 189.

20. Villey, *La formation de la pensée juridique moderne*, 615; Villey, "La nature des choses," 50.

21. Villey, *La formation de la pensée juridique moderne*, 617.

22. Villey, *La formation de la pensée juridique moderne*, 605.

person.[23] If viewed according to this moral mode alone, natural law is devoid of juridical meaning.[24]

The second meaning by which Villey understands the law is decidedly juridical: law is not only a rule of moral conduct but also a juridical norm. Contrary to a common perception among philosophers of law who share his realistic conception,[25] and to occasional formulations of his own arguments,[26] Villey acknowledges that the concept of law also includes a specifically juridical structure when he affirms that "the law should not be entirely expelled from the domain of the right."[27] Thus, Villey's insistence on the thesis that the foundational concept of the juridical domain is that which is juridically right, and not the law, does not imply that the nature of law is outlined exclusively in moral terms.

Contrary to the theory that envisions positive law and subjective rights as specifically juridical extensions of morality, Villey claims that juridicity may be predicated on the content of the moral domain under the specific aspect of the attribution of apportionable things to persons in relations of justice.

23. Villey, "De la laïcité du droit selon Saint Thomas," 211. See also Villey, *La nature et la loi*, 142, and Villey, "Les lieux communs des juristes contemporains et le 'De Cive,'" 315.

24. Villey, *La formation de la pensée juridique moderne*, 615.

25. For example, Hervada criticizes the position he claims to have encountered in Villey's texts, namely, that the law "does not belong to 'right'—it does not contain a juridical entity—but to morality." See Hervada, *Lecciones propedéuticas de filosofía del derecho*, 314–15. In a similar vein, Schouppe understands Villey's concept of law as exclusively pertaining to the moral domain: "For [Villey] the law is a rule of conduct and … pertains to morality." See Schouppe, "El realismo jurídico de Javier Hervada," 49, n. 39.

26. Villey himself confesses his occasional and sometimes imperceptible shifting between the two domains inherent in the concept of law, namely, the moral and juridical. "If I have just said that the term 'law' denotes, for the whole of the doctrine, the source of the juridical order—and if I have elsewhere claimed what seems to be quite the contrary … it is precisely because of the pluriform meanings of this term" (Villey, *La formation de la pensée juridique moderne*, 593). See also Villey, *Le droit et les droits de l'homme*, 88, and Villey, *Philosophie du droit*, vol. 1, 60–61, 126–27.

27. Villey, *La nature et la loi*, 142.

Right is, thus, specialized within morality. And the laws which pertain only to morality should be distinguished from juridical laws; [the concept of] law, in its entirety, is not ... juridical law.[28]

On the other hand, all laws are not juridical laws, that is, *those which prescribe the content of justice*; there also exist simply moral laws which prescribe other virtues.[29]

The moral rule uses a different measure of value than the juridical rule (*judicialis*, [the rule] which expresses the right). The precepts of the Decalogue ... are conformant to their function of being the universal rules of morality, indispensable, immovable, valid at all times and in all places, but it will not [of itself] be in any way sufficient to meet the conditions for the constitution of the right.... The jurist seeks, above all, to know ... the limits between that which is "mine" and that which is "yours."[30]

How does Villey, then, envision the natural law as a "source of the juridical domain?"[31]

It is essentially an unwritten law.... [This] law is the order of nature, the structure of social groups.... [It is] a latent order of which we do not have the formulation, but which we have to search in things, since it is a reason hidden in things. Also, the *modus operandi* of the jurist should not consist of deduction, which takes a given rule as its point of departure, but of a precisely contrary operation—we should seek the rule by taking the observation of nature as our point of departure.[32]

Thus, Villey's account of the juridical status of natural law has several characteristics. As a general premise, it should be noted that he seems to understand natural law in its juridical aspect as a sort of natural nucleus and normative model of all juridical laws.

28. Villey, *La formation de la pensée juridique moderne*, 84.
29. Villey, "De la laïcité du droit selon Saint Thomas," 204–5. Emphasis added.
30. Villey, "De la laïcité du droit selon Saint Thomas," 211.
31. Villey, *La formation de la pensée juridique moderne*, 593.
32. Villey, *La formation de la pensée juridique moderne*, 593.

At one moment, he affirms that "according to classical doctrine, it is true that the just apportionment, that is, the juridical order, corresponds to a law, which is, above all, a natural law."[33]

Next, Villey seems to identify the juridical status of natural law with the order found "in the reflection offered to us by the nature of things,"[34] or the "rationality immanent in things."[35] This rationality indicates the things that are apportioned by nature precisely as *mine* or *yours*,[36] thereby ordering the just relations.[37] The juridical domain is "extracted from the observation of the whole of ... the nature of things" by applying criteria whereby the "things," "goods," "shares" are viewed under the aspect of their attribution to persons by human nature itself.[38] Human nature itself, therefore, performs the primary attribution of certain natural things or basic goods that are owed to the human person as something decidedly *his* according to juridical justice.[39] Beyond indicating the normative structures of human fulfillment and happiness in the domain of individual and social morality, the order of things that are attributed to persons according to their nature is deeply marked by distinctive relations of justice (in French: *riche de justice*)[40] while remaining "charged with normative content."[41]

Nature ... prefigures an order in the ... social universe. It attributes a determinate place for each thing and each man in society. The just is

<hr>

33. Villey, *La formation de la pensée juridique moderne*, 593.

34. Villey, "La méthode du droit naturel," 274.

35. Villey, *La formation de la pensée juridique moderne*, 594.

36. See Villey, *La formation de la pensée juridique moderne*, 605.

37. See Villey, *La formation de la pensée juridique moderne*, 617.

38. See Villey, "La nature des choses," 50.

39. See Michel Villey, *Philosophie du droit*, vol. 2, *Les moyens du droit* (Paris: Dalloz, 1979), 148–49, 154–55.

40. See Villey, "La nature des choses," 53–54. See also Michel Villey, "Le droit naturel et l'histoire," in *Seize Essais de philosophie du droit don un sur la crise universitaire*, 83.

41. Villey, "La nature des choses," 53.

above all a relation which is conformed to this plan of nature.... We affirm that nature has preconstituted certain juridical institutions.[42]

With regard to nature—and I am not referring to that human nature which would be envisioned as merely individual—it is not absurd to follow the tendency to discover harmonious social relations, that is, the just, the right. [It is the task of the jurist] to "read" the nature in each situation and extract the norms which nature contains within itself. And these norms have a value in themselves, because of the nature which they express, that is, simply because they translate in a more or less adequate way the order perceived in nature, without any need for ... a command issued by the state. This is how morality was constituted from antiquity [as the domain] which prohibits certain acts ... and commands certain obligations, insofar as they appear to be contrary or conformant to the ends of our nature. *But this is also the method to which we owe a large part of our juridical realm.*[43]

Another significant characteristic that Villey discerns in the juridical domain of his conception of natural law is its property of being unwritten or nonformulated.[44] He envisions this characteristic in view of the need to distinguish the posterior rational formulations of the juridical domain of natural law from its prior natural promulgation. Because the natural law is promulgated naturally (being "given" to each human person through his or her creation), it inheres, unwritten, in the very nature of each human person.

To understand how the natural law becomes a source of the right, we should view it as a law promulgated naturally—and therefore not by pure creation of human reason—that is then rep-

---

42. Villey, "La philosophie grecque classique et le droit romain," 29.

43. Villey, "Saint Thomas et l'immobilisme," 98. Emphasis added.

44. Villey, "Si la théorie générale du droit, pour Saint Thomas, est une théorie de la loi," 429; Villey, "Droit Subjectif II (Le droit de l'individu chez Hobbes)," 189; Villey, *La formation de la pensée juridique moderne*, 593; Villey, "Le droit naturel et l'histoire," 84; and Villey, "Abrégé du droit naturel classique," 140.

licated in the formulation of positive law.[45] The rationality inherent in the normative structure of natural law is not reducible only to the role that human reason has in its cognition. It is also related to the rationality of the things themselves as the "reflection of the divine order" or of the "eternal law"[46] in both parts of the concept of natural law: the rule of moral conduct *and* the norm of justice. In addition, on Villey's account, the fact that natural law is essentially a nonformulated law also implies that the jurist should discern in every concrete situation which things are attributed by nature to determinate subjects as *theirs*. He should do so by consulting the very nature of things as the primary source of the right, even when its content is already expressed in positive formulations of positive law.[47]

Another element of Villey's contribution to the adequate cognition and understanding of the juridical domain of natural law is contained in his claim that law, including natural law, may provide a "source"[48] for the constitution of the right. As seen before, Villey tends to elaborate this issue by appealing to Aquinas's overlapping doctrine of the law as "not the same as the right, but an expression [*ratio*] of the right."[49] It is no surprise that Villey was heavily influenced by Aquinas's doctrine on the concept of law precisely as addressed in the question on *ius* within his treatise

45. See Villey, "La méthode du droit naturel," 281, and Villey, "Le droit naturel et l'histoire," 76.

46. Villey, "Le droit naturel et l'histoire," 76.

47. Following again the example of Roman jurists, Villey claims that "the *modus operandi* of the jurist must not consist of deduction, which takes a given rule," already fixed as a rational formulation, "as its point of departure, but of a precisely contrary operation—we should seek the rule by taking the observation of nature as our point of departure" (Villey, *La formation de la pensée juridique moderne*, 593).

48. Villey, "Droit Subjectif II (Le droit de l'individu chez Hobbes)," 189; Villey, *La formation de la pensée juridique moderne*, 593; Villey, "La nature des choses," 54; and Villey, "La méthode du droit naturel," 281.

49. *ST* II-II, q. 57, a. 1, ad 2.

on right and justice of the *Secunda secundae* of the *Summa Theologica*, rather than within the broad context of the moral domain in the treatise on law of the *Prima secundae*. Villey rereads the juridical aspect of Aquinas's treatment of law in the *Secunda secundae* as the "expression, indication or the reason of the just relation," namely, as that normative structure that attributes things as rights.[50] Viewed under its aspect of the norm of justice and not only as the rule of conduct, the right is determined by law and is its "objective projection" or "product."[51] If the relation between law and right is understood in these terms, Villey is "prepared to concede" that natural law "is logically pre-existent with regard to right."[52]

In sum, when the natural law is observed under the aspect of attributing certain things as owed in justice to determinate persons, it certainly falls within the range of Villey's reading of Aquinas: "a certain type of law may constitute a source of the right—*aliqualis ratio iuris*."[53]

We have seen that one of Villey's contributions to the cognition of a juridical domain of natural law consists of the process of deriving or specifying the juridical domain from the natural law, considered as its source. It was noted that Villey, following Aquinas (*ST* I-II, q. 99, a. 4), refers to this process as *determination*, a term explicitly borrowed from Aquinas in order to highlight the possible connection between the normative structure of the *ratio* inherent in the nature of things and the constitution of the so-called "rules of the right."[54] The natural law in its moral domain is unsuitable for this connection since, according to Villey, it is

50. Villey, "Droit Subjectif II (Le droit de l'individu chez Hobbes)," 183.
51. Villey, "Droit Subjectif II (Le droit de l'individu chez Hobbes)," 183.
52. Villey, "Droits et règles," 221, n. 5.
53. See Villey, *Philosophie du droit*, vol. 1, 127.
54. Villey, "De la laicité du droit selon Saint Thomas," 211–12.

fallacious to reach conclusions regarding the specificities of the juridical domain (that is, the apportionment of things between persons) from the sole precepts of the natural moral law.[55] In sum, Villey understands determination to be that type of the specification of normative content that puts things or goods that are the object of the precept of natural (moral) or positive law in the focus of the relations of juridical justice.[56] In his view, determination brings about the derivation of natural right from the precepts of natural law.[57]

Although Villey does not detail his understanding of the process of determination at length or with exactitude, he does affirm that through determination, the mutual relation and distinction between the moral and juridical aspects of natural law are clearly delineated.[58] He also claims that in this process, the juridical domain is derived from within its own specific type of autonomous sources[59] rather than automatically from the moral domain. This entails the conclusion that, according to Villey, the process of determination is the means by which the precepts of natural law are constituted for the juridical domain.

What remains to be considered is the fourth basic element of Villey's contribution to the understanding of the juridical domain of natural law, which, as noted earlier, is his continuous reference to Aquinas's concept of so-called *judicial precepts*. Leaving aside for the moment the properties of this concept in the thought of Aquinas, it seems that Villey employs it mostly to highlight the

55. Villey, *La nature et la loi*, 142.

56. Villey, *La nature et la loi*, 142–43.

57. Villey, "Si la théorie générale du droit, pour Saint Thomas, est une théorie de la loi," 429–30.

58. Villey, "Si la théorie générale du droit, pour Saint Thomas, est une théorie de la loi," 430.

59. Villey, "Si la théorie générale du droit, pour Saint Thomas, est une théorie de la loi," 430; Villey, "De la laïcité du droit selon Saint Thomas," 211.

distinctive features of the juridical aspect of law in contrast to its moral aspect. Whereas the concept of the moral precepts refers to rules of conduct in view of the categories of the individual or common good, personal fulfillment, and happiness, in Villey's reading, Aquinas employs the term judicial precepts to primarily express "that which belongs to each person" in view of the fulfillment of justice wherein to each is given "what is owed to him, *suum cuique tribuere*."[60] We have already seen that in one text, Villey views the judicial precepts as a sort of theoretical model or exemplary structural locus, representing a certain overlap between law and right.[61] What is of special interest to Villey is that this type of precept represents a theoretical embodiment of both aspects of his twofold structure of the concept of law: they both retain their preceptive character as rules of conduct and express determinations of duties in justice to others.[62]

It should be noted that, unfortunately, Villey's present contributions are never really systematized in his texts, instead remaining scattered throughout his works. For this reason, they should be viewed more as an assemblage of elements in search of a more systematic treatment. Assembled into a coherent whole, however, they reveal a consistent outline of the main aspects of the juridical status of natural law, which were ultimately abandoned at the margins of Villey's principal juridical-philosophical interests. Javier Hervada's account of these identical issues represents a notable advance in discernment of the elements intuited by Villey, although that is probably due more to his having a philosophical

60. Villey, "Saint Thomas et l'immobilisme," 102. See also Villey, *La formation de la pensée juridique moderne*, 605.

61. Villey, "Si la théorie générale du droit, pour Saint Thomas, est une théorie de la loi," 430.

62. Michel Villey, *Questions de saint Thomas sur le droit et la politique ou le bon usage des dialogues* (Paris: Presses Universitaires de France, 1987), 101, 111.

platform similar to Villey than to an explicit intention of furthering Villey's theses on these precise topics.

Hervada and the Juridical Status
of Natural Law

Since Hervada's arguments on the possibility of predicating a
juridical domain on natural law are far more coherent, unam-
biguous, and systematic than Villey's, I will present his thought
in three distinct subsections.[63] First, Hervada shares Villey's approach regarding the stratification of the primary meanings of the
concept of law according to its moral and juridical aspects. Secondly, in his development of the basic concept of the title of the
right, Hervada reflects on the arguments relative to human nature
as the natural title of rights. Whereas these two subsections posit
certain structural elements that only imply a juridical domain of
natural law, in the third subsection, I will present Hervada's explicit references to this domain extracted from his texts.

The Juridical Aspect of the Legal Norm

In the preceding section, I showed how Villey understands law as
a composite concept that is properly considered under two essential aspects. First, a legal rule has a moral aspect: law is the measure of morality insofar as it is a rule of conduct containing an
order toward the attainment of human fulfillment and happiness.
Secondly, a legal norm has a juridical aspect: law is the measure
of the right, insofar as it attributes certain things to determinate

63. For an earlier analysis of some of the arguments from this section, see Petar
Popović, "A Hervadian Realistic Argument for the Juridical Status of Natural Law," *Ius
Ecclesiae* 31, no. 2 (2019): 567–88.

persons as their *suum* owed in justice by others. Hervada endorses and develops the basic elements of this perspective.

According to Hervada's stratification of the basic aspects of the concept of law, a legal norm has three principal functions, which are as follows:

- *political*, inasmuch as law is essentially a rule that contains the adequate orderedness to the common good within political society;
- *moral*, inasmuch as law is a rule of personal conduct that reflects the order toward the fulfillment of the human person; and
- *juridical*, inasmuch as law is the rule of the right.[64]

Hervada's treatment of the moral and political functions of the legal norm largely overlaps with Villey's understanding of the moral aspect of law regarding individual and social morality.[65] He seems to understand that the moral aspect of law essentially denotes the norm of individual action that expresses the order toward the good of the human person, which consists in man's natural end, the virtues and personal happiness.[66] He envisions the political function of law, however, as the specifically social rule of action that expresses the order of communal human conduct to ward the common good.[67] Commenting on the elements of Aquinas's definition of law—"a rational orderedness of human conduct

64. See Hervada, *Lecciones propedéuticas de filosofía del derecho*, 311.

65. Hervada himself notes this overlap: "To understand Villey's position we should keep in mind that he does not understand the concept of morality as denoting a domain of personal conduct, but instead takes as his starting point the classical meaning of the Greeks, who regarded morality as personal and social conduct.... For Villey, morality comprehends that sphere which we have delimited here as encompassing the object of political philosophy and moral philosophy" (Hervada, *Lecciones propedéuticas de filosofía del derecho*, 315, n. 31).

66. Hervada, *Lecciones propedéuticas de filosofía del derecho*, 312.

67. Hervada, *Lecciones propedéuticas de filosofía del derecho*, 312.

towards the common good"[68]—he affirms that it contemplates law "from the point of view of the development of social life in relation to social ends, to the common good,"[69] an aspect that he explicitly refers to as "the perspective of political philosophy."[70]

On Hervada's account, however, neither the political nor the moral function of law addresses the specific end of the juridical aspect of the legal norm, namely, the order of juridical justice or of that which is juridically right.

This perspective [of political philosophy] is not characteristic of the juridical domain, the key concept of which is not the order, but the apportionment of things, that is of *that which is just*.... When juridical philosophy has adopted the same perspective as political philosophy (as has occurred and occurs so often), it has been incapable of explaining the juridical phenomenon as a whole, and has fallen into reductionism—e.g., the juridical norm as equal to the law enacted by the social power.[71]

According to Hervada, the great majority of treatises in legal philosophy that adopt a jusnaturalist perspective do not observe the legal norm from the perspective of its juridical aspect as a rule of the right but instead adopt as their exclusive starting point the Thomistic definition of law from the *Summa's Prima secundae*. Such philosophical perspectives easily conflate that which is juridically right with that which is prescribed by positive law, without ever really exploring the juridical aspect of the legal norm.[72] In Hervada's view, in order to understand the law in its specifically juridical aspect, it is necessary to observe the legal norm as Aquinas defines it in the *Secunda secundae*, which conceives the

68. Hervada, *Critical Introduction to Natural Right*, 92.

69. Hervada, *Critical Introduction to Natural Right*, 93. See also Hervada, *Lecciones propedéuticas de filosofía del derecho*, 362n.

70. Hervada, *Critical Introduction to Natural Right*, 92–93.

71. Hervada, *Critical Introduction to Natural Right*, 93.

72. See Hervada, *Lecciones propedéuticas de filosofía del derecho*, 313.

law under the aspect of the apportionment of things consequently owed in justice.

The norm is juridical as a function of the *ius* or the right (in the realistic sense). The juridical perspective is not the perspective of the social order, but of the apportionment of things. Consequently, the norm acquires the connotation of juridical because of its relation to ... justice.... Briefly stated, juridical norms are those norms that refer to just conduct, that is, to conduct that is owed (obligatory) because they constitute a duty of ... justice; a norm is juridical when the conduct it prescribes constitutes a just debt.[73]

The distinctive character of the juridical norm may be found in its property of being "related to the thing justly owed,"[74] and thus to juridical justice, beyond also being, in the relevant broader moral context, a norm of good conduct.[75] From the perspective of the juridical aspect of the law, then, we could say together with Hervada that the legal norm has, first, the generic character proper to all laws, which "consists in being an *ordinatio rationis*, a rule or rational structure of human social life," to the extent that a juridical norm cannot fulfill its essence if it is not at the same time "rational" or if it does not constitute or reveal an "order."[76] Secondly, the juridical norm has the specific characteristic of being related to the right.[77] Thus, both of Aquinas's accounts of the law, that of the *Prima secundae* and that of the *Secunda secundae*, are brought together in a new synthesis.

Hervada further explains this specific relation of the legal norm to the right by developing a point that Villey also high-

---

73. Hervada, *Critical Introduction to Natural Right*, 92.

74. Hervada, *Lecciones propedéuticas de filosofía del derecho*, 320.

75. See Hervada, *Critical Introduction to Natural Right*, 91–92. See also Hervada, "Apuntes para una exposición del realismo jurídico clásico," 295.

76. Hervada, *Lecciones propedéuticas de filosofía del derecho*, 362.

77. Hervada, *Lecciones propedéuticas de filosofía del derecho*, 362.

lights in his texts, which is that law is a specific "source"[78] of the right, in continuity with the Thomistic *dictum* on law as the *ratio iuris*.[79] The legal norm is a rule of that which is just, insofar as it "regulates the right and the correlative debt, that is, it indicates what things belong to each person."[80] As such, "If the right is the just thing, that thing which is owed to its titleholder, the norm establishes the statute of the right: it attributes things to a titleholder.... In brief, the norm regulates the right, it is its rule."[81]

For Hervada, law has two specific tasks resulting from its being the source of the right. First, it is the *cause* of the right. The relation in question is one of cause (law) and effect (that which is juridically right).[82] This means that laws apportion certain things by granting their titles of attribution and regulating the corresponding debt—thus, they "create rights."[83] Secondly, law is a *measure* of the right, in the sense that the juridical norm regulates all of the particular aspects and determinations of a concrete right.[84] The relation in question here is one between a measure (law) and the thing measured (right).[85]

Human Nature as the Natural Title of the Right

We have just seen how Hervada views the law, in its juridical aspect, as something approximating what he elsewhere refers to as

---

78. See Hervada, *Lecciones propedéuticas de filosofía del derecho*, 315.

79. Hervada, *Lecciones propedéuticas de filosofía del derecho*, 315, 362.

80. Hervada, *Critical Introduction to Natural Right*, 90. Emphasis added.

81. Hervada, *Lecciones propedéuticas de filosofía del derecho*, 315.

82. Hervada, *What Is Law?* 98.

83. Hervada, *Critical Introduction to Natural Right*, 90; Hervada, *Lecciones propedéuticas de filosofía del derecho*, 316–17; Hervada, *What Is Law?* 99; and Hervada, "Apuntes para una exposición del realismo jurídico clásico," 294.

84. Hervada, *Critical Introduction to Natural Right*, 90; Hervada, *Lecciones propedéuticas de filosofía del derecho*, 317; and Hervada, *What Is Law?* 99–100.

85. Hervada, *What Is Law?* 99.

the title of the right.[86] According to Hervada, the title is that in which the right has its origin, that is, that which attributes the thing to a subject, or that by virtue of which the thing is his own.[87] Among the principal types of different titles, Hervada repeatedly refers to human nature as a possible title of the right.[88] He notes how, since antiquity, the right has ordinarily been divided, according to its title, into natural right and positive right, and he affirms that the former of these "arises from nature."[89]

What does this origin mean? In substance, it means that there are things that are attributed to a person by virtue of the very nature of man—in other words, their title arises from man's very being—and they are measured according to the nature of things.... There are things that are attributed to each man precisely because he is a person. There are things that belong to man by virtue of his nature, for example, his life, his physical integrity, etc.... Each of those things—corporeal and incorporeal—that are attributed to man by nature constitutes a natural right.[90]

Hence, in a realistic conception of right and juridicity, natural rights are those things that are attributed to man by his nature as his own and are owed in justice by all, who are thus indebted to give those rights to their titleholder. The title that attributes things as natural rights is called the "natural title."[91]

<hr>

86. Hervada, *Lecciones propedéuticas de filosofía del derecho*, 317.

87. Hervada, *Critical Introduction to Natural Right*, 26.

88. Hervada, *Critical Introduction to Natural Right*, 26–27; Hervada, *What Is Law?* 52; Hervada, "Apuntes para una exposición del realismo jurídico clásico," 291; and Hervada, *Lecciones propedéuticas de filosofía del derecho*, 205.

89. Hervada, *Critical Introduction to Natural Right*, 51. Here Hervada refers, among other sources, to Aquinas's claim for the existence of natural right: "[Since] the right or the 'just' is a work that is adjusted to another person according to some kind of equality ... a thing can be adjusted [*adaequatum*] to a man ... by its very nature ... and this is called 'natural right'" (*ST* II-II, q. 57, a. 2).

90. Hervada, *Critical Introduction to Natural Right*, 51–52. See also Hervada, *Lecciones propedéuticas de filosofía del derecho*, 523.

91. Hervada, *Critical Introduction to Natural Right*, 54–57. See also Hervada, *Lecciones propedéuticas de filosofía del derecho*, 503–4, and Hervada, *What Is Law?* 68–70.

All the goods inherent to [man's] own being are ... *his* in the most strict and proper sense. With this in mind, it is evident that the set of goods inherent to his being represent *his things*, with which others cannot interfere and which they cannot appropriate.... They are then rights of the person, rights that the person has by virtue of his nature.[92]

In concluding this subsection, I will examine how Hervada connects his doctrine of the juridical aspect of law with the arguments on the natural title before I present in the next subsection various textual instances in which Hervada explicitly refers to the juridical status of natural law. In one such locus, Hervada himself acknowledges this interrelation: "Natural law ... as the rule or measure of rights is a juridical law.... Natural rights obviously do not only have a natural title but also a natural measure ... this natural measure or rule of rights is natural law, since the rule of the right is law."[93]

Therefore, natural law is precisely the normative structure arising from human nature, which represents the natural title and measure of that which is juridically right according to nature. We have seen how Hervada envisions the legal norm, in its juridical aspect, as the title of right, insofar as it indicates what things belong to each person and, thus, "regulates the right and the correlative debt."[94] The precept of natural law, then, possesses the character of a natural title, insofar as it attributes certain things or goods as a person's *suum* owed in justice by others—in other words, as a person's natural rights.[95]

92. Hervada, *Critical Introduction to Natural Right*, 54.
93. Hervada, *What Is Law?* 143.
94. Hervada, *Critical Introduction to Natural Right*, 90.
95. See Hervada, *Lecciones propedéuticas de filosofía del derecho*, 523.

Hervada's Explicit Claims on the Juridical Status of Natural Law

In contrast to Villey, who only incidentally and implicitly lays down certain elements indicating a juridical domain predicable of natural law, Hervada explicitly refers to such a domain on numerous occasions throughout his writings. The precise textual loci in which he explicitly addresses this issue should be read in the immediate context of his accounts on the juridical aspect of the legal norm as the rule of the right and on the natural title of right. In addition, his relevant texts on the juridical domain of natural law testify to his own process of doctrinal development regarding this issue. For this reason, I will follow the chronological thread of argumentation across his works in which he treats this issue.

In the first work of Hervada's mature juridical-philosophical thought, *Critical Introduction to Natural Right*, he already seems to possess clear ideas on the need to postulate a specifically juridical domain pertaining to natural law, although at this point the clarity of his ideas on the present topic is not yet accompanied by the same argumentative precision that he applies to other foundational elements of his theory in this same work.

Early on in the book, he hints at arguments that he will develop in its subsequent sections.

What we call the order of justice, the demands of justice, or the norm of justice is none other than the natural right. And the so-called principles of justice are not distinct from the principles or *precepts of* that [*natural*] *right*.[96]

Expressions such as "the duty of justice," "the demand for justice," and "the norm of justice," denote a duty, a demand, or a law, the ful-

---

96. Hervada, *Critical Introduction to Natural Right*, 10. Emphasis added.

fillment of which is an act of the virtue of justice, that is, an act which denotes a right or a *law—of natural origin* or of positive origin—*of a juridical nature.*[97]

Hervada here mentions the "precepts of natural right" while also speaking of the "law of a juridical nature," which may have a "natural origin." Since in his theory the right and natural right are consistently identified with the just thing itself and are never reduced to a precept, one may conclude with certainty that he has a very clear position on the juridical norms of natural origin that are somehow causally related to natural right. He is certainly not talking about a moral law of natural origin here. In this early stage of the book, he does not yet even mention natural law.[98]

In line with his position on the internal stratification of the concept of law in at least two of its aspects—moral and juridical—Hervada distinguishes two domains of natural law as well.

Natural juridical norms ... are a sector or part of the natural normativity of human life—in its individual aspect as well as in its social aspect—which is given the name of *natural law*; that is why it is appropriate to take note of that law here. However, a detailed study of natural

---

97. Hervada, *Critical Introduction to Natural Right*, 15. Emphasis added.

98. For a book that predominantly addresses the topic of natural rights from a classical Thomistic perspective, the reader may be surprised to discover that Hervada dedicates a relatively small portion of *Critical Introduction to Natural Right* to the topic of natural law. Thomistic accounts of natural rights are usually developed within the framework of Aquinas's discussion of natural law in the *Prima secundae* of his *Summa Theologica*, particularly in I-II, q. 94, a. 2. Natural rights are, then, ordinarily treated as an argumentative extension of the discourse on Thomistic natural law. Hervada's approach in *Critical Introduction to Natural Right* is strikingly different. He starts with the basic elements of what he understands to be the essence of the juridical domain, namely, the right as the thing owed in justice and then moves toward an elaboration of what the concept of natural rights means in classical juridical realism. Even more surprisingly, although he considers natural law to be obviously important for any account on natural rights, his treatment of natural rights is not structured as if it is entirely epistemologically or conceptually dependent on explicit natural-law arguments. Only in the second half of the book does he discuss natural law explicitly, after having laid down the foundations for his account of the juridical domain.

law is not the task of the science of natural rights, but of the moral philosophy. That is why we will only briefly expound on natural law to the extent that we consider it necessary for the study of natural rights.[99]

In reference to the normative structure of the nature of the human person, therefore, which may be identified with the natural moral law, there is a sphere constituted in accordance with the properties of the juridical domain, which Hervada refers to, as seen in the above quote, as natural juridical norms.

In its moral domain, natural law is, according to Hervada, "the set of rational laws that set forth the order of natural tendencies or inclinations towards the ends that are characteristic of the human being"[100] (i.e., toward his individual and social natural ends).[101] Although he dedicates a quantitatively significant portion of his works to natural moral law,[102] Hervada certainly does not envision this aspect of natural law as primarily foundational with regard to the specificities of the juridical dimension.

In *Critical Introduction to Natural Right*, Hervada understands the juridical aspect of natural law as the rule (*ratio*) or set of rules that are the cause and measure of natural rights, because they determine the obligations of so-called natural justice. Hence, this set of rules may be also referred to as "natural juridical law,"[103] which "is that part of natural law that refers to the relations of justice; that is, natural law is natural juridical law insofar as it is a rule of right and only under this aspect."[104]

Thus, natural juridical law represents a discrete feature of the

99. Hervada, *Critical Introduction to Natural Right*, 95.

100. Hervada, *Critical Introduction to Natural Right*, 99.

101. Hervada, *Critical Introduction to Natural Right*, 98.

102. For his presentation of the natural law in its moral domain, see Hervada, *Critical Introduction to Natural Right*, 95–112. For references to natural moral law in his other works, see Hervada, *Lecciones propedéuticas de filosofía del derecho*, 504–6, 584–86; Hervada, *What Is Law?* 148–50, 159–68.

103. See Hervada, *Critical Introduction to Natural Right*, 94, 116–17.

104. Hervada, *Critical Introduction to Natural Right*, 116.

natural law in its specifically juridical aspect, that is, from the perspective of the *ratio* of the right. Hervada says that the precepts such as, for example, "do not kill" or "do not steal," unquestionably "have a moral aspect," but they "do constitute natural juridical law to the extent that they regard the right to life or the right to property."[105] Natural law is the underlying foundational normative *ratio* that determines the specific measure of natural rights, but Hervada highlights that the sole moral aspect of natural law is insufficient to provide the ontological-relational cause of the existence of natural rights.[106] Rather, by establishing certain basic human goods as owed in the perspective of justice, the natural juridical law may be seen as the foundational cause of rights, without ontologically reducing the concept of rights (i.e., the just things or goods themselves) to the concept of law.

In his 1992 work, *Lecciones propedéuticas de filosofía del derecho*, Hervada further elaborates on his line of argument regarding the juridical domain of natural law. When analyzing the concept of natural right in that book, he claims that the concept in question may be viewed from different perspectives, each of them foundational in their own way, but with an inherent conceptual hierarchy among them. Natural right, as the "natural nucleus of a juridical system," may be viewed from the aspect of the "right in the proper and strict sense—as that which is just," but then also "as a norm" or "as a relation."[107] According to Hervada, however, among these perspectives, the primary and proper sense of the concept of natural right is that which is just according to human nature, that is, "the corporeal or incorporeal thing which is adjusted or apportioned to man in virtue of his nature or fun-

---

105. See Hervada, *Critical Introduction to Natural Right*, 116–17.
106. Hervada, *Critical Introduction to Natural Right*, 117.
107. Hervada, *Lecciones propedéuticas de filosofía del derecho*, 518.

damental ontological structure, conjugated with the property of debt and eligibility to make [correspondent] claims inherent in the dignity of the human person,"[108] adding, "This is natural right in the proper sense of the term; the other elements of the natural nucleus of juridicity, such as the natural juridical norms or natural law in its juridical aspect, may be called natural right only in an analogous sense."[109]

Hervada clearly distinguishes the natural law in its juridical aspect from the primary meaning of natural right as the thing or good that is just according to nature. His progression toward a clear terminological differentiation between natural law and natural right is finalized in the arguments he presents in the chapter on "the natural nucleus of right," within a subsection dedicated to the so-called "natural norms."

Human nature ... is constituted as a rule or criterion of personal and social conduct which contains a normative or legal structure—it is a norm of conduct, ordinarily known as natural law. The aspect of this normative structure which has a greater relevance—because of its relation to the perfection and development of the person—is the moral aspect.... We will ... limit ourselves to the study of natural normativity from the juridical point of view, that is, insofar as this natural normativity is, in part, constituted as a natural juridical norm.[110]

The natural juridical norm, or "juridical natural law,"[111] is a set of rules that regulate the right or that which is just. The natural law, "in that which pertains to the juridical domain," is constituted as "the set of natural juridical norms."[112]

---

108. Hervada, *Lecciones propedéuticas de filosofía del derecho*, 523.
109. Hervada, *Lecciones propedéuticas de filosofía del derecho*, 522.
110. Hervada, *Lecciones propedéuticas de filosofía del derecho*, 531.
111. Hervada, *Lecciones propedéuticas de filosofía del derecho*, 532, 586.
112. Hervada, *Lecciones propedéuticas de filosofía del derecho*, 532.

In his 2002 work, *What Is Law? The Modern Response of Juridical Realism*, Hervada contributes some brief yet significant arguments toward a better understanding of the juridical status of natural law. Issued almost twenty years after the publication of the first Spanish edition of *Critical Introduction to Natural Right*, his remarks in *What Is Law?* represent his final thoughts on the doctrinal position advocated in previous works.

First, with regard to the stratification of natural law in its two aspects, moral and juridical, Hervada affirms that the "demands which in themselves or with respect to others flow from the personal nature of humans are what constitute the moral order and the natural juridical order, which is expressed in natural law."[113] At this definitive stage of the development of his argument, he no longer views the juridical domain of natural law from the viewpoint of natural right. Rather, the natural law clearly has a distinct and specific juridical status. Later in the same work, he affirms that although the whole of moral reality, and consequently the natural law, should be viewed as a unity, we may, and should, nonetheless "distinguish aspects in it."[114] Thus, natural law must be viewed also from the aspect of "the rule or measure of rights," that is, as "juridical law."[115] Thus, in Hervada's view, the existence of natural rights calls to our attention the fact that "we have to posit the existence also of the juridical natural law."[116] "This complex of rules of the right," he adds, "constitutes the juridical aspect of natural law, or natural juridical law."[117]

The only possible objection that one could advance to Hervada's account is its underdevelopment in interrelating juridical

---

113. Hervada, *What Is Law?* 116.
114. Hervada, *What Is Law?* 143.
115. Hervada, *What Is Law?* 143.
116. Hervada, *What Is Law?* 143.
117. Hervada, *What Is Law?* 143–44.

natural law with the elements of the Thomistic theory of natural moral law. Whereas Hervada acknowledges the distinction between the moral and juridical aspects of natural law, he does not follow the claim that moral and juridical domains are here "aspects of one and the same law"[118] through to its logical consequences.

Aquinas Revisited

After the survey of the main arguments offered by Villey and Hervada with respect to the juridical status of natural law, a re-reading of some of Aquinas's texts might prove to be helpful in order to check whether he has also at least implicitly contributed to this issue. To be sure, he did not formulate his thoughts on the topic as an explicit *quaestio*. Nonetheless, there are certain textual arguments in which Aquinas does, in fact, make claims that are pertinent to an understanding of the juridical domain as predicable of natural law.

The most important question in the *Summa Theologica* with respect to such arguments is found in the *Secunda secundae*: "whether the precepts of the Decalogue are precepts of justice [*praecepta iustitiae*]."[119] Out of the four objections presented by Aquinas at the beginning of the article, the first two are of particular importance for my present analysis. The first objection actually denies that the precepts of the Decalogue may be constituted as precepts of justice, since the Decalogue, belonging to the genus of law, prescribes the acts of all virtues and not of justice alone. The second objection concentrates instead on the relation

118. Hervada, *What Is Law?* 145.
119. *ST* II-II, q. 122, a. 1.

between two types of precepts—moral precepts and judicial precepts. While the judicial precepts pertain to justice, the precepts of the Decalogue necessarily belong to the moral precepts.

In the *respondeo*, Aquinas affirms that the precepts of the Decalogue clearly belong to the genus of law and are, indeed, "the first principles of the law" that "natural reason assents to at once, as to the principles that are most evident."[120] Aquinas then makes the claim that it is "altogether evident that the notion of duty" (*manifestissime autem ratio debiti*), which is "essential to a precept," is a notion that "appears in justice" (*apparet in iustitia*).[121] Now, justice considers "those matters where man is directed toward the other."[122] He then concludes that since, "in matters that refer to another it appears manifestly [*manifeste apparet*] that a man is under obligation to render to another that which is his due," then, in his view, "the precepts of the Decalogue *must needs pertain to justice*."[123]

In the response to the first objection, Aquinas acknowledges that "the intention of the law is to make all men virtuous," but this intention, he adds, is realized "in a certain order": namely, "by first of all giving them precepts about those things where the notion of duty is most manifest [*est manifestior ratio debiti*]."[124] We have seen that in the *respondeo*, he states that the notion of duty appears *manifestissime* in justice. Hence, the precepts of the Decalogue may be constituted as precepts of justice (*praecepta*

---

120. *ST* II-II, q. 122, a. 1.

121. *ST* II-II, q. 122, a. 1. "The notion of duty is not so patent in the other virtues as it is in justice. Hence the precepts about the acts of other virtues are not so well known to the people as are the precepts of the acts of justice. Wherefore the acts of justice especially come under the precepts of the Decalogue, which are the primary elements of the law" (*ST* I-II, q. 100, a. 3, ad 3).

122. *ST* II-II, q. 122, a. 1.

123. *ST* II-II, q. 122, a. 1. Emphasis added.

124. *ST* II-II, q. 122, a. 1, ad 1.

iustitiae), insofar as they specifically address duties of justice toward others.

Before advancing the claim that Aquinas's argument regarding the precepts of justice may refer to the present analysis of the juridical status of natural law, it is necessary to address two additional issues. First, it must be verified that in Aquinas's doctrine, the precepts of the Decalogue may be, in some way, reducible to natural law. Second, it must be demonstrated that his reference to justice with regard to *praecepta iustitiae* may at least partly be taken to include the specific issues of juridical justice.

Aquinas addresses the first issue through an argument that may be combined from various textual loci of his *Summa Theologica*. In the first place, he claims that

all the moral precepts belong to the law of nature, but not all in the same way ... for there are certain things which the natural reason of every man, of its own accord and at once, judges to be done or not to be done—e.g., "Honor thy father and thy mother," and "thou shalt not kill, thou shalt not steal"—and these belong to the law of nature absolutely.[125]

Given the examples he cites from the Decalogue, it is possible to conclude from this article that Aquinas understands the precepts of the Decalogue as exemplary moral precepts that belong to the natural law in an absolute way. He further writes in an article dedicated to the question of whether it is right to distinguish other moral precepts of the law besides the Decalogue,

Now of [the moral precepts] there are three grades: for some are most certain, and so evident as to need no promulgation ... wherefrom no man can have an erroneous judgment about them. Some precepts are more detailed, the reason of which even an uneducated man can easily

125. *ST* I-II, q. 100, a. 1.

grasp; and yet they need to be promulgated, because human judgment
… happens to be led astray concerning them: these are the precepts of
the Decalogue. Again, there are some precepts the reason of which is
not so evident to anyone, but only the wise; these are moral precepts
added to the Decalogue.[126]

The precepts of the Decalogue thus belong to the second level
of precepts, which need to be promulgated even though they, as
Aquinas says, can be gathered at once from the first general principles "with but slight reflection." According to Aquinas, however,
the Decalogue also contains those very "first general principles"
(the moral precepts that belong to the first level) as "principles
in their proximate conclusions."[127] This argument enhances the
overlap between the content of natural law and the precepts of
the Decalogue. In conclusion, when Aquinas speaks about the
precepts of the Decalogue as potential principles of justice, one
can understand the Decalogue to mean those legal norms that
are, in a way, structurally reducible to natural law, and which, in
other ways, encompass all moral precepts as "principles in their
proximate conclusions."[128]

The second issue orbits the question of whether Aquinas's reference to justice with regard to *praecepta iustitiae* may at least
partly be taken to include the specific issues of juridical justice.
When answering the question of "whether the mode of virtue falls
under the precepts of the law," Aquinas affirms that "the mode of
doing acts of justice, which falls under the precept, is that they be
done in accordance with the right [*secundum ordinem iuris*]."[129]
This argument is as important as it is concise. When this text is
read in connection to his firm position that right is the object

126. *ST* I-II, q. 100, a. 11.
127. *ST* I-II, q. 100, a. 3.
128. *ST* I-II, q. 100, a. 3.
129. *ST* I-II, q. 100, a. 9, ad 1.

of justice,[130] with justice defined as the "perpetual and constant will to render to each his own right,"[131] it is sufficiently clear that Aquinas gives an affirmative answer to the above question.

Having settled the two additional issues, it is possible to conclude that Aquinas's argument on the constitution of the principles of natural law as precepts of justice comprises his doctrine on the juridical status of natural law, at least implicitly.

Before I conclude this chapter, I still have to address Aquinas's response to the second objection from question 122, article 1, of the *Summa*'s *Secunda secundae*. The objector, as noted, claims that the precepts of the Decalogue are, in fact, moral, not judicial, precepts, and, as such, they are not intrinsically connected to matters of justice. The real question that interests me here is whether, as Villey claimed, the correct way to establish the juridical status of natural law is that of considering the precepts of *lex naturalis* within the context of Aquinas's doctrine on the judicial precepts. In his response, Aquinas claims that judicial precepts are *determinationes* of moral precepts, thereby reconfiguring judicial precepts' telic aspect to concern primarily the domain of justice.[132] But Aquinas is quite clear in his response that judicial precepts, although they "are determinations of the precepts of the Decalogue," are not themselves contained in the Decalogue.[133] It seems that although judicial precepts do, in fact, pertain to justice, their particular function does not make them suitable for the paradigmatic example of the potential overlap between the moral and juridical domains for which Villey advocated regarding natural law.

Aquinas's concept of judicial precepts has the essential func-

---

130. *ST* II-II, q. 57, a. 1.
131. *ST* II-II, q. 58, a. 1.
132. *ST* II-II, q. 122, a. 1, ad 2.
133. *ST* II-II, q. 122, a. 1, ad 2.

tion of denoting those precepts of the Old Mosaic Law that "derive their force from their institution alone [and not from the very dictate of natural reason alone, as is the case with 'moral precepts'], since before they were instituted, it seemed of no consequence whether things were done in this or that way."[134] It is precisely in virtue of their institution, and not because of any overlap with the genesis of various degrees of moral precepts, that the judicial precepts are *determinationes* of the "precepts of the Decalogue."[135] Moreover, in Aquinas's system of precepts, the judicial precepts of the Old Mosaic Law are abolished by the New Law.[136]

All of these arguments lead to the conclusion that the content and function of judicial precepts, notwithstanding their link to the domain of justice, makes them unsuitable for delineating a conceptual overlap between the moral and juridical domains within natural law. Such conceptual overlap may instead be found, as we have seen, in Aquinas's arguments in favor of the constitution of the precepts of the Decalogue as the *praecepta iustitiae*. One can read Aquinas's claim that "the determination of the common precepts of that justice [*communis praecepti de iustitia*] which is to be observed among men is effected by the judicial precepts"[137] as corroborating my present interpretation of the function of judicial precepts. Indeed, judicial precepts serve to determine certain aspects of the moral precepts with greater precision and to "'fill in the blanks' when more than one way of doing so might be reasonable."[138] They do not, however, primarily determine a juridical domain as predicable of natural law.

---

134. *ST* I-II, q. 100, a. 11. See also *ST* I-II, q. 104, a. 1.

135. *ST* I-II, q. 100, a. 11, ad 2.

136. *ST* I-II, q. 104, a. 3.

137. *ST* I-II, q. 99, a. 4.

138. J. Budziszewski, *Commentary on Thomas Aquinas's Virtue Ethics* (Cambridge: Cambridge University Press, 2017), 268.

A final thought regarding Aquinas's implicit doctrine on the juridical status of natural law is reserved for the question of whether this doctrine actually establishes a way for an alternative reading of what is known as the *lex injusta non est lex* natural-law argument. According to the standard reading of this argument, on its most general level, any positive law or declaratory enactment of subjective human rights that would illegitimately hinder a precept of natural moral law is thereby immoral and thus *lex injusta*. I will not here engage in a detailed analysis of Aquinas's position, such as examining the degree to which an immoral or unjust positive law is deficient with regard to its obligatory effect on citizens, or whether such a law still retains the characteristics which Raz refers to as the systemic moral properties of law.[139] Surely, the great majority of Aquinas's contemporary commentators make a detailed case for the incorrectness of the proposition that an immoral and thus unjust law somehow *eo ipso* ceases to be any kind of law at all.[140]

I instead suggest an alternative and complementary Thomistic reading, in line with the realistic conception of right and juridicity, regarding the modalities in which immoral laws might also be said to be unjust. In a nutshell, I argue that the unjust character of positive laws does not arise immediately from their immorality. Rather, a positive law is unjust because it does not respect the order of justice established by natural law in its strictly juridical

139. For the details of Aquinas's doctrine on this issue, see *ST* I-II, q. 92, a. 1, ad 4; q. 95, a. 2; q. 96, a. 4; and q. 96, a. 6.

140. See, for example, Finnis, *Natural Law and Natural Rights*, 354–62; Finnis, *Aquinas*, 272–73; Finnis, "A Grand Tour of Legal Theory," 105; George, "Natural Law and Positive Law," 161; Robert P. George, "Religious Liberty and Political Morality," in *In Defense of Natural Law*, 131; and Robert P. George, "Kelsen and Aquinas on the Natural Law Doctrine," in *St Thomas Aquinas and the Natural Law Tradition: Contemporary Perspectives*, ed. John Goyette, Mark S. Latkovic, and Richard S. Myers (Washington, D.C.: The Catholic University of America Press, 2004), 251–59.

aspect. Such would be the case when the order of things that are attributed to the titleholders by the relevant precepts of natural law as their *suum* owed in justice is then repristinated in positive laws in a defunct way with regard to the attribution of those same things or with regard to their precise measure.[141]

This reading is in line with Aquinas's understanding of *ius* and of the juridical status of natural law as well as with his doctrine of unjust laws. In his view, "the force of law depends on the extent of its justice": "In human affairs a thing is said to be just, from being right [*rectum*] according to the rule of right reason [and] the first rule of reason is the law of nature."[142]

Next, Aquinas claims that laws may be unjust by being contrary to the human individual or common good according to three perspectives:

Now laws are said to be just, both from the end, when, to wit, they are ordained to the common good—and from their author, that is to say, when the law that is made does not exceed the power of the lawgiver—and from their form, when, to wit, burdens are laid on the subjects, according to an equality of proportion and with a view to the common good ... so that on this account, such laws as these, which impose proportionate burdens, are just and binding in conscience, and are legal laws.[143]

Aquinas thus introduces a further qualification, at least to the third perspective in which laws are said to be just, namely, that of the imposition of disproportionate burdens. This further qualification is the distinction that he recognizes in laws that are

141. For example, the good of human life may be repristinated in positive laws in a defunct way because it is somehow not attributed to its true titleholders but to other persons, or because it is attributed to its titleholders only partially with regard to the content or natural time frame of this good.

142. *ST* I-II, q. 95, a. 2.

143. *ST* I-II, q. 96, a. 4.

in accordance with the human good: they are "just" laws (*iustae sunt*), they are morally "binding in conscience" (*obligant in foro conscientiae*), and they are "legal laws" (*sunt leges legales*).[144]

In sum, a thing may be said to be unjust with regard to natural law when it is contrary to the human good in a way that is not entirely reducible to the question of whether it is morally binding or legal. We have already seen how Aquinas arrives at the conclusion that the precepts of the natural law are constituted as precepts of justice (*praecepta iustitiae*), insofar as they specifically address duties in justice toward others.[145] Therefore, I propose a complementary reading of Aquinas's understanding of just or unjust laws that centers on the question of whether these laws are in accordance with the human good not only within the moral domain of natural law but also through its juridical aspect—otherwise known as the natural norms of justice.[146]

---

144. *ST* I-II, q. 96, a. 4.

145. *ST* II-II, q. 122, a. 1.

146. It seems that John Finnis is, to a certain degree, aware that something is missing in the passage between the claim that a certain positive law is immoral and the claim that the law in question is also unjust. He seems to advocate relieving such conceptual tension by assigning precedence to the category of *immoral* over *unjust* when predicated on positive law. In one textual locus, Finnis affirms that "justice and injustice are predicated on laws only by an analogy (of attribution), for justice is the 'steady and undeflected will [*of a person*] to give to others what they are entitled to.'" See John Finnis, "Just Votes for Unjust Laws," in *Collected Essays*, vol. 4, *Philosophy of Law*, 438, n. 6. He then adds that precisely this fact, among other things, "creates significant strains in extending the traditional and sound idea of intrinsically immoral acts to categories of laws and to the positive obligation to make laws against murder and abortion."

4

At the Intersection between *Ius* and Morality

Bringing Together the Thomistic Natural-Law Traditions

As evidenced in the previous chapter, Aquinas, Villey, and Hervada each advance certain claims concerning the juridical status of natural law, but their respective accounts of this topic seem to be outlined on the margins of their main theoretical interests, predominantly in fragmented textual arguments that resemble incomplete elements of a theory in need of further elaboration and development.

It would certainly be opportune to merge Aquinas's, Villey's, and Hervada's arguments on the realistic account of right and juridicity with the natural-law theories of other Thomistic authors presented in the first chapter, because the Thomistic traditions may prove to be complementary when it comes to foundations of the juridical phenomena. It is my conviction that the arguments for the juridical status of natural law should be adequately examined in light of the Thomistic tradition of the moral status of natural law, and vice versa. Such examination is necessary for the correct understanding of the shared preceptive substructures of the principles of natural law in both domains, moral and juridical. To be sure, my present effort cannot exhaustively address all issues that necessarily arise from these levels of analysis. For this reason, I will limit myself only to an outline of certain essential elements of the overlap and distinction between the moral and juridical domains of natural law.

First, I will sum up the elements of the argument according to which the natural law may be considered to be the natural *title* of the right. Secondly, I will analyze the main traits of the things that are constituted as *res iusta*, rights, or juridical goods. Thirdly, I will present the structure of natural law as a *sui generis* juridical norm. Since the juridical perspective reconstitutes the telic properties of the natural moral norm according to the specific ends of the juridical domain, I will also analyze the normative structure of the precepts of natural law considered precisely as *natural* juridical norms. Finally, I will advance the claim that given the line of argument followed throughout this chapter, it is possible to coherently and adequately refer to the juridical aspects of natural law under the rubric of *natural norms of justice.*

The theoretical account of the juridical status of natural law would surely benefit from examples of its application to practical issues, so as to facilitate the reader's understanding of the theory's conceptual reach *in concreto*, at the level of its practical significance for existential matters. Natural rights, as well as their juridical foundations in the precepts of natural law, are ontologically linked to lived instantiations of the just things or goods owed in justice. This is why I will later offer two examples of how the theory of the natural norms of justice may be understood in light of practical issues regarding certain natural rights, within the perspective of the potential violation of these norms and rights through certain unjust acts.

Natural Law as the Natural Title of the Right

As we have seen, in juridical realism's account of law and rights, the law's juridical aspect is necessarily connected to the realistic conception of right (*ius*). One of the basic forms of this structural connection is manifested in the category of the title of the right, which is the determinate cause, source, or origin that creates the right by attributing a thing to a person as something owed in justice by others.

In the case of natural rights, the title of things that are attributed to a person for the constitution of the right is human nature or, more specifically, a precept or cluster of precepts of natural law that presents itself to us as a natural title. As seen before, an argument concerning the juridical title was intuited by Villey and further conceptualized by Hervada. The cognitive starting point in both Villey's and Hervada's juridical epistemology is the thing or good itself that is "in search of" its juridical title for the purposes of tracing out its constitution as the right.

By contrast, from the juridically relevant ontological point of view, the starting point is that state of affairs wherein, through the properties pertaining to attribution and obligatoriness, the right originates, and this is precisely the title of the right or, in the case of natural rights, the natural title. The search for the natural title of the right leads to the precept (or cluster of precepts) of natural law that, in fact, attributes a whole array of things or goods to the person precisely as something distinctly *his*, a *suum* that is consequently owed by others in justice as their *non suum*.

Since the domain of the right is, as seen above, constituted as a peculiar structural moment within the context of morality—thus interrelating the juridical domain to the moral domain as a specific part to the whole—the norm of natural law in which the right originates (its title), under the aspect of the whole, is essentially the norm of natural moral law. To inquire into the conditions according to which the norm of natural law may be said to be established also as a juridical norm, I must now consider the properties that bring the precept of natural moral law under the focus of that specific viewpoint that constitutes the juridical domain within the broader context of morality.

In order for a precept of the natural moral law to be constituted as a juridical norm, it must be viewed under the following two aspects:

- as the origin of attribution of a thing or good to determinate persons in the manner of something distinctly *theirs*, and
- the consequent obligatoriness of the precept, which arises from the fact that the thing or good in question is owed by others according to the precise measure by which it constitutes the titleholder's *suum* and the debtor's *non suum*.

When the immediate object of the precept of natural law—the concrete human good—is viewed under the aspect of the properties of juridicity, rather than that of the fulfillment of the whole moral domain in light of this particular good's collocation within the context of man's natural end or happiness, the precept itself is reconstituted as a juridical norm. It then represents the title of natural right.

The precept of natural law is thus structurally connected to the thing or good that it constitutes as the right through its inherent preceptive reference to all the properties of juridicity. This means that, first of all, the precept of natural law must refer to things or goods that can form part of an external dimension (i.e., outwardness) in at least some of their manifestations. In addition, the thing or good constituted by the precept of natural law as a person's *suum* must be something apt to obligate other persons to be indebted with regard to this *suum* (i.e., other-directedness). The *res* in question must also stand within the power sphere of another person's at least potential interference with the titleholder's *suum* (i.e., obligatoriness).

At the same time, the precept of natural law must have as its immediate object a thing or good that is, at least in some of its essential and determinable aspects, apportionable to a person, which here means that the thing or good must be susceptible to becoming a right by being apt to be attributed to a person as his *suum* as well as to constitute a relation of debt with other persons as debtors with respect to the titleholder. Finally, this thing or good, which is attributed to a person as titleholder and correlatively owed in justice to him by others, must be apportioned to the titleholder according to a certain kind of equality. In the case of natural rights, as we have seen, things or goods are attributed and thereby owed in justice, equally to every member of the human species. This is because natural rights are based on those things or goods that constitute particular objects of the precepts of natural law and that, as parts conducive to the whole (or universal) human good, are equally instantiated in each human person by their nature.

For example, the precept (or cluster of precepts) of natural moral law establishes the good of life as perfective of the human person with regard to his natural end or his whole human good.

The normative structure of this moral precept has as its object, among other elements, those aspects which form part of the imperative of preserving and fulfilling this natural human good. At the same time, this moral precept attributes the good of life to its titleholder in the outward domain and with regard to all other people as its debtors (*erga omnes*). Since others could potentially interfere with this good at any time, obligations in justice are established between them and the titleholder of the good of life according to the equality that demands the respect of the same good in other persons. The relevant precepts of natural law are thereby constituted as juridical norms.

This reconstitution of the precept of natural moral law as the juridical norm is supported, as noted by both Villey and Hervada, in the doctrine on the two aspects of the concept of law in Aquinas. The natural law, which falls under Aquinas's definition of law in general as "an ordinance of reason for the common good, made by him who has the care of community, and promulgated"[1] is reconstituted—while retaining all of the elements from the definition—as the "*ratio* of the right"[2] that "adjusts" certain things or goods to persons *ex ipsa natura rei*.[3] This means that natural rights—the natural human goods owed in justice that have the natural law as their title—are determinable and measured for the juridical domain according to the very nature of things (*natura rei*) or goods outlined in the preceptive *ratio* of the natural law. In other words, things or goods become rights by virtue of a natural title, the precept of natural law, which is itself the very measure of the *ratio* instilled in the nature of these things or goods. The juridical domain is constituted within the setting of the moral

1. *ST* I-II, q. 90, a. 4.
2. See *ST* II-II, q. 57, a. 1, ad 2.
3. See *ST* II-II, q. 57, a. 2.

sphere, which in turn has its underlying foundational *ratio* in the ontological givenness of the thing or good in question. As seen, both Hervada and Villey note these premises,[4] though without fully developing them into systematic conclusions.

The realistic account of the natural juridical law as the attributional natural title and the measure of natural rights represents a *novum* from the viewpoint of contemporary legal theories rooted in the tradition of Thomistic natural law. Those theories envision the juridical status of natural law entirely within the framework of an unmediated and automatic passage from natural moral law to the domain of the right and obligations in justice, without any differentiation between moral and juridical aspects of that law. By enclosing the normative structure of the demands of justice deriving from human nature exclusively within the moral domain, the phenomenon of natural legality ultimately amounts to an extra-juridical question. According to the realistic juridical tradition of Thomistic legal theory, the precept of natural law retains its normative identity as the ordinance of reason while also becoming the *ratio* of justice. The normative content of practical reasonableness inherent in the moral ordinance of the precept of natural law becomes the measure of natural rights. Human goods, such as life, freedom of conscience, freedom to form and perform an act of faith, bodily and psychological integrity, and other natural human *res* or goods become owed in justice as natural rights.

Hence, a precept of natural law or the relevant cluster of its precepts is the immediate title of natural rights in all cases where

4. "There are things that are attributed to a person by virtue of the very nature of man—in other words, their title arises from man's very being—and they are measured according to the nature of things" (Hervada, *Critical Introduction to Natural Right*, 51). Villey envisions the juridical domain of natural law to be dependent on the "rationality immanent in things," which indicates the things that are apportioned by nature precisely as *mine* or *yours*, and is thus an ordinance of just relations. See Villey, *La formation de la pensée juridique moderne*, 594, 605, 617.

additional determination of a title is not necessary for the constitution of natural right. Hervada notes that there are also natural rights that originate in human nature, in the sense that they find their justification in the precepts of natural law, while still needing *in concreto* positive titles that give rise to fully determined measures of particular rights, for example, the natural right to property. This right is situated among the normative structural presuppositions of human nature (i.e., in the cluster of natural-law precepts relevant for the particular human good of the personal property–based mode of possession of things). These precepts determine the capacity for possession and the actuality of ownership as a human good with regard to the fruit of a person's work, the convenience of support for the material existence of the person and the communities to which he belongs, the adequate use of personal property in view of the common good, etc. *In concreto*, however, the right to property always has a specific additional title that determines those details regarding the measure of this right that do not immediately arise from human nature, such as contracts, wills, etc. Hervada refers to these presuppositions of human nature as the "natural foundation" of the right.[5]

5. "We understand the foundation of the right to be that in virtue of which the titleholder is capacitated to possess a title" (Hervada, *Lecciones propedéuticas de filosofía del derecho*, 232). "The foundation [of the right] is that by virtue of which a subject may be the subject of a right or certain rights. The foundation qualifies one to hold a right, but does not grant it.... The distinction [between the title and foundation of the right] is very important in those rights that are closely based on human nature, because it would be easy to confuse the title with the foundation. At times, human nature is the title and foundation at the same time; at others it is only the foundation. For example, the rights of ownership; ownership is based on human nature, but every concrete ownership has a positive title (inheritance, purchase, work, occupation, donation, etc.), such that nothing is possessed by way of nature" (Hervada, *Critical Introduction to Natural Right*, 26). See also Hervada, *Lecciones propedéuticas de filosofía del derecho*, 232–34, and Hervada, *What Is Law?* 54–55. In the case of the right to property and other similar relations between the foundation of the right and its natural title, Hervada uses the term "proximate natural

Juridical Natural Law and the Constitution of Juridical Goods

The reconstitution of the precept of natural moral law and the ordinance of reason contained therein as a juridical norm is not the only element of the intersection between the right and morality that follows the *sui generis* "part-whole" paradigm for the interrelation of the two domains. The thing itself—or, better yet, the good—also shares in the peculiar shift of perspective from the moral domain of natural law to that of its juridical status. Exploring the nature of this shift may prove helpful for understanding natural law's juridicity.

We have seen that the *ipsa res iusta*, or the just thing itself, denotes the primary meaning of right in the realistic juridical tradition. The word "thing" essentially points to the ontological consistency of the real givenness of a certain thing, in the broadest sense of the term, and its being a right (i.e., the object of justice). "Things" become rights not through an ontological alteration, a process of idealization, or a mental fiction but rather, according to Thomistic juridical realism, through the practical verification of certain properties pertaining to their relational perspective, the so-called properties of juridicity. Even so, they always remain the same "things."

The question I now intend to explore is whether the things that are just according to nature may rightfully be called *natural*

---

foundation," which is that type of foundation in which the natural title is established in an immediate way. He also distinguishes the proximate foundation from the "mediate foundation" and "ultimate foundation." The "mediate foundation" of rights is always the human condition of being a person whose ontological structure capacitates him to have rights in general, whereas the "ultimate foundation" of the right is observed on the level of a sapiential or metaphysical contemplation of the juridical reality—which, ultimately, brings us to the topic of the relation between the juridical domain and God. See Hervada, *Lecciones propedéuticas de filosofía del derecho*, 233, 583–89.

juridical goods. Beyond the mere terminological shift, can we posit some doctrinal background to the concept of the specifically juridical good? That these natural human things are constituted and ordinarily referred to as goods, or more precisely, human goods, in the broader domain of morality is already a well-researched matter.[6]

Interestingly, Hervada himself uses the term *good* on various occasions precisely to denote the *res* that is constituted as the right, although without explicit doctrinal justification of the usage of the concept of good in the juridical sense.

Therefore, all the goods inherent to [the person's] own being are the object of his dominion, are *his* in the most strict and proper sense. With this in mind, it is evident that the set of goods inherent to his being represent *his things,* with which others cannot interfere and which they cannot appropriate except through force or violence, which would infringe on the ontological status of the person; they are then rights of the person, rights that the person has by virtue of his nature.

6. Seldom has the term *human good* received such frequent and developed usage as in the moral and legal philosophy of John Finnis. Without entering into the details of his account, Finnis's understanding of the human good is grounded in the argument he claims to have inherited from Aquinas that "the basic forms of good grasped by practical understanding are what is good for human beings with the nature they have." Finnis then adds that Aquinas "considers that practical reasoning begins not by understanding [human] nature from the outside, as it were, by way of psychological, anthropological, or metaphysical observations and judgments defining human nature." Instead, according to Finnis's reading of Aquinas, "by a simple act of non-inferential understanding one grasps that the object of the inclination which one experiences is an instance of a general form of good, for oneself (and others like one)." The author then concludes that "the practical principles which enjoin one to participate in those basic forms of good, through the practically intelligent decisions and free actions that constitute the person one is and is to be, have been called in the Western philosophical tradition the first principles of natural law" (Finnis, *Natural Law and Natural Rights,* 34, 97). A basic bibliography of the critiques of various arguments made by Finnis may be found in the first chapter of this book. However, my elaboration of the concept of human good and its reconfiguration as a juridical good is relatively emancipated from contemporary Thomistic debates on the origin of moral obligation, since in the present study, I am focused exclusively on the intersection between the moral and juridical domains.

They are natural rights of man in the strictest sense of the word. These rights or goods, which belong to the person because they make up his being ... engender in others the duty of respect.[7]

As we have stated, those goods inherent to the being of man constitute rights with a natural title.[8]

The doctrinal background that Hervada omits, however, may be found in Aquinas's texts, in which his reference to the juridical good is located in his broader interest regarding the question of whether any aspect of the good pertains to the juridical domain. Aquinas is quite clear in his claim that it, in fact, does. Human virtues in general, he says when quoting Aristotle on this subject, "render a human act and man himself good," and this, he claims, "can be applied to justice."[9] In his view, justice "regards a certain special aspect of good" (*quandam rationem boni specialem*).[10] The right as the object of justice represents an aspect of this specific juridical orderedness to human good, which consists in giving to each his own right.

The connection between the object of the virtue of justice and the concept of the good may be further explained by the element of operative intentionality referred to in the definition of justice—the perpetual and constant will to render to each his own right. Since on Aquinas's account, the proximate principle of action is the appetitive power, he concludes that "justice must be in some appetitive power of its subject."[11] And this appetitive power, says Aquinas, is the intellective appetite that can have the good as its object—the will.[12] The will of the human person inclines to the

---

7. Hervada, *Critical Introduction to Natural Right*, 54.

8. Hervada, *Critical Introduction to Natural Right*, 59.

9. *ST* II-II, q. 58, a. 3.

10. *ST* II-II, q. 79, a. 1.

11. *ST* II-II, q. 58, a. 4. See also *ST* II-II, q. 58, a. 5, ad 2.

12. *ST* II-II, q. 58, a. 4.

object of juridical justice on apprehending that this object regards a certain special aspect of good.[13]

What are the essential characteristics of this "certain special aspect of good" that pertains to the right as the object of justice?

First of all, Aquinas maintains that the good of justice is essentially *the good of the other person*. Justice, he says, differs from other virtues precisely with regard to its other-directed object: "[whereas] the other virtues are commendable in respect of the sole good of the virtuous person himself, … justice is praiseworthy in respect to the virtuous person being well disposed toward another."[14] He concludes this argument by saying that justice is somewhat (*quodammodo*) the good of another person (*bonum alterius*).[15] The *other*, whose good is the object of the virtue of justice, may be either another individual together with his particular good, or a community of persons and its common good.[16] Justice, therefore, regards goods either as "due to one's neighbor" (*bonum sub ratione debiti ad proximum*) or "in relation to the community" (*facere bonum debitum in ordine ad communitatem*).[17] In sum, a person establishes the equality of justice through the fulfillment of the good that consists in rendering to another his due (*reddendo alteri quod ei debitur*).[18] The right, as the object of juridical justice, is essentially the good of another, other-directed good, be it another individual or a community as a group-person.

Another important special aspect of the juridical good regards the mode in which things are owed and, consequently, as Aqui-

---

13. See *ST* II-II, q. 58, a. 4, ad 2.
14. *ST* II-II, q. 58, a. 12.
15. *ST* II-II, q. 58, a. 12.
16. *ST* II-II, q. 58, a. 5; II-II, q. 58, a. 7.
17. *ST* II-II, q. 79, a. 1.
18. *ST* II-II, q. 79, a. 1.

nas says, "done in accordance with the right."[19] Aquinas argues that juridical justice refers to a specific kind of equality that must be established in relations of justice.[20] He claims that "a person establishes the equality of justice by doing good, i.e., by rendering to another his due,"[21] or, as he elsewhere specifies, "his own right."[22] This passage should be read together with his previously cited claim that a thing is said to have the "rectitude of justice … without taking into account the way in which it is done by the agent."[23] The good of justice is thus considered under a special aspect: "justice is concerned with operations and things which are external," not with the internal "passions" of the subjects.[24]

In other words, some things are apportioned in a relation of justice in such a way that in order to attain the juridical good (i.e., to give the right to the titleholder in its juridically relevant outward aspects), the internal dispositions of these persons are relatively irrelevant. The orderedness to the good that is the object of justice is delineated by the imperative that the concrete measure of the titleholder's *suum* is primarily respected in its outward aspects. Thus, the right denotes that aspect of the good that is desired and accomplished in a way that transcends the internal aspect of subjective dispositions in which the act of justice is done by the agent. Again, from the perspective of the juridical domain, a person is not primarily interested that others have morally perfective subjective dispositions regarding his life, bodily integrity, property, or inheritance. Rather, this person is primarily interested that his life, bodily integrity, property, or inheritance is not interfered with. That which is juridically right or juridically good

---

19. *ST* I-II, q. 100, a. 9, ad 1.
20. See *ST* II-II, q. 57, a. 1; II-II, q. 57, a. 2; and II-II, q. 58, a. 2.
21. *ST* II-II, q. 79, a. 1. Emphasis added.
22. *ST* II-II, q. 58, a. 1. Emphasis added.
23. *ST* II-II, q. 57, a. 1. Emphasis added.
24. *ST* II-II, q. 79, a. 1, ad 1.

is not to be confused with the moral good or envisioned as fully separate with regard to moral good. Rather, it actually secures the attainment of the moral good in its outward and other-directed aspects relevant for the domain of justice.

What do all these elements of the argument for the juridical aspect of the good tell us about the juridical status of the natural law and the natural human goods which are the objects of its precepts?

When speaking about whether "to do good" is a part of justice, Aquinas affirms that justice regards a special aspect of the good, namely, "the good as due in respect of divine or human law."[25] Now, we can understand this claim to also include the natural law, since Aquinas defines natural law essentially as the "participation of the eternal law in the rational creature."[26] He adds that the mode of doing acts of juridical justice, which falls under the precept, is that they be done in accordance with the right (*secundum ordinem iuris*).[27] In other words, the natural juridical good is fulfilled when the right, attributed by the precept of natural law, is rendered to its titleholder according to its measure contained in the *ratio* of the precept itself.

The precept of natural law does more than establish an ordering to the particular human moral good that is in accordance with the whole human good and is therefore essential for human personal fulfillment. It also establishes its telic object according to the distinct criteria of the juridical domain. There, the good that is owed is not the whole human good but that aspect of the *bonum humanum* that concerns the *good of justice*: to give to each his own right. In this sense, the *res* in question is the juridical

25. *ST* II-II, q. 79, a. 1; *ST* II-II, q. 79, a. 3. Emphasis added.

26. *ST* I-II, q. 91, a. 3. Aquinas affirms also that there are things which are "naturally just," and, thus, "contain the very order of justice." See *ST* I-II, q. 100, a. 8, ad 1.

27. *ST* I-II, q. 100, a. 9, ad 1.

good of the other, that is, the titleholder. The overlap between moral and juridical good is not merely coincidental. Rather, the underlying *ordinatio* or *ratio* of the good at both levels of human goods is ontologically and axiologically the same. The difference is only in the extent to which the primary focus of the juridical level of the good in question, outlined by the properties of juridicity, exhausts its peculiar share in the general *ratio* of the good.

Lastly, Carlos José Errázuriz rightfully notes that the term juridical good has a greater potential to convey the essentials of the realistic conception of right to a contemporary audience because it transcends the possible conceptual difficulty inherent to the premodern ontological setting wherein rights were understood as things. This understanding should pose no problem for a contemporary conceptualization of rights as essentially the things themselves to which we can assign a structural priority with regard to their elaborations as subjective claim-rights. The benefit of theoretical tools for reconnecting rights more closely to their real objects could prove to be a welcome and easily acceptable upgrade for contemporary legal mentality. Finnis, for one, clearly understands that Aquinas meant to denote "acts, objects, and states of affairs"[28] when he defined right as the just thing itself. Errázuriz warns, however, that the sole reference to the concept of *res* in the explanation of the focal point of *ius*, without the simultaneous reference to the concept of juridical good, could prove awkward to contemporary ears and be easily misunderstood to denote exclusively material objects.[29]

The realistic concept of right as juridical good is not premised on the necessary return—justified only in terms of "wanting to

---

28. See Finnis, *Natural Law and Natural Rights*, 206.

29. Carlos J. Errázuriz M., "L'essenza del diritto alla luce delle proposte di Sergio Cotta, Michel Villey e Javier Hervada: riflessioni conclusive," *Forum. Supplement to Acta Philosophica* 5, no. 2 (2019): 714–16.

put the clock back"[30]—to premodern ontological categories. Instead, it restates the perennial aspects of the premodern tradition for the contemporary context deeply marked by the variety of good-based theories of law.

Natural Law as the Set of Natural Juridical Norms

Although both aspects of natural law's goodness, moral and juridical, contain the same elements enumerated in Aquinas's definition of *lex* from the *Prima secundae*,[31] it is of extreme importance to understand the ways in which the structure of natural law essentially differs from that of positive human law. Positive law is ontologically reducible to a written rational formula (or, under certain circumstances, an unwritten one, as in the case of a custom) that, according to Aquinas's definition of law, contains an ordinance of reason promulgated by him who has the care of the community in view of the common good. The promulgation of a rational written formula by the public legislative authority has the effect of rendering the order expressed in this rational formula enforceable and coercible upon people under the legal and, as John Finnis says,[32] presumable and defeasible moral obligation to obey it. In contemporary juridical culture, it is precisely the structure of positive human law that is commonly taken as the paradigmatic model for the concept of law, or at least as the primary analogue most proximate to the essence of this concept.

The normative structure of juridical natural law, however, is

---

30. See Finnis, *Natural Law and Natural Rights*, 209.

31. *ST* I-II, q. 90, a. 4.

32. See Finnis, *Natural Law and Natural Rights*, 245–52, 299–368.

not essentially reducible to the model of positive law understood as a positivized rational formula. In addition, the normative structure of natural law pertains to a different mode of promulgation than that of a positivized formula developed by human reason. Even the rationally formulated expressions of the juridical aspect of natural law, developed in the human mind or artifactually expressed in positive law, are not themselves juridical natural law. An abstract rational rule, formulated in the human mind within the process of cognition of the demands of justice and the right in the nature of things, is not itself the cause of the obligations of natural justice.

The precept of juridical natural law has the essential structure of what may be referred to as a *natural* norm. It is not the rational formula worked out from the *ratio iuris* but the *ratio* itself of the natural order of justice as it is instilled in all the focal points of its promulgation *ex ipsa natura rei* taken together. The precept of natural law, be it a moral rule of human conduct or a rule of the right (*ratio iuris*), has the structure of multilayered modes of promulgation, which, both ontologically and epistemologically, transcend the paradigm of positive law represented by the model of the abstract rational formula.

If one confuses the natural norm of justice arising from human nature with the rationally formulated rule that expresses it, the immediate consequence is that, although the rational formula contains the elements of the natural norm, the formula remains posited as somehow extrinsic to reality. The rule that is rationally formulated in the human mind may, so to speak, "contain" the juridical natural norm as it is expressed and promulgated in nature, and thereby have a declaratory function with regard to the natural norm, but the juridical natural norm, being promulgated through human nature and making reference to the order of justice arising from nature, is constitutive of the right (*ratio iuris*). This natural norm, as shown above, is the natural title of the right, since it constitutes certain human goods as owed in justice, which is to say, as juridical goods.

Thus, the natural law possesses a juridical domain precisely as the law promulgated *by* human nature, instilled *in* nature. The juridicity of human nature is not primarily a "product" of human reason expressing the demands of justice arising from human nature through abstract rational formulas or, subsequently, through positive law. Likewise, the normative aspect of the natural juridicity of the human person is not generated solely by subsequent elaboration through human rational categories in the form of abstract ideas that assert the existence of the juridical phenomenon in the reality of things. Such a position can be adequately termed *idealistic*, since it would necessarily understand juridicity as arising exclusively from the rational formula containing that which is just. Instead, in a realistic conception of right and juridicity, it is reality itself—the nature of the variety of things in the context of outward and other-directed human relations—that establishes certain human goods as juridical goods. The juridical phenomenon is primarily founded on the order of reason (*ratio*) instilled in nature, which indicates an order of attributions (to an individual or communal subject) of things owed in justice by others.

A realistic juridical conception of law and rights thus reconsiders the paradigmatic model of predicating the juridical phenomenon only on the positive legal norm or some other legal-normative structure that frames the demands of justice exclusively in the form of abstract rational formulas. Such formulas may well be correct and may even reflect the order of natural juridical justice. They may "contain" and refer to natural rights, or establish positive rights, but until we predicate juridicity on the natural norm itself, the abstract rational formulas that contain the juridical order—expressed in positive law or in norm-based instantiations of moral or purely legal subjective rights—are ultimately posited at a level that is extrinsic to the reality of things themselves, at least from the specifically juridical perspective.

In other words, the order constituted by natural law in view of the attainment of natural juridical goods is not essentially found in the formula of human reason that the norm of positive law expresses. Where, then, is this order to be found? What is the significance of the focal points of the promulgation of the precepts of natural law for the present study, namely, for the juridical status of these precepts?

Again, the focus of my study is not the analysis of the origin and purely moral significance of the normative orderedness toward the human good for juridical purposes, although that approach is ordinarily adopted in many contemporary Thomistic presentations of the natural-law theory that mainly focus on Aquinas's question 94, article 2, in the *Primae secundae*. Rather than analyzing the moral aspect in the orderedness of the *ratio* toward human good instilled across the focal points of promulgation of the natural law, I am primarily interested in an additional layer of inquiry on which these focal points are brought into focus as elements of the natural juridical norm. In sum, my intention is to analyze the domain in which the natural preceptive orderedness toward the human good is shifted to the perspective of justice.

The natural law possesses an inherent juridical status precisely as a natural norm. A quick survey of the Thomistic tradition of natural-law doctrine should help to understand just how the dynamics between the focal points of the promulgation of the precepts of natural law gives rise to a norm that can only be called natural. In his analysis of the Thomistic natural-law theory, Russell Hittinger notes how Aquinas organizes his natural-law theory according to a threefold answer to the question of what natural law is *in* (i.e., what are the focal points of its peculiar promulgation as a natural norm). In Aquinas's view, a natural-law theory should necessarily include a specific interrelation of all three focal points of promulgation: the order arising from the *divine mind,* the order in *human nature,* and the order in the *human mind.*[33] In Hittinger's view, Aquinas's realistic hermeneutical key for approaching the interrelation between these three foci is the distinction between what comes first in the order of being and what comes first in the epistemological order, and the structural priority of the former over the latter.[34] Aquinas outlines this argument in the first question in the *Summa Theologica* that addresses the issue of the essence of the concept of law:

Since law is a kind of rule and measure, it may be in something in two ways. First, as that which measures and rules: and since this is proper to reason, it follows that, in this way, law is in the reason alone. Secondly, as in that which is measured and ruled. In this way, law is in all those things that are inclined to something by reason of some law: so that any inclination arising from a law may be called a law, not essentially but by participation as it were.[35]

33. See Hittinger, introduction to *The First Grace,* xvi, xviii–xxiii; Hittinger, "Natural Law and Catholic Moral Theology," 4–12; and Hittinger, "Authority to Render Judgment," 95–98. I have already noted in the first chapter that Aquinas's distinction of the essential focal points of promulgation of natural law sets up the structural context for subsequent theories of natural law. Each post-Aquinas theory of natural law could be categorized according to its systematic gravitation toward some of the focal points of the promulgation of natural law, even to the exclusion of others. Since modernity, the general direction of the interrelation of the three foci of natural law has increasingly leaned toward the marginalization and, in contemporary legal philosophy, the exclusion of the order in the divine mind. In that context, the epistemological (the order in human reason) and natural (the order in human nature) foci have become architectonic. See Hittinger, "Natural Law and Catholic Moral Theology," 9.

34. See Hittinger, introduction to *The First Grace,* xvi.

35. *ST* I-II, q. 90, a. 1, ad 1.

According to Hittinger, law is in the intellect that "actually performs the act of measuring and ruling" in an essential way, whereas it is only derivatively in that which is "measured and ruled."[36] He harbors no doubt whatsoever that for Aquinas, the order in the divine mind[37] is primary in the order of being with regard to natural law—which means it is the primary and essential focal point of what the natural law is *in*.[38]

Nowhere does Thomas *define* natural law in anything but theological terms. Indeed, in answer to the objection that for there to be both an eternal law and a natural law was needless duplication, Thomas responds: "this argument would hold if the natural law were something diverse from the eternal law, whereas it is nothing but a participation thereof." Natural law is never (and I must emphasize *never*) defined in terms of what is first in the (human) mind or first in nature.[39]

At the same time, in Aquinas's view, the internal structural logic of natural law is characterized by a principle that Hittinger labels as "metaphysical continuity"[40] between the various orders

36. See Hittinger, "Authority to Render Judgment," 96.

37. "Just as in every artificer there pre-exists a type [*ratio*] of the things that are made by his art, so too in every governor there must pre-exist the type [*ratio*] of the order of those things that are to be done by those who are subject to his government. And just as the type [*ratio*] of the things yet to be made by an art is called the art or exemplar of the products of that art, so too the type [*ratio*] in him who governs the acts of his subjects bears the character of a law.... Wherefore as the type [*ratio*] of the Divine Wisdom, inasmuch as by It all things are created, has the character of art, exemplar or idea; so the type [*ratio*] of Divine Wisdom, as moving all things to their due end, bears the character of law" (*ST* I-II, q. 93, a. 1).

38. "If we ask whether natural law is first in things or in the human mind, Thomas gives the surprising answer that, properly speaking, it is neither.... For his part, Thomas denies that natural law can be reduced to what is prior as order constituted in the human species" (Hittinger, introduction to *The First Grace*, xxii). "Since law is properly and essentially in the intellect of the legislator, natural law is 'in' the divine mind" (Hittinger, "Authority to Render Judgment," 97).

39. Hittinger, "Natural Law and Catholic Moral Theology," 9. The internal quotation from Aquinas is taken from *ST* I-II, q. 91, a. 2, ad 1.

40. Hittinger, "Natural Law and Catholic Moral Theology," 9.

of law and the focal points of their promulgation. According to this principle, the order of being is made known—*promulgated*—through its effects in the order of cognition, where the order of human nature and human reason may be, in certain ways, epistemologically more proximate to the perspective of the cognizing person.[41] In the article of the *Summa Theologica* dedicated to the question of "whether there is in us a natural law," Aquinas applies to natural law his doctrine on the modalities in which a law may be in something. He affirms that since "all things subject to divine providence are ruled and measured by the eternal law … all things partake somewhat of the eternal law … from its being imprinted on them … and this participation of the eternal law in the rational creature is called the natural law."[42] Elsewhere, Aquinas makes explicit the principle of metaphysical continuity between various orders of law in the claim that "we cannot know the things that are of God as they are in themselves, but they are made known to us in their effects."[43] In Hittinger's words,

Evidence for the "[natural] law" is gathered from order inherent in nature and in the human mind, but law is predicated not merely of the effects but rather chiefly of the divine mind.... The fact that we first perceive ourselves discovering or grasping a rule of action does not mean that the human mind is the first in the causal order, or in the ultimate order of being.... Thomas defines the [natural] law from the standpoint of its causal origin (that is, what makes it a law), not in terms of a secondary order of causality through which it is discovered (human intellect).[44]

---

41. "One may doubt that natural law can be reflectively analyzed very thoroughly without grappling with the question whether epistemic priority implies ontological priority" (Hittinger, "Natural Law as 'Law,'" 295, n. 66).

42. *ST* I-II, q. 91, a. 2.

43. *ST* I-II, q. 93, a. 2, ad 1.

44. Hittinger, "Natural Law and Catholic Moral Theology," 8.

Interestingly enough, Aquinas holds that the very stratification (or metaphysical continuity) of legal orders that are hierarchically operative in the order of being and the order of cognition is essentially linked to the concept of promulgation. In Thomistic theory, promulgation is the structural moment necessary for the understanding and operativity of the concept of law, and it is one of the four essential elements of the very definition of law (next to its being an ordinance of reason, posited by those who possess legislative authority in a political community, and expressing an order for the attainment of the common good).

In order that a law obtain the binding force which is proper to a law, it must needs be applied to the men who have to be ruled by it. Such application is made by its being notified to them by promulgation. Wherefore promulgation is necessary for the law to obtain its force.[45]

Hittinger points out that in the Thomistic tradition, promulgation, within any order of law, is essentially a *communicatio*—the act of one mind by which a rule of reason for action is made known to another, and is thus participated or shared in by this other.[46] Along similar lines, Stephen L. Brock, commenting on the above-quoted article on promulgation from the *Summa*, notes that "promulgation is the act by which the law first becomes a law in act and not merely in the lawgiver's intention."[47]

Aquinas addresses the objection that "natural law needs no promulgation" by affirming that "the natural law is promulgated

---

45. *ST* I-II, q. 90, a. 4.

46. See Russell Hittinger, "The Legal Renaissance of the 12th and 13th Centuries: Some Thomistic Notes," *Doctor Communis* 1–2 (2008): 67.

47. Brock, *The Light That Binds*, 47. In Brock's view, the moment of promulgation is of paramount importance—indeed, "the only possible basis"—for a consistent distinction between the various kinds of law (eternal, natural, positive). See Brock, *The Light That Binds*, 48. He claims that it "seems reasonable to conclude" that each kind of law indicates a distinct and *sui generis* mode of promulgation.

by the very fact that God instilled it into man's mind so as to be known by him naturally."[48] Hittinger concludes from this that natural law is a law not only because it is ontologically in human persons but also because it is a natural norm according to the mode of promulgation in the order of cognition:[49] "Hence, natural law is real law because basic moral norms are actually made-to-be-known (promulgated) to the rational creature who grasps the divine law 'naturally' (*naturaliter*)."[50]

Therefore, with regard to natural law, the promulgation of the natural norm at the level of the order of being—primarily, in the order in divine reason—is accomplished through the effects of

48. *ST* I-II, q. 90, a. 4, ad 1.

49. Hittinger, "Authority to Render Judgment," 97.

50. Hittinger, "Natural Law as 'Law,'" 52. I will not enter in the details of the Thomistic debate on whether and to what degree the cognition of natural law also includes a determinate knowledge of the eternal law (the normative order in the divine mind), especially with regard to the cognition of the Lawgiver. Hittinger claims that it was Aquinas's firm doctrine that the cognition of natural law enables men to "reason from the effect in us to a superior cause," that is, "from the *signum* (as an effect) to the legislative point of origin in order to confirm the divine pedigree [of natural law]." See Hittinger, introduction to *The First Grace*, xx, and Hittinger, "Natural Law as 'Law,'" 52. In Hittinger's view, Thomas "did not stipulate that the recipient of the law necessarily has to know the ultimate legislative point of origin" in much detail. Thomas firmly maintains that "a human agent ought to know ... that moral norms bind by virtue of something other than our own mind" and that the very "movement of the mind from the effect (moral truth) to the cause (God) is something that, in principle, falls to human reason" (Hittinger, "Natural Law as 'Law,'" 53–54). According to Hittinger, however, Thomas also claims that "the promulgation is effective even if the creature has only the foggiest idea of law's origin in the divine mind," since already at the level of its promulgated effect in the order of human nature and human reason "the knowledge of moral right and wrong testifies to the fact of a legislated law" (Hittinger, "Natural Law as 'Law,'" 52–53). Hittinger here comments on the crucial text in which Aquinas makes explicit the mode of cognition of the natural law in the claim that "we cannot know the things that are of God as they are in themselves; but they are made known to us in their effects" (*ST* I-II, q. 93, a. 2, ad 1). Stephen L. Brock elaborates on Hittinger's claims by affirming that the peculiar mark of the law promulgated naturally is the very fact that its promulgation "does not essentially require a notification of the promulgating authority": we grasp the truth of the precepts of natural law and their normative quality "before we attain any clear knowledge of their authoritative origin" (Brock, *The Light That Binds*, 63–64).

this order: in the foci of the order of human nature and the order of human reason. The order of cognition of natural law is identical to the order of its promulgation, and both participate or share in the order of reason of the divine legislator. Brock concurs with Hittinger's thesis that the natural law "gets its very name from the manner in which its promulgation is accomplished"[51]—"natural law is a law naturally promulgated."[52] According to Brock, it "is not another law besides the eternal law" but "only another promulgation of God's law, besides the first and eternal promulgation of that law," or "a derivative expression" of eternal law "naturally impressed by God upon his rational subjects."[53] In his view, a distinction in promulgations between eternal and natural law "need not entail a diversity in the thing promulgated";[54] instead, the initial or primary promulgation in the order of divine reason is subsequently promulgated through secondary acts of natural promulgation.[55] For this reason, in the order of cognition, we perceive natural promulgation's secondary acts: promulgation in the order of human nature and in the order of the human mind. Brock claims, however, that these natural orders "can be only a secondary and instrumental source of law, something promulgating law only in the secondary way."[56] Thus, natural promulgation is an act by which the order contained in the eternal law is "transmitted to those who are to be ruled by it."[57]

Brock notes that the question of what the natural promulgation of law might precisely consist of "requires study."[58] For the

---

51. Brock, *The Light That Binds*, 49.
52. Brock, *The Light That Binds*, 50.
53. Brock, *The Light That Binds*, 36.
54. Brock, *The Light That Binds*, 51.
55. See Brock, *The Light That Binds*, 50–51.
56. Brock, *The Light That Binds*, 51–52.
57. Brock, *The Light That Binds*, 52.
58. Brock, *The Light That Binds*, 49.

purposes of the present study, it will suffice to give only a brief and summary overview of the mode of natural promulgation, or the promulgation of a natural norm, as this is expressed in the foci of human nature and the human mind.

First of all, Brock correctly notes that it is not possible to clearly distinguish these two foci of natural law's promulgation, given that human reason forms a constitutive part of human nature. Neither is it clear how to conceive of human nature if it is presented as distinct from or in contrast to human reason. Surely there have been, and perhaps still are, natural-law theories that claim natural law is predominantly or almost exclusively promulgated through human reason, and that neglect to consider the broader metaphysical framework or the order of causality expressed through other traits of human nature.[59] In Hittinger's view, Aquinas firmly establishes that the human mind participates or shares in the promulgation of the natural law on account of its operative "share" in the active principle of the eternal law. The human mind on this account is a "measured measure" (*men-*

59. See again, for example, the admonitory note in the 2009 document of the International Theological Commission: "Reacting to the danger of physicalism and rightly insisting on the decisive role of reason in the elaboration of the natural law, some contemporary theories of natural law neglect, indeed reject, the moral significance of the prerational natural dynamisms. The natural law would be called 'natural' only in reference to reason, which would define the whole nature of man. To obey the natural law would therefore be reduced to acting in a rational manner, i.e., to applying to the totality of behaviors a univocal idea of rationality generated by practical reason alone. This amounts to wrongly identifying the rationality of natural law with the rationality of human reason alone, without taking into account the rationality immanent in nature" (ITC, *In Search of a Universal Ethic*, 79, n. 75). For a presentation of the inclusion of the role of human reason and prerational natural dynamisms in the perspective of the nature of the human person, see my research on the dialogue between Karol Wojtyła's Thomistic Personalism and the Thomistic doctrine of natural law in Petar Popović, "Securing the Foundations: Karol Wojtyła's Thomistic Personalism in Dialogue with Natural Law Theory," *Nova et Vetera* 16, no. 1 (2018): 231–57. See also Petar Popović and Piotr Maj, "The Personalistic Value of the Human Act in the Philosophy of Karol Wojtyła," *Anthropotes* 32, no. 2 (2016): 357–84.

sura mensurata) rather than the "measuring measure" (*mensura mensurans*) that is a quality pertaining to the divine mind.[60] The natural promulgation of the order that is first in the mind of the divine legislator, according to the Thomistic doctrine, "imprints on man a directive principle of human actions."[61] This promulgation of what is first in the mind of the divine legislator is metaphysically pertinent to the order in the human mind (*mensura mensurata*), as well as to the broader metaphysical framework or the order of causality expressed through other traits of human nature. Hence, natural law is naturally promulgated also through prerational natural dynamisms and all other expressions of rationality that are "immanent"[62] in both the psychoaffective and corporeal aspects of human nature.[63]

The Thomistic definition of the natural law would then, according to Brock, contain the following elements: "an ordination

60. See Hittinger, "Authority to Render Judgment," 97. See also *ST* I-II, q. 91, a. 3, ad 2: "Human reason is not, of itself, the rule of things: but the principles impressed on it by nature are general rules and measures of all things relating to human conduct, whereof the natural reason is the rule and measure, although it is not the rule and measure of things that are from nature." See also *ST* I-II, q. 93, a. 2, ad 3: "The types of the divine intellect do not stand in the same relation to things as the types of the human intellect. For the human intellect is measured by things, so that a human concept is not true by reason of itself, but by reason of its being consonant with things.... But the divine intellect is the measure of things."

61. *ST* I-II, q. 93, a. 5, ad 1.

62. ITC, *In Search of a Universal Ethic*, 79, n. 75.

63. "The doctrine of the natural moral law must, therefore, maintain at the same time both the central role of reason in the actualization of a properly human plan of life, and the consistency and the proper meaning of the prerational natural dynamisms" (ITC, *In Search of a Universal Ethic*, 79). Pope John Paul II labels the "rationality 'immanent' in nature," in specific reference to the corporeal or bodily trait of human nature, as "anticipatory signs." While analyzing the elements of the order in human nature as a constitutive part of a natural promulgation of the eternal law, John Paul II, in his peculiar language of Thomistic personalism, affirms that "the person, by the light of reason ... discovers in the body the *anticipatory signs*, the expression and the promise of the gift of self, in conformity with the wise plan of the Creator." See John Paul II, Encyclical Letter *Veritatis splendor* (August 6, 1993), 48.

of divine reason, for the common good of the universe, promulgated to man by God as governor of the universe, through the instilling of the natural light of the human intellect."[64] The natural law thus represents the normative orderedness of moral necessities contextualized in the nature of the human persons, which originates in the mind of the divine legislator. This orderedness is shared in by human persons through its impression—natural promulgation—in their order of being across multiple dynamisms focalized in various traits of their rational nature.

Having thus summarized at least the basic Thomistic elements for the doctrine on the focal points of promulgation of natural law, I wish to conclude this section with some remarks regarding the link between these elements and the juridical status of natural law as a natural norm. In one textual locus, Aquinas mentions that "it belongs to the law to direct human acts according to the order of justice [*secundum ordinem iustitiae*]."[65] If this claim is read with the natural law in view, the link between the legality of natural law and the order of juridical justice becomes clearer. When a precept of natural law is considered under the aspect of the attribution of certain natural human goods to persons as their titleholders and their obligatoriness in the relational perspective, which includes other determinate subjects as debtors regarding these goods, one may refer to this normative structure also as a natural norm that pertains to the order of juridical justice. Given the shift of focus regarding the aspect of the good as the object of the natural norm— that is, the shift from individual and common moral good to that of the juridical good—I will henceforth refer to the juridical status of the precepts of natural law also as natural norms of justice.[66]

---

64. Brock, *The Light That Binds*, 2.

65. *ST* I-II, q. 91, a. 5.

66. I have already signaled in the first chapter that this precise expression appears in some of Hittinger's texts and that it seems to conceptually overlap with a slightly different

The natural norms of justice are constituted according to the distinct orders relative to the focal points of their promulgation. We have seen that Aquinas understands natural law as primarily and essentially a normative participation in the order of the divine mind. This means that the eternal law aims to assign or attribute certain things as foundational human goods in the orderedness toward human fulfillment. This attribution proceeds through the impression, by way of natural promulgation, of the very same normative content that originated in the order of the divine mind. The natural norms of justice thereby have their juridical antecedents in the precepts of eternal law, within the order in the divine mind that anticipates natural promulgation. In this way, the order in the divine mind already assigns or attributes certain human individual or common goods to human persons as owed in justice by others, thereby constituting them as juridical goods. By the same token, the eternal law already possesses a juridical domain with regard to human nature, insofar as it is to be shared in by natural law in the perspective of justice.

The normative aspect of the natural juridicity of the human person is, then, according to a Thomistic framework of the division of the orders of law, already preestablished by eternal law. Consequently, this natural promulgation of the eternal law—its impression in the focal points of the human person's order of be-

---

terminology ("norms of natural justice") used in the official English translation of the ITC document. See Hittinger, "Natural Law and Catholic Moral Theology," 8, and Hittinger, "Natural Law as 'Law,'" 51. See also various occurrences of the term norms of natural justice in ITC, *In Search of a Universal Ethic*, 83, 88–92. Hittinger and the International Theological Commission have not themselves engaged in providing this terminology (neither each of its elements nor their conjunction in one expression) with doctrinal background to support it. This is probably why Hittinger avails himself of the expression only occasionally, and why the ITC document easily switches to a different terminology in its various translations. A realistic conception of right and juridicity, and the observation of natural law from the viewpoint of this conception, however, offer doctrinal tools that support the sufficiently clear and precise applicability of the expression natural norms of justice to the juridical domain of natural law.

ing—"naturalizes" the norms of justice that already exist in the order of the divine mind: "there must pre-exist the type [*ratio*] of the order of those things that are to be done."[67] The legal structure of the order within this *ratio* may be observed according to its aspect of being a *ratio iuris*. In other words, the ordinance of divine reason may represent the primary promulgation of the norm of justice to the extent that it preexists the respective natural norm of justice that apportions things or goods as natural rights in the order of juridical justice through secondary or natural promulgation.

Through secondary or natural promulgation, the natural norms that assign or apportion things as goods owed according to the order of justice also have the status of being a *ratio iuris*, a natural norm of the right whose measure is determined by the *rationabilitas* inbuilt in the norm itself. The difference between the two orders of promulgation, as we have already seen in Brock, is most intelligible if we focus on the peculiarity of the act or form of promulgation rather than on the "thing promulgated."[68] Nonetheless, from the perspective of natural juridical justice, both orders of promulgation ultimately give origin to norms that apportion natural rights and determine their measure, even prior to their conceptualization in abstract rational formulas according to the model for the promulgation of positive law.

Practical Issues, Natural Rights, and Natural Norms of Justice

My account of the natural norms of justice introduces certain new elements into what is usually understood to be the "standard" contemporary central claim of Thomistic natural jurispru-

---

67. *ST* I-II, q. 93, a. 1.
68. See Brock, *The Light That Binds*, 51.

dence[69] concerning the role of natural law at the law-morality intersection. In my opinion, this standard approach is incomplete to the degree that it does not offer an integral account of the juridicity inherent in natural law. Instead, in the framework of the realistic conception of the natural norms of justice, the focus on natural law is narrowed from the broader domain of morality to the relational perspective of the thing or good that is apportioned as a *suum* owed in justice. The standard contemporary reading of the law-morality intersection in Thomistic natural jurisprudence would benefit from an upgrade that would remove it from exclusive appeals to morality as the foundations of law and direct it instead toward a specifically juridical argument of identifying the features of the natural law in the perspective of justice.

Developing a case for natural law's inherent juridicity entails highlighting those aspects of it that of themselves already form a genuine juridical argument, thus bringing what is (according to the standard reading) an exclusively moral account of natural law to its logical consequences in the juridical domain. Allow me to quickly summarize the crucial passages in the development of this argument.

At the starting point of juridical epistemology, within a realistic account of the natural norms of justice, we encounter certain natural human things, goods, *res* (such as life, bodily integrity, various instantiations of legitimate personal freedom, etc.) attributed to the human person. A first moment in realistic juridi-

---

69. The reference to the "standard" contemporary central claim of Thomistic natural jurisprudence intends to denote the common reading of the law-morality intersection on the part of those authors who adhere to Aquinas's natural-law theory but embrace only its specifically moral domain for the constitution of the legal domain, without integrating into their respective accounts Aquinas's premodern realistic conception of *ius*. According to this standard reading, then, the two dimensions, moral and juridical, are somehow intercommunicative, although the natural law falls entirely under the realm of morality and is structurally separate from the juridical dimension.

cal epistemology should be to identify the juridical title of these things, meaning that which constitutes a particular thing as a right. The crucial point here is to discover whether the normativity conducive to the identification of these goods as desirable objects in the perspective of the attainment of the whole human good may be reducible to morality alone or already somehow delineates the existence of a juridical domain. Such an analysis must especially consider whether the human goods in question, beyond being attributed as perfective of human beings and their personal fulfillment in the moral domain, are also apportionable as outward and other-directed goods that belong to a person as his own—*mine,* rather than *yours, suum* as opposed to *non suum*—according to a measure that delimitates them from the sphere of violation of other persons. If so, they would therefore constitute a relation of debt in the juridical domain.

To the extent that human goods are apportioned to persons according to the properties of juridicity, the telic feature of these goods shifts perspectives from the exclusively moral domain to also include the specific ends denoted by the concept of juridical good. The precepts of natural law that establish these goods as genuinely desirable for the attainment of the whole human good are reconstituted as natural norms of justice and represent the juridical title of the constitution of those human goods as natural rights. In the shift of coextensive perspectives from the establishment of morality toward the constitution of the natural right, the natural juridical goods retain their essential telic orderedness toward the fulfillment of the whole human good, but only within the range outlined by the obligatoriness characteristic for the juridical domain.

The natural juridical good itself—that is, the natural right (*ius naturale*)—then becomes the focal point of the juridical phenomenon and juridical relations. If the constitution of natural law as natural norms of justice were not taken into consideration, the standard legal discourse of natural-law jurisprudence would continue to operate only with the concept of moral norms that generate claims of a moral nature—valid ones, certainly—with regard to human moral goods. The morally legitimate spheres of respect for the demands of the safeguarding of human goods within the framework of the attainment of telic moral perfection would then, according to this reading, necessarily require recognition in the legal domain.

It is not difficult to see how certain contemporary authors steeped in Thomistic natural-law jurisprudence, such as John Finnis, seek to seal and secure the juridical argument primarily by exploring legitimate ways to transpose basic moral principles into positive law or into adequate formulations of subjective individual rights, legal or moral. By contrast, in a realistic account of the natural norms of justice, the transposition of metajuridical moral principles into their preceptive juridical extensions is secured already at the level of natural law itself, without necessary recourse to establishing its juridical status through, so to speak, extrinsic extension. The normative structure of the basic moral precepts that identify basic human goods as aspects of the whole human good may be seen as already intrinsically juridical. Thus, a realistic account of natural norms of justice, by focalizing the core of the juridical phenomenon in the concrete givenness of the natural *res* in question, is grounded in a juridical anthropology that reveals how both natural law and natural rights form part of the juridical domain.

Furthermore, in a realistic account of the natural norms of justice, the individuation of the concrete focal points of juridicity (i.e., the natural juridical goods) must be considered foundational in every search for a just juridical solution to complex cases in which several juridical goods, or people's value-based accounts of them, are in deep conflict. This brings us to another general characteristic of a realistic account of the natural norms of justice, namely, that of their actual and immediately effective juridical validity, even prescinding from their translation into positive law. Certainly, the range of this argument is very broad and cannot be discussed at length here.[70] In connection to my present effort, however, it should at least be affirmed that because the natural norms of justice point to certain things or goods according to their juridical status, those norms themselves, as well as the goods to which they refer, are already entirely within the juridical domain. Both natural norms of justice and natural goods owed in justice are already juridically "actual" and not merely "potential," since they create real relations of debt between their titleholders and potential violators of those relations, that is, their debtors. The more specific questions regarding positive-law determinations and the elucidation of conclusions from the natural norms of justice are certainly crucial issues and should be clarified at their proper level of analysis, which likewise exceeds the scope of this work. However, these issues do not diminish the fact that the natural norms of justice are genuinely juridical norms; they point to the things that are just, that is, owed in justice, according to nature.

At this juncture, to facilitate an understanding concerning the argument on the existence and the distinctive features of the nat-

70. Jeremy Waldron attempts to envision, for purely speculative purposes, an "idea of the positive presence of natural law among us" in a putative situation of the absence of positive law or human institutions: "so, when we ask what the law of nature is like, we must expect it to contain not just a set of deontic norms, but norms that it makes sense to enforce and norms concerning which we can imagine serious, sober, and reasonably conclusive thought about appropriate punishment for violations" (Waldron, "What is Natural Law Like?" 79, 87).

ural norms of justice, it will be helpful to revisit these features in the examples of certain practical issues regarding concrete juridical goods. Hence, I will reread these theoretical passages in the light of examples of two concrete natural rights or natural juridical goods. I have decided to present the constitution, through the natural norms of justice, of two natural juridical goods that are well known and still heavily debated in contemporary juridical culture. These presentations will necessarily be carried out summarily, only to shed light on the theoretical and practical significance of a realistic account of natural norms of justice. Through examining the tension between a particular juridical good and the possibility that its apportioned measure—and the relations of justice arising from it—may sustain interference, I hope to facilitate an adequate understanding of the theoretical nuances in the passages that shape the realistic conception of the natural norms of justice.

The Life of the Unborn Child

As we have seen earlier, in a realistic juridical account of law and rights, the starting point of juridical epistemology is the simple fact that certain things or goods are apportioned according to a measure to determinate subjects. Human life is one such thing (*res*), or good. Life is a *res* that is connatural to human persons: it is a basic natural human good[71] of our personal and interpersonal existence.

To whom is this fact attributed or apportioned? To answer this question, I presuppose and take for granted the scientific and philosophical-anthropological fact that the initial moment of hu-

---

71. Even H. L. A. Hart includes "the most characteristic provision of law and morals: *Thou shalt not kill*" as the first truism within his conception of the minimum content of natural law. See Hart, *The Concept of Law*, 194–95.

man life takes place at the very moment of fertilization. With this in mind, it is possible to say that the good of life is apportioned to the actual individual substance in which the fact of human life is biologically instantiated in its inherent corporeal-spiritual expression through rational human nature (the objective ontological aspect of the good). That same rational human nature is, in turn, to be instantiated in a conscious and self-conscious subjective lived experience of the individual person (the subjective personalistic aspect of the good).[72] From its initial moment, this complex good of human life already inherently bears the instantiation of particular traits implied by the aspects of the human person outlined above, although some of these (such as full consciousness) exist only or mainly in potentiality, to be fully developed during the course of human life.[73]

How exactly is the good of human life apportioned to the person? The actuality of human life not only has a factual structure but also bespeaks a preceptive one. A cluster of precepts of natural law connected to this particular human good contains the orderedness of the *ratio* according to which the good of life falls within the scope of the whole human perfective good, in the perspective of human fulfillment. Thus, life is constituted as a human moral good.

Now, in the standard contemporary Thomistic reading of the law-morality intersection, the constitution of the juridical

72. In this determination of the subject of attribution of the fact of life, I am relying on a synthesis of the "objective" and "subjective" aspects of philosophical anthropology as laid out by Karol Wojtła in his methodological approach of Thomistic personalism. See, for example, Karol Wojtyła, "Subjectivity and the Irreducible in the Human Being," in *Person and Community: Selected Essays*, trans. Theresa Sandok (New York: Peter Lang, 1993), 209–17.

73. This is why Robert P. George refers to the instantiation of human life in the unborn child from the moment of fertilization as the "actual" human life "with potential." See Robert P. George, *Conscience and its Enemies: Confronting the Dogmas of Liberal Secularism* (Wilmington, Del.: ISI Books, 2013), 179.

domain, with respect to the human moral good of life, may be recapitulated in the following argument: Since the good of life is a basic human good whose safeguarding is an imperative of practical reasonableness, any positive law or declaratory enactment of subjective human rights that would illegitimately hinder this human good or would likewise hinder the relevant precept of natural moral law, is thereby immoral and thus unjust, which constitutes the grounds for overturning the presumptive moral obligation to obey this law. In such a reading, precepts of natural moral law and the human good of life to which they refer must be, so to speak, "juridicized" by means of subsequent legal formulations, through positive law and the formal recognition of subjective human rights.

In a realistic conception of right and juridicity, however, the pertinent question is whether the preceptive attribution of the *res*—in this case, of the good of life—also establishes the elements of a genuinely juridical title. As we have seen, the attribution of the *res* to the titleholder in view of establishing a right (*res iusta*) shares in the normative identity of the precept of natural moral law. If that were not the case, we would not know where to begin in determining its apportionment and basic measure, or how to even understand the essence of the juridical good as a *res*, or a thing-in-itself-as-it-really-is. But the focus of the natural juridical good is narrower in comparison to natural human good. In order to verify the features of the juridical domain regarding the good of human life, we should therefore verify the criteria of this narrower focus (i.e., the existence of the properties of juridicity).

Beyond constituting an aspect of the whole human good, the good of human life may certainly also be considered as apportionable to a person as *his own*, his *suum*, and not indiscriminately as though it were anyone's or everyone's. Life is certainly a human reality with a sufficient outward manifestation to be, as such, a part of the juridical domain. It is also an interpersonal reality, to which other persons are oriented in manifold manifestations of the opportunities for respect or possible violation of this *res*. Finally, life is susceptible to becoming the object of relations of justice, creating *erga omnes* obligations in justice regarding the integral respect of its instantiation in the personal existence of its titleholder. To the extent that the properties of juridicity are verified with regard to the cluster of precepts of natural law relative to the human good of life, those precepts are reconstituted as natural norms of justice, while the human good of life is reconstituted as a juridical good, a natural right, *res iusta ex ipsa natura rei*.

In this way, in a realistic conception of right and juridicity, human life is constituted as a natural right and hence as a focal point of the juridical domain even before it is recognized as such by positive law. Applied to the initial question on the juridical status of life of the unborn child, the instantiated actuality of human life from the moment of fertilization has the immediate consequence that through natural norms of justice, life becomes a juridical good at the very moment of fertilization and does so as a natural right that is effective *erga omnes*. In view of this argument, generally speaking, abortion and abortion policies not only violate the moral human good of the life of the unborn child but moreover constitute a violation of a natural right and the relations of justice arising from it.[74]

---

74. One can draw a parallel with the distinction between a premodern and modern conception of the *ius* in connection to this topic. As noted, Villey on various occasions deems the peculiarity of the term *ius altius non extollendi* (right not to elevate one's immovables) to reveal the existence of a discontinuous watershed of contrasting conceptions of *ius* between premodern and modern juridical mentality. He is amazed to discover that this right, according to the Roman source-texts, refers to a titleholder who is the owner of a building that was not supposed to be elevated, rather than to the owners of neighboring buildings. In a modern and contemporary subjectivist concep-

Once the status of human life as a natural juridical good or natural right is established, each evaluation of different juridical goods in potential conflict in a particular state of affairs must ensure the protection of the good of life as a natural right and not merely as a moral imperative. Thus, the natural juridical good of human life is placed in the order of juridical justice not as a "moral right" that merely replicates the moral order relevant to the human good of life but rather as a genuinely juridical natural right reconstituted in accordance with the specific properties of juridicity.

Alternate accounts of the law-morality intersection tend to resolve the tension of the competing goods in the juridical domain by favoring individual personal autonomy as the overarching juridical-anthropological value.[75] Juridical arguments that lead

---

tion of rights talk, the latter would be the titleholders of the claim to negative servitude. Today, we would probably reconfigure the argument and decide to focus on the primary juridical good in question—the view from neighboring buildings—and elaborate our juridical argumentation starting with this focal point. Still, just as that premodern argument might seem almost unintelligible outside of a realistic conception of right, a claim to have a "right to abort" would sound equally unintelligible in a premodern juridical mentality. We could speculate that Aquinas, if confronted with this putative right, would not quite understand what it actually means. Perhaps he would reformulate the argument and affirm that the life of the unborn child constitutes the primary juridical good and that, consequently, the titleholder of this right, the unborn child, would have the right not to be aborted. The juridical sphere of all the other acting persons who could, at least potentially, interfere with the primary juridical good of life of the unborn child would be structured according to the right not to abort. For contemporary jurisprudential usage of the expression "right not to abort" as applied to relations of justice that have as their focus the mother of the unborn child and her connected claims for the reconstruction of relevant parts of legal systems in order that the unborn children's right not to be aborted and her right not to abort may be considered a natural right and recognized as a juridical focal point of legal systems, see, for example, Christophe Foltzenlogel, Claire de La Hougue, and Grégor Puppinck, "La prévention de l'avortement: garantir le droit de ne pas avorter," in *Droit et prévention de l'avortement en Europe*, ed. Grégor Puppinck (Bordeaux: LEH Édition, 2016), 73–105; Grégor Puppinck, "Abortion and the European Convention of the Human Rights," *Irish Journal of Legal Studies* 3, no. 2 (2013): 146, 190–92; and Grégor Puppinck, "Abortion in European Law: Human Rights, Social Rights and the New Cultural Trend," *Ave Maria International Law Journal* 4, no. 1 (2015): 38.

75. The preference for the central role of the value of individual personal autonomy

to the conclusion on the overarching value of individual human autonomy in the debates on the permissibility of abortion usually reference several different juridical goods: the radically underspecified right to so-called reproductive self-determination, privacy, equality of the sexes, freedom of religion and of conscience to form one's own opinion regarding the fact of life of the unborn child, etc. Their common denominator is the fact that they are all envisioned and developed independently from the juridical good of human life of the unborn child, within the context of a juridical anthropology that considers juridical goods to be detachable from one another, like *sui generis* autonomous monads, under the umbrella of the equality of personal autonomy. If and when they are eventually brought in connection to the value of human life of the unborn child, these monad-like juridical goods are essentially understood as competing values in contrast with the good of human life.

In a most extreme conception, which seems to have become the mainstream line of argument in the juridical cultures of many contemporary legal systems, the juridical value of the human life of the unborn child is itself observed from the standpoint of the overarching value of an unencumbered individual personal autonomy. Legal systems employing such a conception recognize the human life of the unborn child as made dependent (up to a determinate phase of the development of the fetus) on the factual, moral, and, consequently, juridical value assigned to it by the individual personal autonomy of other implicated subjects, predominantly of the mother. They usually assign rather weak,

---

is a common feature in these authors' theoretical accounts, even though they largely diverge with regard to the line of argument of reaching such preference. Thus, Raz arrives at the centrality of the value of equal personal autonomy through his comprehensive perfectionist doctrine, Rawls through a constructivist political conception of justice, and Dworkin through his account of the foundations of law in principles of political morality.

fragmented, or merely putative conceptions of legal personalities of the unborn child as legal fictions, constructed in abstraction from reality. Thus, the juridical good of the human life of the unborn child, far from being taken into consideration and respected as a natural right, ends up either unrecognized or subordinated to the overarching juridical-anthropological value of individual autonomy of other persons.

In a realistic conception of right and juridicity, the natural juridical good of human life is, instead, apportioned to its titleholder, the unborn child, by the natural norms of justice. This good is objectively posited and juridically effective even prior to the determinations of positive law; it is not modeled according to subjective and ultimately contingent balance of interests and personal beliefs as expressions of the individual autonomy of persons that are not the titleholders of the child's good of life.

The Freedom in Forming and Performing the Act of Personal Assent in Matters of Faith

Realistic juridical epistemology identifies certain states of affairs that represent the starting point for understanding the juridical status of the act of personal assent in matters of faith or of the transcendent truth about the existence of God, as well as for understanding the juridical aspect of the issues arising from the impact of that truth on the life of the person who forms and performs such an assent. First, the act of assent itself in matters of faith falls within the scope of the broader search for the good of intellectual and practical truth in all areas of human life, which includes the transcendent truth, the truth of societal life, of individual moral life, of natural and social sciences, and so forth. Next, the truth sought regarding the existence of God and the impact of this search on a person's life is a transcendent truth. It transcends secular matters, providing them with a cluster of theological metavalues that structure the deep meaning of human existence and of all the aspects of secular realities.[76] This state of affairs regarding the act of assent in matters of faith explains why such an act is certainly foundational for a person's life-structuring self-determination.

In what way are the inherent features and presuppositions for such an act apportioned to the human person? Again, before turning to the question of the properties of its juridical attribution, we need to first understand the basic axiological grammar of this act by revealing the essentials of its moral attribution. At the level of individual morality, the search for truth, especially for life-structuring truth, is certainly morally perfective of the human person.[77] Furthermore, since the act in question is the act of personal self-determinative assent, its structure is truly perfective if it is authentically personal (i.e., if personal assent is not substituted by someone else's assent and if the person is not deprived of the self-determinative freedom to give assent to a life-structuring truth).[78] Thus, the moral good of the act of assent with regard

76. This general property of the scope of transcendent truth may be applied to all kinds of personal conclusions regarding this truth, including atheism or any kind of assent to the proposition that the only transcendent truth is the lack thereof.

77. The Thomistic account of the anthropological core of religious freedom argues that the basis of the natural right to a free act of personal assent in matters of transcendent truth is the natural-law preceptive structure of the rational inclination to search for the truth about God, a search that represents an aspect of the whole human good of persons. See, for example, Russell Hittinger, "Religion, Human Law, and the Virtue of Religion: The Case of *Dignitatis Humanae*," *Nova et Vetera* 14, no. 1 (2016): 156, 169–70, 175.

78. "The natural inclination to grasp the human good of such acts of truth seeking in reference to an ultimate good ... could not be alienated without loss of dignity.... The human acts of pursuing, assenting to and acting rightly upon the truth are of their very nature personal acts that cannot be outsourced. Such acts perfect the human person precisely because they are free and upright." See Russell Hittinger, "An Issue of the First Importance: Reflections on the 50th Anniversary of *Dignitatis Humanae*," *Journal of Law*

to the transcendent truth is locked in a peculiar tension between personal self-determinative freedom, on the one hand, and the properties of transcendent truth that appeal to this freedom by structuring its potentialities, on the other. Already at the level of individual morality, the freedom inherent in the act of personal assent to transcendent truth is not an empty negative liberty, left to the subjective disposition of the person. This freedom is, instead, inherently structured to coexist in dynamic interplay with the features of the search for transcendent truth itself.[79]

In what way does the normative aspect of the morally perfective resolution of the tension between personal self-determinative freedom and the properties of transcendent truth relate to the juridical domain? Again, the juridical status of the natural human good is constituted wherever the properties of juridicity may be predicated on the preceptive structure that establishes the orderedness toward this good—which, in the present case, is the good of the truth in matters of faith and its structural prerequisites. The properties of outwardness and other-directedness are certainly predicable of such an act, since the initially internal act of assent to transcendent truth is essentially life-structuring and thus necessarily expressed through an array of external manifestations. Moreover, the integrity of the act itself, and of its external manifestations, may be interfered with by others through mani-

____

and Religion 30, no. 3 (2015): 472. "The principal justifying argument from natural reason [that is, natural law] is this: *so important* is it for each human being to seek, find and live according to *the truth* about God and man—religious truth—that coercion, since it prevents, distorts, or tends to render inauthentic that search for religious truth, is wrongful." See John Finnis, "Religion and Public Life in Pluralist Society," in *Collected Essays*, vol. 5, *Religion and Public Reasons* (Oxford: Oxford University Press, 2011), 49.

79. For a more complex account of the underlying anthropological-moral framework for the tension between freedom and truth inherent in the dynamics of the act of the personal assent of faith, see David L. Schindler and Nicholas Healy, *Freedom, Truth and Human Dignity: The Second Vatican Council's Declaration on Religious Freedom* (Grand Rapids, Mich.: William B. Eerdmans Publishing Company, 2015).

fold forms of violence or modes of individual or social pressure.

The next question is whether the human good in the structure of the act of assent, inherently locked in the interplay between personal self-determinative freedom and the properties of transcendent truth, may be apportioned to the human person as something that is specifically *mine,* as opposed to *yours,* everyone's, or anyone else's. Can it constitute genuine relations of justice, resulting in the juridical obligations of others to respect the apportioned *res*? The general answer seems to be a qualified "yes," vested with a further qualification regarding the various subsidiary arguments dependent on whom exactly are the possible debtors with regard to the juridical good in question. If the potential interferer is a random individual person, then, certainly, the internal tension of self-determinative freedom in the act of assent to transcendent truth is something that is apportionable and attributable as wholly *mine* as opposed to *yours.*

On the other hand, the features of the search for values regarding transcendent truth may also constitute a peculiar part of the essential common good of certain group-persons, for example, a family, the Catholic Church, or the political community. It seems that, in parallel with the present analysis of properties of juridicity, it is necessary to briefly inquire, beyond matters of merely individual morality, into certain effects of basic moral values stemming from the social ontology of group-persons.

The transmission of values regarding all the structuring aspects of human life, including transcendent truth, undoubtedly forms part of the common good of the family, as it belongs to what was previously referred to as the intrinsic common good; it is the precise element of the desired form of order that concerns communal action, or the common good of shared action. When apportioned within a family, it is attributed in the form of the interplay between the right of parents to educate their children in accordance with their religious and philosophical beliefs and the right of children to the freedom of conscience and belief. The resolution of the tension between personal self-determinative freedom and the properties of transcendent truth always remains something that is apportioned to the individual human person as *mine* and not anyone else's. Parents are certainly not in the category of "anyone else" with regard to their child, given that the child has yet to reach maturity with regard to both his freedom and his personal assent in matters of faith. With regard to children, the juridical good of the truth in matters of faith, along with its structural prerequisites, is structured within a family in the context of the transmission of values from parents to children as a part of the intrinsic common good of the family. This juridical good is apportionable to the child and his parents as their respective things owed in justice, or rights, within the broader context of the intrinsic common good of the family as a group-person. Within this context, the measure of the respective rights of the child and those of the parents regarding this juridical good are not to be exclusively observed in light of their structural mutual clash or potentially contrasting and conflicting claims.

Similar arguments could be made with regard to the interrelation between the structure of the act of assent in matters of faith and the transcendent truth when such interrelation is played out in the context of the attainment of the essential common good of the Catholic Church. The act of assent to a transcendent truth that one discovers to be identical with the authentic teachings of, for example, the Catholic Church, as well as the decision to become a member of that church as an external expression of this assent, is morally and juridically locked into the above-described interplay between personal self-determinative freedom and the properties of transcendent truth. This self-determinative, life-structuring act of assent to transcendent truth, in view of its external expressions, is a *res* that is apportioned as *mine* as opposed to anyone else's. The personal agency of the titleholder of this juridical good cannot be substituted or expropriated by somebody else's acts of interference, since the access to the proper level of the resolution of the tension intrinsic to this act is apportioned only to the titleholder.

In response to this personal assent to transcendent truth, however, the group-person of the Catholic Church has its own juridically constituted right to secure the integrity of its doctrine and demand, with juridical bonds, that the person's act of assent be in accordance with what the church integrally believes. Therefore, the juridical good of the person's freedom to form the act of assent to transcendent truth is further structured as a *res iusta* by the right of the church as a group-person to safeguard the integrity of its doctrine in a series of relations of justice toward its members.[80] The relations of justice in the Catholic Church are juridical expressions of those relational realities that constitute the substratum of its intrinsic common good as a group-person with the determinate desired form of order of such-and-such communal action. In other words, the individual person's juridical good of the truth in matters of faith and its structural prerequisites is

---

80. For this aspect of the structure of religious liberty within the Catholic Church, see Carlos J. Errázuriz M., "Esiste un diritto di libertà religiosa del fedele all'interno della Chiesa?" *Fidelium Iura* 3 (1993): 79–99. For insightful debates on the matter, see Thomas Pink, "The Right to Religious Liberty and the Coercion of Belief: A Note on *Dignitatis Humanae*," in Keown and George, *Reason, Morality and Law*, 427–42; Finnis, "Reflections and Responses," 566–77; Martin Rhonheimer, "Benedict XVI's 'Hermeneutic of Reform' and Religious Freedom," *Nova et Vetera* 9, no. 4 (2011): 1029–54; Thomas Pink, "The Interpretation of *Dignitatis Humanae*: A Reply to Martin Rhonheimer," *Nova et Vetera* 11, no. 1 (2013): 77–121; and Martin Rhonheimer, "*Dignitatis Humanae*—Not a Mere Question of Church Policy: A Response to Thomas Pink," *Nova et Vetera* 12, no. 2 (2014): 445–70.

further structured for members of the Catholic Church by its juridical good of the faith as the expression of the common good of
its specific societal union.[81]

How is the juridical good of truth in matters of faith, along
with its structural prerequisites, envisioned with regard to mul-
tiform relations with the political community organized in the
state? Keeping in mind the preceding analysis, one may arrive
at an answer to that question by first answering two preliminary
questions. First, does the adherence to a transcendent truth constitute an essential common good of the political community, or
is political society somehow only instrumental with regard to the
person's act of religious assent? Second, does the political community possess the necessary jurisdiction and cognitive tools to
take a definitive stand with regard to transcendent truth?

A Thomistic answer to the first question, in synthesis, is that
the primary common good of the political state is essentially
found in its function of furthering, facilitating, aiding, and directing the exercise of individual natural rights, as well as the exercise
of group rights arising from the common goods of communities
distinct from the state (e.g., families and churches), in accordance
with the principle of subsidiarity. If legislation, policies, or other
acts of the political state were to outsource the natural-law integrity of personal acts of assent in matters of faith or denature the
common-good order that is proper to the communities distinct
from the state, they would go directly against both the individual
good and common good of the state and other communities.[82]

---

81. For more details on the juridical good of faith and the juridical status of the common good of the Catholic Church, see Popović, *The Goodness of Rights and the Juridical
Domain of the Good*, 263–91.

82. This concise argument does not seek to resolve the issue, which is still the object
of debate in Thomistic natural-law theory, on the status of the political community as a
necessary society, or the issue of whether the political common good is (a) rooted in a basic human good arising from man's natural inclinations to live in society or (b) merely an

With regard to the second question, any synthesis of a Thomistic natural-law position would argue for the claim that the goal or purpose of the personal act of assent in matters of faith "transcends the terrestrial common good."[83] This position is contextualized within the following state of affairs: the political community lacks jurisdictional competence with regard to the source of transcendent truth, because the things that comprise the individual good and the common good of societies, such as families and churches, constitute the proper loci of the resolution of the tension between personal self-determining freedom and transcendent truth. As Hittinger correctly notes, however, the po-

instrumental good. The narrow scope of the present argument intends to focus only on the question of whether the natural-law precepts that establish aspects of religious freedom in terms of human individual or common goods also constitute the limits to state actions and policies regarding these goods. For a more nuanced development of this line of argumentation regarding religious freedom, see Hittinger, "An Issue of the First Importance," 461–74; Hittinger, "Religion, Human Law, and the Virtue of Religion," 151–77. For a detailed argument on Catholic social doctrine's historical and doctrinal shift in emphasis toward a conception of the political common good as instrumental with regard to individual natural rights and the group rights of societies "higher" or "lower" than the state, see Hittinger, "Social Pluralism and Subsidiarity in Catholic Social Doctrine," 389–98; Hittinger, "The Coherence of the Four Basic Principles of Catholic Social Doctrine," 105–19; Russell Hittinger, "Reasons for Civil Society," in *Reassessing the Liberal State: Reading Maritain's Man and the State*, ed. Timothy Fuller and John P. Hittinger (Washington, D.C.: The Catholic University of America Press, 2001), 11–23; and Russell Hittinger, "Introduction to Modern Catholicism," in *The Teachings of Modern Roman Catholicism on Law, Politics and Human Nature*, ed. John Witte Jr. and Frank S. Alexander (New York: Columbia University Press, 2007), 15–25. The contrasting points in the debate between John Finnis and Lawrence Dewan on the general nature of the political common good as either "public" and contextually supportive of the "private" good and thus "limited and in a sense instrumental" (Finnis) or as a "basic human good" (Dewan) do not alter the essence of the present argument. Even Dewan, who advocates that the political common good arises from the basic human good of societal life, affirms that "a different relation of the household or family to the political society than one finds in Finnis ... need not at all violate any 'principle of subsidiarity,' which means simply authentic causal hierarchy: there really is a role proper to the lower thing, and it belongs to the higher thing to foster, not destroy the lower thing." See Lawrence Dewan, "St. Thomas, John Finnis, and the Political Good," *The Thomist* 64, no. 3 (2000): 373–74. For Finnis's line of argument, see *Aquinas*, 219–54.

83. See Hittinger, "Religion, Human Law, and the Virtue of Religion: The Case of *Dignitatis Humanae*," 169.

litical community's jurisdictional incompetence does not entail a complete epistemological incompetence regarding the value of transcendent truth for individuals, families, and churches.[84]

Thus, the political community may indeed recognize that its specific common good includes the task of safeguarding the integrity of personal acts of assent in matters of faith, and, accordingly, the task of facilitating the outward and other-directed expressions of those acts. The political community is also sufficiently epistemologically competent to be mindful of the multileveled group-identities of human persons, which include not only the category of "citizen" but also categories such as believers, nonbelievers, and, generally, members of societies other than the state, with their respective distinct common goods.[85]

When all the above claims, arising from the relevant cluster of precepts of natural law and the social ontology of group-persons and their respective common goods, are filtered through the verification of the properties of juridicity, these claims are constituted as the natural norms of justice. The juridical good that is thereby constituted is, in the present example, the natural *res iusta* of the integrity of the act of personal assent in matters of faith regarding the resolution of the inherent tension between freedom and the structuring properties of transcendent truth. The political community is juridically incompetent to outsource the resolution of this tension

---

84. See Russell Hittinger, "The Declaration on Religious Freedom, *Dignitatis Humanae*," in *Vatican II: Renewal within Tradition*, ed. Matthew L. Lamb and Matthew Levering (Oxford: Oxford University Press, 2008), 369, 380, n. 38.

85. "Where government emphasizes one [among the persons' categories of group-identity] so heavily that the others fade from view, the person can be put at war with himself.... When the state looks upon persons *only* as citizens, and strives to form a body politic in its various dimensions exclusively according to that point of view, it can be a species of ... 'negative confessionalism.'" See Russell Hittinger, "Political Pluralism and Religious Liberty: The Teaching of *Dignitatis Humanae*," in *Universal Rights in a World of Diversity: The Case of Religious Freedom*, ed. Mary A. Glendon and Hans F. Zacher (Vatican City: Pontificia Academia Scientiarum Socialium, 2012), 54.

from the human person or from relevant group-persons. Possible limits to this juridical good may be determined only by the cluster of the natural norms of justice which delineate its measure.[86] Thus, actions, policies, and legislative enactments of the political community may refer to and enforce limits to this juridical good only in the case that their titleholders overstep its determined measure, violate juridical goods apportioned to others, and, generally, introduce acts of injustice within the setting of the political common good, "in the name of" what is appealed to as "religious freedom."

The content of the natural right of integrity of the act of personal assent in matters of faith (i.e., religious freedom) cannot be reduced to mere respect for an empty negative liberty or the juridical claim to be merely "left alone," without any conceptual relation to transcendent truth. The individual human good that lies at the foundation of this natural right, along with the related aspects of the common good of group-persons, and the political common good of the state actually reveal that the structures of this right presuppose a positive "freedom *for*" inclination in view of the search and attainment of truth in matters of faith. Thus, any concrete outcome regarding the human person's "freedom *for*" type of inclination to transcendent truth may not, in the order of juridical justice, be demanded by the political state. Moreover, a determinate content pertaining to the realm of the individual's moral due with regard to the search for transcendent truth cannot be juridically demanded by the political community as a precondition to the recognition of the right to religious freedom.

On the other hand, the juridical good of integrity of the act of personal assent in matters of faith includes the demand that the political community abstain from denaturing religious freedom by

---

86. "External limits on [religious] freedom are not drawn from principles completely alien to those that ground religious liberty itself" (Hittinger, "The Declaration on Religious Liberty, *Dignitatis Humanae*," 368).

treating it in its acts and policies as an empty negative liberty. Instead, this right should be politically conceptualized according to its structural relation to necessary features of the search for transcendent truth in such a way that the political community never oversteps the boundaries of its jurisdictional incompetence with regard to the source of this truth.[87] This means that the political community may not in any way—outside of the juridical implications of the political common good—juridically preclude the existence or any of the purely transcendent characteristics of religious truth by means of laws, policies, or other actions violating the relations of justice that arise from the right to religious freedom.

In concrete cases, the political community may recognize a realistic set of circumstances according to which a specific religious view is historically, culturally, or morally significant for determinate issues in a particular country, but it may be neither "faithful" nor "agnostic" with regard to transcendent truth to the degree that it actually violates the natural right to the integrity of the act of personal assent in matters of faith.[88]

87. "The negative prohibition [of interference or coercion] implied by 'incompetence' [of the civil authority in religious matters], in other words, necessarily presupposes and is based upon the positive recognition of the transcendent nature of religion that is owed by the state" (Schindler and Healy, *Freedom, Truth and Human Dignity*, 122).

88. "The state's government and law cannot justly teach that no religion is true.... And if a state does not teach that but its arrangements give rise, as a side effect, to widespread belief that the state's government has adopted them because it holds that no religion is true, the government has a significant duty to do what it reasonably can to rebut that inference." See John Finnis, "Religion and State," in *Collected Essays*, vol. 5, *Religion and Public Reasons*, 100. Beyond their differences in other issues regarding religious freedom, I believe that Finnis's argument is compatible with Joseph Boyle's claim that "political society is morally obliged to create the social space for people to fulfill their obligation to seek the truth in religious matters and live accordingly [and] it cannot do this if political life is conducted as if a certain outcome of this inquiry—whether a particular type of belief or nonbelief—were correct; for such political action skews public life in ways that hinder rather than facilitate this inquiry, and inevitably and unfairly coerces some to support actions whose rationales are incompatible with deep elements in their worldviews." See Joseph Boyle, "The Place of Religion in the Practical Reasoning of Individuals and Groups," *The American Journal of Jurisprudence* 43, no. 1 (1998): 22.

＞ 5

Walls of Separation
or Prospective Points
for Dialogue?

One possible way to approach the various different currents in legal philosophy and their often contrasting or mutually exclusive central claims is to envision them as a world of dialectic discontinuity that excludes the possibility for any type of common ground. In the present study, however, we have encountered on more than one occasion authors who have not hesitated to view the law-morality intersection through the conceptual lens of their fellow legal philosophers from the "competing" camps. Perhaps no sudden theoretical "conversions" occurred in that process, but these authors probably gained a better understanding of contrasting conceptual positions and perhaps even strengthened their own essential claims in light of the theoretical accounts of their "adversaries." Once the points of mutual divergence have been well established, certain aspects of theoretical accounts may even reveal themselves to be situated on the outer ridges of the borders of these "walls of separation," within the scope of prospective points of dialogue.

In this brief final chapter, I will attempt to summarize both the walls of separation and the prospective points of dialogue between a realistic account of the natural norms of justice and those competing approaches to the law-morality intersection that were presented in the first chapter. To this end, it might first be useful to enumerate briefly the central claims of a realistic account of the natural norms of justice.

The first claim is that the Thomistic account of natural law provides the juridical-anthropological basis for the necessary point of contact between the juridical domain and morality.

The second claim is that juridicity may be predicated on the precepts of natural law by putting in focus the fact that these precepts apportion certain natural human goods to persons as their titleholders within the scope delineated by the properties of juridicity, thereby constituting these goods as natural juridical goods, or natural rights owed in justice. In this way, the precepts of natural moral law are reconstituted as the natural norms of justice.

The third claim is that the natural norms of justice constitute natural rights that possess an authentically juridical status even in abstraction, apart from and prior to any enactments of positive law and legal recognitions of subjective natural rights. Natural norms of justice and natural rights are neither fictional entities nor purely moral ones awaiting to be "juridicized" by further legal enactments, nor otherwise imperfect juridical phenomena bereft of "actual" juridical value.

The fourth claim is that natural rights, or natural juridical goods, are functional as the focal point for any question regarding their status in various practical issues related to the order of juridical justice. Accordingly, natural rights must be evaluated as foundational in every search for a just juridical solution to theoretical, complex cases in which several juridical goods, or people's value-based accounts of them, are in deep conflict with one another.

A Response to Hart, Raz, and Dworkin

Given the contrasts between their main ideas regarding the law-morality intersection, Hart's, Raz's, and Dworkin's theories are not easily gathered into a single group of arguments. Interestingly, however, if we confront each of them with the central claims of the realistic conception of the natural norms of justice, a common denominator emerges.

All three authors are preoccupied with revealing what they understand as permissible ways—be they necessary (Raz, Dworkin) or merely contingent (Hart), purely formal and systemic (Raz), or minimally substantive (Hart, Dworkin)—for morality to be somehow pertinent and perhaps even foundational to the legal dimension. As we have seen, they dedicate a large portion of their texts on the law-morality intersection to the more formal questions of systemic moral features (Raz), principles of natural justice (Hart), or the procedural aspects of the justifying legal principles of political morality (Dworkin). These formal or procedural issues represent common ground with Thomistic natural-law theory, which itself shares an interest in the systemic features of the rule of law, the obligatoriness of positive law, and the overlapping issues between legal and political philosophy.[1]

---

1. As an example of an author steeped in Thomistic natural-law theory who addresses these arguments, see Finnis, *Natural Law and Natural Rights*, 260–96, 351–68.

The crux of the analysis of the law-morality intersection, however, is to be found elsewhere. Above and beyond the question of the formal or procedural validity of law, what is it that, ultimately, renders a law substantively unjust? We could speculate that the replies of these three authors, from the rather complex standpoints of their respective systems, would predominantly gravitate around the issues such as the minimal content of natural law (Hart), the principle of personal autonomy (Raz), or the liberal conception of equality (Dworkin). This strikes me as an intentionally "weak" juridical anthropology and epistemology, or, as it was referred to in the first chapter, a minimalist natural-law theory. As we have seen, Hart professes that the classical natural-law theory contains debatable and disputable "obscurities and metaphysical assumptions" that are "unacceptable to most modern secular thought."[2] In Raz's view, the theory of natural law fails to epistemologically support a general consensus on the status of natural law as the anthropological core of the juridical phenomenon at the law-morality intersection. Natural-law claims are reducible to "belief-based" support for the normativity of law.[3] Dworkin explicitly distances himself from the "orthodox natural-law theory," which establishes a juridical anthropology on foundations that are decidedly stronger than his "liberal conception of equality."[4]

These juridical-epistemological positions certainly seem to be *prima facie* in deep contrast to the core arguments of the theory of natural norms of justice. However, it could be useful to disentangle some of the main arguments of the proponents of such positions from the whole of their respective theories by examining

2. Hart, "Problems of the Philosophy of Law," 111; Hart, *The Concept of Law*, 191–92.
3. See, for example, Raz, *Practical Reason and Norms*, 169–70.
4. See Dworkin, *Taking Rights Seriously*, 339, 341, 344.

these particular arguments in light of individual central claims of a realistic account of the natural norms of justice just outlined.

Regarding the first central claim, Hart does, in fact, posit his own version of the contingent or nonessential minimum content of natural law: it consists of certain "natural necessities" that point to rules of conduct that "any social organization must contain if it is to be viable"[5] and are "so fundamental that if any system did not have them there would be no point in having any other rules at all."[6] Within the confines of his own theoretical account, Raz never actually denies that a person could legitimately and reasonably endorse a natural-law argument as his background support for legal normativity. Rather, he appears to hold that a person could endorse such an argument as long as it does not contradict the principle of personal autonomy as the overarching substantive principle of the entire legal system, and as long as it does not outweigh positive laws as exclusionary reasons for action. In my reading, Dworkin's argument on the procedural issues of the justifying legal principles of political morality could, in theory, also be permissive of similar personal endorsements, provided that its public legal recognition does not in any way hinder his liberal conception of equality. Admittedly, these minimalist or individualist claims are far from an adherence to the first central claim of the realistic account of the natural norms of justice, but they demonstrate that it is not possible to speak of a completely closed wall of separation.

With regard to the second central claim of the realistic account of the natural norms of justice, Ronald Dworkin asserts that the "most extreme of the natural lawyers ... say that there can be no difference between principles of law and principles of mo-

---

5. Hart, *The Concept of Law*, 193.

6. Hart, "Positivism and the Separation of Law and Morals," 80. See also Hart, "Problems of the Philosophy of Law," 112.

rality,"[7] denying "the difference between legal and moral arguments in hard cases."[8] Given the presentation of their accounts in the first chapter, one may take for granted that the thoughts of Hart and Raz are, at least to some extent, echoed in this position. However, the second central claim does not rest on the argument for identity between moral and legal arguments. Quite the contrary, for according to this claim, juridicity is predicated on human nature through the verification of the properties of juridicity. Therefore, the moral domain is not, as such, comprehensively "smuggled" into the legal domain. To the possible objection that this realistic claim is a mere conceptual sleight of hand that introduces elements of substantive morality into the law, it is possible to respond that these elements are, in the ultimate analysis, introduced into the juridical domain by the givenness of human nature itself in the relational perspective of justice, as described in previous chapters of this work.

So, besides the basic juridical-epistemological question of "what is the impact of the moral domain on the law," or "what is the moral status of the law," there is another similarly essential set of questions that is not entirely and explicitly answered in the texts of these authors. These questions are "what is the pertinence of that which is juridically right to the moral domain?" and "what is the juridical aspect of moral goods and moral principles?" The answers to these questions ultimately gravitate toward issues pertaining to the contemporary debate in legal philosophy concerning whether the concept of law is exhausted in human *artifactual* enterprise or whether it also permits the inclusion—or, indeed, a foundational role—of what I have referred to as juridical goodness, or what may be called the "natural nucleus" of juridicity.[9]

---

7. Dworkin, *Taking Rights Seriously*, 341.

8. Dworkin, *Taking Rights Seriously*, 344.

9. For an overview of the main arguments of the artifactual theory of law, see Luka

Now, I do not claim that Hart, Raz, or Dworkin would fully endorse an artifactual theory of law and completely discard a realistic account of right and juridicity, although I believe they would find the former theory to be quite proximate to their own positions. I intend only to highlight that the above "what is" questions are not presented from all possible angles in their respective theories, and neither have they been fully explored and settled within today's discussion on the artifactual nature of law. Therefore, it may be that the effort to establish a field for dialogue rather than a wall of separation will in coming years coalesce around not only the issues regarding the goodness of law but also the question of the juridicity of goodness itself.

Arguably, then, Hart, Raz, and Dworkin would allow for certain points of a limited dialogue with regard to the first two claims of Thomistic juridical realism, under the condition that the natural law be conceptualized as a module within a putative, broader common platform concerning various reasonable "belief-based" accounts of the law-morality intersection. I will analyze the details of this line of dialogue in the next section in my final assessment of Rawls's theoretical account that proposes such a common platform.

However, the third and fourth central realistic claims present a genuine stumbling block for theories such as Hart's, Raz's, and Dworkin's. This is because the last two claims introduce elements that are incompatible even with this type of limited and conditional dialogue. If juridicity is predicated on human nature, then natural right is nothing less than an authentic, real juridical right. If the juridical domain is constituted prior to and in abstraction from positive law, then it establishes, within relations of justice, certain juridical goods as foundational and necessary criteria for just positive law and for all concrete juridical solutions. These

Burazin, Kenneth Einar Himma, and Corrado Roversi, *Law as an Artifact* (Oxford: Oxford University Press, 2018).

claims surely exceed the level of the juridical-anthropological argumentation that Hart, Dworkin, and Raz would be prepared to reconsider.

An Assessment of Rawls's Priority of the Right over the Good

Rawls's account of juridicity within the framework of his political conception of justice, essentially marked by the idea of the priority of the right over ideas of the good, constitutes a contrasting account to a realistic conception of the natural norms of justice. We have seen how his concept of justice is wholly fixed in an aprioristic way with regard to the juridical domain, whereas this domain is outlined *a posteriori* in the basic structure of society. According to Rawls's political conception of justice, the fundamental idea of the priority of right over ideas of the good itself constitutes a moral value that Rawls identifies with the political common good. Thus, he recognizes a certain prejuridical moral domain as inherent in his political conception of common-good justice that, with its inbuilt foundational criterion of the priority of right over good, defines the framework of the right as the object of justice in the basic structure of society.

The framework that Rawls delineates is problematic in numerous aspects when confronted with the realistic account of the natural norms of justice. Simply said, whereas for Rawls the juridical domain is constructed according to the model of political morality in abstraction from substantive good, in Thomistic juridical realism, the natural norms of justice situate the good, individual or common, in the juridical domain.

Perhaps Martin Rhonheimer's assessment of Rawls's political

philosophy may prove to be helpful in detailing certain difficulties inherent in the attempt to establish natural rights as juridical goods while sustaining some elements of the validity of Rawls's principle of priority of right over good. Rhonheimer affirms that his own views "differ from Rawls."[10] "I never accepted his dichotomy between the 'right' and the 'good,'" he explains,[11] and he questions Rawls's "right-good" dichotomy on the level of substantial morality: he considers "a conception of the good of the person … as far as it is politically relevant, to belong to natural law."[12] He also claims that natural law is politically relevant precisely as "a natural legal doctrine," identifying it with the German term *Naturrecht*[13] and articulates many critiques to Rawls's system, almost all of which are grounded in his restatement of the aspects of natural law.[14]

Hence, it is all the more surprising to find out that Rhonheimer seems to endorse Rawls's idea of the *political* (as opposed to morally substantive or, as Rawls would say, comprehensive) priority of the right over the good. Within his "partly sympathetic confrontation"[15] with Rawls's political liberalism, Rhonheimer's understanding of a "natural legal doctrine" (i.e., the politically relevant aspect of natural law) is tailored to a vision of the political common good wherein the political priority of right over good is somehow inbuilt. Rhonheimer seems to generally follow Rawls's fundamental idea of the political conception of justice:

10. See Martin Rhonheimer, "Rawlsian Public Reason, Natural Law, and the Foundation of Justice: A Response to David Crawford," in *The Common Good of Constitutional Democracy*, 268, n. 9.

11. Rhonheimer, "Rawlsian Public Reason," 268, n. 9.

12. Rhonheimer, "Rawlsian Public Reason," 287.

13. See Rhonheimer, "Rawlsian Public Reason," 287–88.

14. See, for example, Rhonheimer, "Rawlsian Public Reason," 267, 273–74.

15. See Martin Rhonheimer, "The Political Ethos of Constitutional Democracy and the Place of Natural Law in Public Reason: Rawls's *Political Liberalism* Revisited," in *The Common Good of Constitutional Democracy*, 191.

Constitutional essentials and the public conception of justice must be shaped in a way that allows all peacefully to cooperate for mutual advantage in society as free and equal citizens. This is also the idea of the *political* priority of the right over the good.... It seems to me that, with this, Rawls not only expresses the modern political ethos of constitutional democracy in its quintessential form, but also formulates a principle of reasonableness that seems to be nothing other than what we all understand to be the basis of any workable and just political order.[16]

True, Rhonheimer's understanding of such political priority is, to a degree, narrower than Rawls's. In Rhonheimer's conception, the right, which is prior to the good, does not seek to preclude "the question of right reason or of truth from the political agenda," but rather to create "a public platform on which conflicting views about truth and right reason can be settled in what modernity has learned to be the only politically reasonable way, that is, without jeopardizing social peace, cooperation, and basic liberties."[17]

However, it remains unclear to what extent even this narrow idea of the political priority of the right would preclude the good that is instantiated in natural rights understood as juridical goods. This doubt is certainly enhanced by Rhonheimer's neglect of the political-philosophical relevance of a realistic juridical philosophy wherein that which is juridically right is predicated on the (individual or common) good by the natural norms of justice. In his account, the ultimate reason why a good constituted by natural law forms part of the juridical domain does not arise from the argument for juridicity as predicated on the individual or common good.[18] Instead, he justifies the inclusion of the good in the

16. Rhonheimer, "The Political Ethos of Constitutional Democracy," 228.

17. Rhonheimer, "The Political Ethos of Constitutional Democracy," 241–42.

18. An argument for something resembling natural juridical goods, constituted by the natural norms of justice as a foundational criterion for the political conception of

juridical domain with the claim that the individual or social good, based on natural law, is referred to the specific political common good and reconstituted according to political reasons.[19]

A realistic account of the natural norms of justice cannot admit an account of political common-good justice and natural rights that is founded on the constructivist idea of the priority of right over ideas of the good. This does not mean, however, that a realistic account is unable to recognize certain valid postulates of political philosophy. Quite the contrary, in a realistic account of the natural norms of justice, postulates of political philosophy are deeply rooted in the principle of respect for natural juridical goods. In other words, the postulates of political philosophy

---

justice, is, beyond the occasional mention of "natural legal doctrine," practically absent from Rhonheimer's "partly sympathetic confrontation" with Rawls's system. "To determine, therefore, which natural-law reasons are also public reasons—that is, reasons that can show that something must, or should, be also publicly endorsed by legal and political means—we need in every case a *further* argument that not only refers to 'natural law as such'—to its being the moral law—but also shows why such and such a norm of natural law refers to a political good and is therefore politically relevant and thus a candidate for also being ... publicly endorsed (e.g., by statutes or otherwise enforced by the juridical system). I cannot see what this has in common with viewing natural law 'from the perspective of and according to the conditioning and internal logic of the core principles of liberalism'" (Rhonheimer, "Rawlsian Public Reason," 282). It seems that Rhonheimer's "further argument," which refers to something more than "natural [moral] law as such," is predominantly formulated in terms of the political priority of right over good, not in terms of necessary juridical goods as natural rights.

19. "But public reason includes natural law in a restricted and limited way, that is, it includes natural law insofar as it is politically relevant. Yet, what exactly is the criterion for 'political relevance?' Natural law is politically relevant insofar as it refers to the common good of political society.... Positive law does not repress certain acts simply because they are immoral or opposed to natural law. The reason why [for example] murder—deliberate homicide—is declared to be a crime and punished by public authority is a specifically political one: it is necessary in order to allow citizens to live together in peace and security and, thus, to prevent society from disintegrating.... To be apt for public justification, natural-law reasons must first be converted into public reasons. They become public reasons only insofar as they can be justified in terms of referring to the common good of political society" (Rhonheimer, "The Political Ethos of Constitutional Democracy," 239–40).

are rooted in a conceptual framework wherein the (individual or common) good possesses an inherently juridical status, whose *ratio* is determined by the natural norms of justice.

How Juridical Is the "Standard" Thomistic Natural-Law Argument on the Law-Morality Intersection?

Throughout the course of this work, I have already addressed many aspects of a critique to the "standard" contemporary Thomistic natural-law position on the law-morality intersection and therefore do not intend to repeat them here. These arguments, in line with the scope of this work, gravitate toward the second central claim of a realistic account of the natural norms of justice: contrary to the so-called standard position, natural law does not remain on a purely moral level prior to its structural extension into the juridical categories of positive law and enactments determining subjective natural rights.[20] Rather, the natural law may be said to inherently possess a juridical status, and I am convinced that this realistic claim, rather than posing a wall of separation between the two positions, may instead represent a field for dialogue with the standard reading. This dialogue would certainly contribute to a better understanding of the levels of law's goodness as well as of the various instantiations of the juridical realm of goodness.

On the other hand, this dialogue also entails an invitation for a realistic juridical conception of law and rights to adequately in-

20. The first central claim of the realistic account of the natural norms of justice is shared by both the so-called standard and the realistic approaches rooted in Thomism. The last two claims are accepted by the standard position only to the extent that they are envisioned in abstraction from the second central realistic claim, since it is precisely this claim that is the basis of the contrasts between the two approaches.

terrelate the starting point of juridical epistemology with the origins of the moral "ought" as indicated by the precepts of natural moral law. We have seen that the attribution of certain natural realities (*res*) to persons as titleholders of rights is not reducible to a merely attributional state of affairs (e.g., to the mere fact that life is attributed to somebody). It is, instead, outlined within a basic understanding of the moral value of the natural thing-in-itself. The juridical epistemology of natural juridical goods must find its starting point in the understanding of how a certain natural reality or state of affairs falls within the scope of the individual or common human good. Natural right does not originate in a value-neutral habitat but rather within the context of what I have called the "part-whole" setting of the juridical and moral domains. This is why the general tendency of the standard Thomistic natural-law position to focus on the domain of morality is extremely valuable for finding the correct framework for understanding the juridical domain of individual and common goods.

Nonetheless, the dialogue between the juridical and the moral Thomistic natural-law positions should be also oriented toward the identification of the salient features of the juridical domain, which is not just any part of the moral domain. Although the juridical epistemology of natural juridical goods includes an initial moral insight into the thing-as-it-is-in-itself that is necessary to understand its basic axiological qualities, juridicity is predicated on a certain human natural *res* only insofar as these basic axiological qualities are attributed to the person in a way that meets the specific conditions of the juridical domain. I have referred to these specific conditions as the properties of juridicity. Since these constitute the natural human goods within a domain of *ius* that is distinct from morality, the juridical validity of these goods depends neither on the full range of factors relevant for the moral constitution of natural human goods nor on the theoretical status of the debates on the moral foundation of these goods.

How Difficult Is It to Establish a Dialogue with the So-Called "Third Pillar of Jurisprudence"?

My earlier brief analysis of the American and Scandinavian "legal realisms" has led me to comment that certain aspects of these approaches may seem almost as if they were envisioned on the "other side" or, in fact, "outside" of the conventional approach to the law-morality intersection. In this concluding subsection of this chapter, I will revisit this comment and its implication for what might prove to be a theoretical wall of separation between a realistic conception and the broader trend to which these two legal realisms belong.

The conventional approach to the law-morality intersection is formulated within a binary framework of contrasts between various strands of positivistic thought and versions of the natural-law theory. In contrast to this conventional approach, however, some authors have perceived the existence of a wholly distinct line of argument regarding the issues on the law-morality intersection and have insisted its development can be traced throughout the last two centuries of legal philosophy. This line of argument amounts to what is sometimes called a *third pillar of jurisprudence,* in the sense that, in the words of Brian Z. Tamanaha, it represents a "longstanding and coherent alternative to natural law and legal positivism."[21] Alternatively, it has been called "social le-

---

21. Brian Z. Tamanaha, "The Third Pillar of Jurisprudence: Social Legal Theory," *William & Mary Law Review* 56, no. 6 (2015): 2237.

gal theory,"[22] since its essential proposition is that the dominant argument for understanding the nature of law is its distinctively social function. The essential nature of law is exhausted in its property of being "an instrument to achieve individual and social purposes infused with, and buffeted by, social forces."[23]

Social legal theory is grounded on the widespread perception that law is a social institution, with social influences and consequences, that is used instrumentally.[24]

The common thread that unites this jurisprudential tradition can be pared down to two propositions: law is social in nature and is best understood through an empirically focused lens.[25]

That this theoretical line of argument is not ordinarily treated in legal philosophy textbooks as a separate autonomous account of the law-morality intersection does not diminish its pertinence for a correct understanding of major conceptions of law in Montesquieu, Friedrich von Savigny, Rudolph von Jhering, Eugen Ehrlich, Max Weber, and others.[26]

Social legal theory, however, does not amount to a theory of the nature or concept of law. It is, rather, a "social 'perspective' or 'orientation' toward law."[27] As such, it is well equipped to es-

22. Tamanaha, "The Third Pillar of Jurisprudence," 2238. "Henceforth I will refer to the third branch of jurisprudence as 'social legal theory.' Another fitting label would be 'social historical legal theory,' with a nod to both theoretical strains that embody it, but I prefer 'social legal theory' for concision and because variations of it already circulate [law and society scholars frequently use the labels 'socio-legal' and 'sociolegal']" (2262).

23. Tamanaha, "The Third Pillar of Jurisprudence," 2260.

24. Tamanaha, "The Third Pillar of Jurisprudence," 2262.

25. Tamanaha, "The Third Pillar of Jurisprudence," 2266.

26. Tamanaha, "The Third Pillar of Jurisprudence," 2237–262. "I believed then, and still do, that this theory and its accompanying narrative had dominated Western thinking about the relation between law and social change for the last two centuries, although in strictly legal writing the theory is usually inexplicit: it lurks as a set of background assumptions rather than being explicitly set forth and argued for." See Robert W. Gordon, "'Critical Legal Histories Revisited:' A Response," *Law & Social Inquiry* 37, no. 1 (2012): 202.

27. Tamanaha, "The Third Pillar of Jurisprudence," 2262.

tablish genuine theoretical dialogue with positivistic accounts or with natural-law theories.[28] It is, at least in principle, open to the development of various points of contact with the central claims of a realistic account of the natural norms of justice.

With that said, in sketching out these introductory remarks on the social legal theory, it was my principal intention to highlight that this third pillar of jurisprudence contains within it the potential for the development of a radical current that is almost hermetically closed to any dialogue with both legal positivism and the natural-law theory. The methodological premises and doctrinal outcomes of the social legal theory may be inherently incompatible with the conventional approaches to the law-morality intersection when they are imbued with an accompanying philosophical narrative that pushes the tensions within the three-pillar jurisprudential framework to the extreme. By "extreme," I mean that the main premises of the social legal theory may radically absolutize the social aspect of law to the exclusion of the properties of the concept of law that are ordinarily predicated both in a positivistic account and in natural-law theory. Thus, the main motivation for my present analysis is reflected in the fact that some elements of this radical current of social legal theory are present and operative in today's mainstream legal culture.

The radicalization of the social function of the concept of law represented a dominant feature of some recent legal doctrines usually grouped under the rubric of "critical legal theory."[29] Ac-

---

28. Such dialogue may move in the direction of positivistic or natural-law accounts taking into serious consideration that law is a social institution (e.g., Raz's source thesis or a Thomistic account of positive law as a system of social *determinationes* of the precepts of natural law). On the other hand, "social legal theory can incorporate natural law and legal positivist theories themselves within its own framework," and thus reframe them "through the social legal theory lens" (Tamanaha, "The Third Pillar of Jurisprudence," 2270–271).

29. "Indeed, sociological insights have been deeply integrated into the works of …

cording to a prominent advocate of this doctrinal approach, Roberto Unger, the core claims of the theory merge elements of the social legal theory with the background philosophical narratives of postmodern jurisprudence and versions of neo-Marxist postulates in an effort to resolve practical issues connected to multiple forms of social inequality.[30] In what is often seen as doctrinal continuity with the legal realists' strand of social legal theory,[31] critical legal theory, which was operative during the 1970s and 1980s, adopted a postmodernist stance according to which any deterministic—that is, positivistic or natural-law-based—expla-

adherents of Critical Legal Studies (CLS)." See Brian Z. Tamanaha, "Pragmatism in U.S. Legal Theory: Its Application to Normative Jurisprudence, Sociolegal Studies, and the Fact-Value Distinction," *The American Journal of Jurisprudence* 41, no. 1 (1996): 317.

30. "For what did critical legal studies stand?... A first current of ideas was the radicalization of legal indeterminacy. Call it the indeterminacy or *deconstruction* approach to critical legal studies. Its antecedents lay in antiformalist legal theories, in literary deconstruction, and in *structuralist* approaches to the history of shared forms of consciousness. It viewed past or contemporary doctrine as the statement of a particular vision of society while emphasizing the contradictory character of doctrinal argument and its susceptibility to doctrinal manipulation. Its characteristic thesis was the radical indeterminacy of law.... A second tendency in critical legal studies combines functionalist methods with radical aims in the study of law. Call it the *neo-Marxist* approach. Its point of departure has been the thesis that law and legal though reflect, confirm, and reshape the divisions and hierarchies inherent in a supposedly universal and indivisible type or stage of social organization." See Roberto M. Unger, *The Critical Legal Studies Movement: Another Time, A Greater Task* (London: Verso, 2015), 26, 28. Emphass added.

31. For claims in favor of the continuity between legal realism and critical legal theory, see Mark V. Tushnet, "Critical Legal Theory," in Golding and Edmundson, *The Blackwell Guide to the Philosophy of Law and Legal Theory*, 81; J. Stuart Russell, "The Critical Legal Studies Challenge to Contemporary Mainstream Legal Philosophy," *Ottawa Law Review* 18, no. 1 (1986): 3–8. However, some authors who are more inclined to advocate a moderate social legal theory affirm that such continuity is wholly unwarranted, for example, "CLS [i.e., 'critical legal studies'] movement adopted Legal Realism as an intellectual parent and attributed a family resemblance to it that it never possessed." See Wouter de Been, *Legal Realism Regained: Saving Realism from Critical Acclaim* (Redwood City: Stanford University Press, 2008), 1. "Legal realism is distinct from critical legal studies that reduce law to ideology and view law as structurally indeterminate in principle." See Gregory Shaffer, "The New Legal Realist Approach to International Law," *Leiden Journal of International Law* 28, no. 2 (2015): 196.

nation of the nature of law was suspect as a matter of principle.[32] Given that it was a radical version of the social legal theory, the primary concern of critical legal scholars was not focused on "the question 'What is law?,' or, 'What is the connection between law and morality?,' although their narrower concerns ultimately intersected with these more traditional questions."[33] Instead, their approach to issues on the law-morality intersection, in addition to following postmodernist principles, was fueled also by the systematic option for the "humanist Marxism rediscovered in the 1960s," which they found "valuable in completing their social theory."[34] The social standpoint from which legal theory should be viewed, according to the adherents of the critical legal theory, is one that, in Tamanaha's words, systematically unveils how "beneath a facade of neutrality, law fundamentally serves and enforces social hierarchies of power."[35] The enterprise of "unveiling" the unjust substructures in the law is accomplished by critical legal scholars with the aid of deconstructionist and poststructuralist tools, borrowed from thinkers such as Jacques Derrida and Michel Foucault.

According to most accounts, by the mid-1990s, critical legal theory had ceased to highlight the broader themes of social inequalities, such as working-class solidarity, poverty, and lack of a communitarian perspective regarding those and other social issues, instead becoming fragmented in various atomized direc-

---

32. de Been, *Legal Realism*, 11. "In law, postmodernism signals the movement away from interpretation premised upon the belief in universal truths, core essences, or foundational theories." See Gary Minda, *Postmodern Legal Movements: Law and Jurisprudence at Century's End* (New York: New York University Press, 1995), 3. For a presentation of "critical legal theory" as decisively postmodernist, see Minda, *Postmodern Legal Movements*, 106–27.

33. Tushnet, "Critical Legal Theory," 81.

34. Tushnet, "Critical Legal Theory," 83.

35. Tamanaha, "The Third Pillar of Jurisprudence," 2261.

tions, specified according to the particular interests of socially disadvantaged group-identities, delineated especially by race, ethnicity, sex or sexual orientation, and disabilities or different types of social (e.g., educational) exclusion.[36] In sum, it has gradually grown to become a doctrine in legal philosophy whose predominant focus is a juridical reading of the practical social issues ordinarily known under the heading of "identity politics."

The background philosophical narrative and methodological presuppositions of the critical legal theory, as well as that of its presently fragmented instantiations, may render this segment of the third pillar of jurisprudence radically sealed off from any prospective for dialogue with a realistic conception of the natural norms of justice. The postmodernist stance of critical legal theory is in deep contrast to the first central claim of the realistic conception of the natural norms of justice, since, as a matter of principle, it discards any mention of natural law as inherently deterministic. In addition, the neo-Marxist stance on critical legal theory undercuts the second central realistic claim—the very possibility that juridicity could be predicated on the moral domain—since the realistic conception of natural juridical law would, under neo-Marxist logic, amount to an "institutional oppression." In sum, a realistic account of the natural norms of justice could be seen by critical legal scholars as a conception of right and justice that is deconstructable as epistemologically unwarranted and inherently unjust in its claims to safeguard the social hierarchies of power "imposed" by nature.

36. See Gordon, "'Critical Legal Histories Revisited:' A Response," 204; Tushnet, "Critical Legal Theory," 88; and Robin West, *Normative Jurisprudence: An Introduction* (Cambridge: Cambridge University Press, 2011), 115–22.

Conclusion

According to a realistic conception of right and juridicity, the right is that precise thing that is apportionable to its titleholder as something that is distinctly *his* and is, in the outward and intersubjective dimensions, owed (hence, the obligatoriness of the right) by others (hence the other-directedness of the right) in a relation of justice. We can trace each right back to an attributional cause that situates the thing or good within a realm of application *in concreto* of the properties of juridicity, and this attributional cause thus becomes the origin of the predication of the juridical phenomenon to a particular thing or good; it is called the title of the right. If the attributional cause is human nature itself, or, more precisely, the precept or cluster of precepts of natural law, then this normative structure takes the form of natural norms of justice. When the focus on a precept of natural law is shifted from its orderedness toward the whole human good in the moral domain of human fulfillment to its function of attributing certain human goods to persons by constituting obligatoriness in the order of juridical justice, this precept is thereby constituted as a natural norm of justice. In this way, that natural human good that is the proximate object of the orderedness of the natural law to the human person's attainment of the whole human good is reconstituted by the natural norms of justice as a juridical good or a natural right.

In this study, I have demonstrated that all the essential elements of the doctrine on the natural norms of justice are already present in the line of tradition rooted in a realistic conception of the right and juridicity. This tradition began with Aristotle and was pursued in the doctrine of the Roman jurists. Thomas Aquinas's arguments on law, natural law, the right, natural right, and justice already possess sufficient elements for a further systematic elaboration of the juridical status of natural law as a specific overlap of juridical and moral domains, of the right and the moral "ought."

Since Hervada and Villey were both interested in unveiling the full range of doctrinal consequences inherent to the rediscovery of a premodern meaning of *ius*, they could not have bypassed the issue of the relation between this realistic conception of *ius* and *lex naturalis*. Perhaps their treatment of this issue was more *en route* and tangential than a primary focus of their academic interests, but their discovery of the elements at the intersection of the right and morality, of natural right and natural law, was very original.

After making an effort to harmonize Villey's and Hervada's arguments on the juridical status of natural law, I outlined certain directions where their line of argumentation could be taken further by interrelating it with relevant original Aquinas texts or their interpretation by contemporary authors. The result of this study looks very much like a rereading of valid "old" ideas and their elements, one which seeks a novel synthesis as an answer to new contemporary questions.

Perhaps Aquinas's neglecting to provide an explicit treatment of what is here termed the natural norms of justice should be ascribed to the fact that my study's main question did not form part of his conceptual realm when he elaborated the concepts of law, right, and justice. In a medieval *rei*-centric juridical culture—wherein juridicity was essentially envisioned as already somehow given in concrete *res*, whereas morality was understood to be instilled in the *rationabilitas* of the nature of the very same *res*—many of the contemporary nuances in the distinction between the right and morality were not yet even expressly posited as questions. We have seen, as Villey and Hervada both highlight, that Aquinas is in principle quite familiar with the general characteristics of this distinction. He scatters the implications of his perception of the right-morality distinction throughout a number of texts to the extent that he even mentions the precepts of justice in the context of precepts of natural law. The juridical culture that shaped Aquinas's mentality, however, did not have to deal with questions such as whether there is a necessary connection between *ius* and substantive morality, or whether we may envision a conception of justice as divided from, prior to, or in opposition to ideas of the good. Those and similar questions have, however, become foundational for contemporary juridical culture.

New questions may require a restatement of old ideas in light of changed circumstances, but this does not, of itself, invalidate those ideas. On the contrary, new questions may serve as a means to illuminate certain aspects of the old answers that did not have the occasion to emerge in previous contexts. A realistic conception of right and juridicity, as well as the correlative argument concerning the natural norms of justice, constitutes a reproposal of a platform in juridical argumentation that, in my estimation, has the capacity to successfully bridge the nuanced gap between the old and the new. If this study contributes to constructing such a bridge, I will consider that an ample reward for my efforts.

Bibliography

Books and Scholarly Articles by Michel Villey

Villey, Michel. *Recherches sur la littérature didactique du droit romain.* Paris: Les Éditions Domat–Montchrestien, 1945.

———. *Le droit Romain: Son actualité* (reprint from 1945). Paris: Presses Universitaires de France, 2012.

———. "L'idée du droit subjectif et les systèmes juridiques romains." *Revue historique du droit français et étranger* 24 (1946): 201–28.

———. "Du sens de l'expression *jus in re* en droit romain classique." *Revue internationale des droits de l'Antiquité* 2 (1949): 417–36.

———. "La philosophie grecque classique et le droit romain." In *Leçons d'histoire de la philosophie du droit*, 23–36. 2nd ed. (reprint from 1962). Paris: Dalloz, 2002.

———. "Abrégé du droit naturel classique." In *Leçons d'histoire de la philosophie du droit*, 109–65. 2nd ed. (reprint from 1962). Paris: Dalloz, 2002. English translation: "Epitome of Classical Natural Law (Part I)." Translated by Guillaume Voilley. *Griffith Law Review* 9, no. 1 (2000): 74–97; "Epitome of Classical Natural Law (Part II)." Translated by Guillaume Voilley. *Griffith Law Review* 10, no. 1 (2001): 153–78.

———. "Les Institutes de Gaius et l'idée du droit subjectif." In *Leçons d'histoire de la philosophie du droit*, 167–88. 2nd ed. (reprint from 1962). Paris: Dalloz, 2002.

———. "De la laicité du droit selon Saint Thomas." In *Leçons d'histoire de la philosophie du droit*, 203–19. 2nd ed. (reprint from 1962). Paris: Dalloz, 2002.

———. "Les origines de la notion de droit subjectif." In *Leçons d'histoire de la philosophie du droit*, 221–50. 2nd ed. (reprint from 1962). Paris: Dalloz, 2002.

———. "Law in the Liberal Arts—Law and Values—A French View." *Catholic University Law Review* 14, no. 2 (1965): 158–70.

———. *La formation de la pensée juridique moderne.* Edited by Stéphane Rials. Paris: Presses Universitaires de France, 2013. First published in 1968 by Montchrestien (Paris).

———. "Une définition du droit." In *Seize Essais de philosophie du droit dont un sur la crise universitaire*, 15–37. Paris: Dalloz, 1969.

———. "La nature des choses." In *Seize Essais de philosophie du droit dont un sur la crise universitaire*, 38–59. Paris: Dalloz, 1969.

———. "Le droit naturel et l'histoire." In *Seize Essais de philosophie du droit dont un sur la crise universitaire*, 73–84. Paris: Dalloz, 1969.

———. "Saint Thomas et l'immobilisme." In *Seize Essais de philosophie du droit dont un sur la crise universitaire*, 94–106. Paris: Dalloz, 1969.

———. "Morale et droit." In *Seize Essais de philosophie du droit dont un sur la crise universitaire*, 107–20. Paris: Dalloz, 1969.

———. "Droit subjectif I (La genèse du droit subjectif chez Guillaume d'Occam)." In *Seize Essais de philosophie du droit dont un sur la crise universitaire*, 140–78. Paris: Dalloz, 1969.

———. "Droit subjectif II (Le droit de l'individu chez Hobbes)." In *Seize Essais de philosophie du droit dont un sur la crise universitaire*, 179–207. Paris: Dalloz, 1969.

———. "Droits et règles." In *Seize Essais de philosophie du droit dont un sur la crise universitaire*, 221–33. Paris: Dalloz, 1969.

———. "La méthode du droit naturel." In *Seize Essais de philosophie du droit dont un sur la crise universitaire*, 263–81. Paris: Dalloz, 1969.

———. "Sur les essais d'application de la logique déontique au droit." *Archives de philosophie du droit* 17 (1972): 407–12.

———. "Si la théorie générale du droit, pour Saint Thomas, est une théorie de la loi." *Archives de philosophie du droit* 17 (1972): 427–31.

———. *Critique de la pensée juridique moderne (douze autres essais).* Paris: Dalloz, 1976.

———. *Philosophie du droit.* Vol. 1. *Définitions et fins du droit.* 2nd ed. Paris: Dalloz, 1978.

———. *Philosophie du droit.* Vol. 2. *Les moyens du droit.* Paris: Dalloz, 1979.

———. "Les lieux communs des juristes contemporains et le 'De Cive.'" *Revue européenne des sciences sociales* 20, no. 61 (1982): 305–24.

———. *Le droit et les droits de l'homme.* Paris: Presses Universitaires de France, 1983.

———. *Questions de saint Thomas sur le droit et la politique ou le bon usage des dialogues.* Paris: Presses Universitaires de France, 1987.

———. *Réflexions sur la philosophie et le droit: Les carnets de Michel Villey.* Edited by Marie-Anne Frison-Roche and Christophe Jamin. Paris: Presses Universitaires de France, 1995.

———. *La nature et la loi: une philosophie du droit.* Paris: Les Éditions du CERF, 2014.

Books and Scholarly Articles by Javier Hervada

Hervada, Javier, "Reflexiones en torno al matrimonio a la luz del derecho natural." *Persona y Derecho* 1 (1974): 27–140.

———. *Critical Introduction to Natural Right.* Translated by Mindy Emmons. 2nd ed. Montréal: Wilson & Lafleur Ltée, 2020. First published in 1981 as *Introducción crítica al derecho natural* by EUNSA (Pamplona).

———. "Apuntes para una exposición del realismo jurídico clásico." *Persona y Derecho* 18 (1988): 281–300.

———. Avant-propos to *Le réalisme juridique*, by Jean-Pierre Schouppe, vii. Bruxelles: E. Story-Scientia, 1987.

———. *Lecciones propedéuticas de filosofía del derecho.* 4th ed. Pamplona: EUNSA, 2008. First published in 1992 by EUNSA (Pamplona).

———. *Historia de la ciencia del derecho natural.* 3rd ed. Pamplona: EUNSA, 1996.

———. *What Is Law? The Modern Response of Juridical Realism: An Introduction to Law.* Translated by William L. Daniel. Montréal: Wilson & Lafleur Ltée, 2007. First published in 2002 as *Qué es el derecho? La moderna respuesta del realismo jurídico: una introduccíon al derecho* by EUNSA (Pamplona).

———. "Las raíces sacramentales del derecho canónico." In *Vetera et nova: Cuestiones de Derecho Canónico y affines (1958–2004)*, 297–319. 2nd ed. Pamplona: Navarra Gráfica Ediciones, 2005.

———. "El derecho natural en el ordenamiento canónico." In *Vetera et nova: Cuestiones de Derecho Canónico y affines (1958–2004)*, 605–18. 2nd ed. Pamplona: Navarra Gráfica Ediciones, 2005.

———. "La definición clásica de la justicia." In *Vetera et nova: Cuestiones de Derecho Canónico y affines (1958–2004)*, 633–43. 2nd ed. Pamplona: Navarra Gráfica Ediciones, 2005.

———. "Le droit dans le réalisme juridique classique." In *Escritos de derecho natural*, 275–78. 3rd ed. Pamplona: EUNSA, 2013.

Classical Texts

Aquinas, Thomas. *Commentary on Aristotle's Nicomachean Ethics*. Translated by C. I. Litzinger, OP. Notre Dame, Ind.: Dumb Ox Books, 1993.
———. *Summa Theologiae*. Vol. 1. Translated by Fathers of the English Dominican Province. New York: Benziger Brothers, 1947. For a concordance between the Latin text and a different English translation, I consulted Thomas Aquinas, *Summa Theologiae*. Vol. 28, I-II, 90–97. Translated by Thomas Gilby, OP. London: Eyre & Spottiswoode, 1966; *Summa Theologiae*. Vol. 29, I-II, 98–105. Translated by David Bourke and Arthur Littledale. London: Eyre & Spottiswoode, 1969.
———. *Summa Theologiae*. Vol. 2. Translated by Fathers of the English Dominican Province. New York: Benziger Brothers, 1947. For a concordance between the Latin text and a different English translation, I also consulted Thomas Aquinas, *Summa Theologiae*. Vol. 37, II-II, 57–62. Translated by Thomas Gilby, OP. London: Eyre & Spottiswoode, 1975; *Summa Theologiae*. Vol. 38, II-II, 63–79. Translated by Thomas Gilby, OP. London: Eyre & Spottiswoode, 1975; *Summa Theologiae*. Vol. 39, II-II, 80–91. Translated by Kevin O'Rourke, OP. London: Eyre & Spottiswoode, 1964; *Summa Theologiae*. Vol. 41, II-II, 101–122. Translated by T. C. O'Brian. London: Eyre & Spottiswoode, 1972.
Aristotle. *Nicomachean Ethics*. Translated by Terence Irvin. 2nd ed. Indianapolis, Ind.: Hackett Publishing Company, 1999.
Watson, Alan, ed. *The Digest of Justinian*. Vol. 1. Philadelphia: University of Pennsylvania Press, 1999.
Watson, Alan, ed. *The Digest of Justinian*. Vol. 4. Philadelphia: University of Pennsylvania Press, 1998.

Documents of the Catholic Church

International Theological Commission. *In Search of a Universal Ethic: A New Look at the Natural Law*. 2009.
John Paul II. *Veritatis Splendor*. Encyclical Letter. August 6, 1993.

Secondary Sources: Books, Chapters in Books, Scholarly Articles, and Papers

"Extracto del *curriculum vitae* del profesor Javier Hervada." *Ius Canonicum: Escritos en honor de Javier Hervada: volumen especial* (1999): xxi–xxx.

Adams, James L. "The Law of Nature in Greco-Roman Thought." *The Journal of Religion* 25, no. 2 (1945): 97–118.

Alexander, Gregory S. "Comparing the Two Legal Realisms—American and Scandinavian." *The American Journal of Comparative Law* 50, no. 1 (2002): 131–74.

Arrieta, Juan I. "Laudatio al prof. Javier Herada Xiberta." *Ius Ecclesiae* 14, no. 3 (2002): 611–14.

Bachiochi, Erika. "Safeguarding the Conditions for an Authentic Human Ecology." *Position Papers*, February 2017.

Bird, Otto. "How to Read an Article of the *Summa*." *The New Scholasticism* 27, no. 2 (1953): 129–59.

Bjarup, Jes. "The Philosophy of Scandinavian Legal Realism." *Ratio Juris* 18, no. 1 (2005): 1–15.

Boyle, Joseph. "The Place of Religion in the Practical Reasoning of Individuals and Groups." *The American Journal of Jurisprudence* 43, no. 1 (1998): 1–24.

Brock, Stephen L. "Natural Inclination and the Intelligibility of the Good in Thomistic Natural Law." *Vera Lex* 6, no. 1–2 (2005): 57–78.

———. "The Primacy of the Common Good and the Foundations of Natural Law in St. Thomas." In *Ressourcement Thomism. Sacred Doctrine, the Sacraments, and the Moral Life: Essays in Honor of Romanus Cessario, O.P*, edited by Reinard Hütter and Matthew Levering, 234–55. Washington, D.C.: The Catholic University of America Press, 2010.

———. "Natural Law, Understanding of Principles and Universal Good." *Nova et Vetera* 9, no. 3 (2011): 671–706.

———. *The Philosophy of Saint Thomas Aquinas: A Sketch*. Eugene, Ore.: Cascade Books, 2015.

———. *The Light That Binds: A Study in Thomas Aquinas's Metaphysics of Natural Law*. Eugene, Ore.: Pickwick Publications, 2020.

Budziszewski, J. *Commentary on Thomas Aquinas's Virtue Ethics*. Cambridge: Cambridge University Press, 2017.

Burns, Tony. *Aristotle and Natural Law*. New York: Continuum International Publishing Group, 2011.

Chroust, Anton-Hermann, and David L. Osborn. "Aristotle's Conception of Justice." *Notre Dame Law Review* 17, no. 2 (1942): 129–43.

Crozier, J. B. "Legal Realism and a Science of Law." *The American Journal of Jurisprudence* 29, no. 1 (1984): 151–67.

D'Entrèves, Alexander P. *Natural Law: An Introduction to Legal Philosophy*. 2nd ed. New Brunswick: Transaction Publishers, 1994.

de Been, Wouter. *Legal Realism Regained: Saving Realism from Critical Acclaim*. Redwood City, Calif.: Stanford University Press, 2008.

Del Pozzo, Massimo. *L'evoluzione della nozione di diritto nel pensiero canonistico di Javier Hervada*. Roma: EDUSC, 2005.

Del Vecchio, Giorgio. *Justice: An Historical and Philosophical Essay*. Translated by Lady Guthrie. New York: The Philosophical Library, 1953.

Delos, Jean. "Notes et appendices." In *Somme Théologique. La Justice: Tome Premier (II-II, Questions 57–62)*, by Thomas Aquinas. Paris: Desclée & Cie, 1948.

Demelemestre, Gaëlle. "La réception de l'interprétation française des théories du droit naturel dans le monde anglo-saxon." *Archives de philosophie du droit* 58 (2015): 393–428.

Dewan, Lawrence. "St. Thomas, John Finnis, and the Political Good." *The Thomist* 64, no. 3 (2000): 337–74.

Doig, J. C. *Aquinas's Philosophical Commentary on the Ethics: A Historical Perspective*. Dodrecht: Kluwer Academic Publishers, 2001.

Dufour, Alfred. "In memoriam Michel Villey." *Persona y Derecho* 20 (1989): 284–88.

Dworkin, Ronald. *Taking Rights Seriously*. 2nd ed. Cambridge, Mass.: Harvard University Press, 1978.

———. "'Natural Law' Revisited." *University of Florida Law Review* 34, no. 2 (1982): 165–88.

———. *A Matter of Principle*. Cambridge, Mass.: Harvard University Press, 1985.

———. *Law's Empire*. Cambridge, Mass.: Belknap Press of Harvard University Press, 1986.

———. "Thirty Years On." Review of *The Practice of Principle: In Defense of a Pragmatist Approach to Legal Theory*, by Jules Coleman. *Harvard Law Review* 115, no. 6 (2002): 1655–687.

———. "Rawls and the Law: Keynote Address." *Fordham Law Review* 72, no. 5 (2004): 1387–405.

———. *Justice in Robes*. Cambridge, Mass.: Belknap Press of Harvard University Press, 2006.

———. "Justice for Hedgehogs: Keynote Address." *Boston University Law Review* 90, no. 2 (2010): 469–77.

———. *Justice for Hedgehogs*. Cambridge, Mass.: Belknap Press of Harvard University Press, 2011.

Ehrlich, Eugen. Foreword to *Fundamental Principles of the Sociology of Law*, lix. Translated by Walter L. Moll. New Brunswick, N.J.: Transaction Publishers, 2002.

Errázuriz M., Carlos J. "Esiste un diritto di libertà religiosa del fedele all'interno della Chiesa?" *Fidelium Iura* 3 (1993): 79–99.

———. *Justice in the Church: A Fundamental Theory of Canon Law*. Translated by Jean Gray. Montréal: Wilson & Lafleur Ltée, 2009.

Escrivá Ivars, Javier. *Relectura de la obra científica de Javier Hervada: Preguntas, diálogos y comentarios entre el autor y Javier Hervada*. Vol. 2, *Derecho natural y filosofía del derecho*. Pamplona: Servicio de Publicaciones de la Universidad de Navarra, 2009.

Farrell, Dominic. "Wanting the Common Good: Aquinas on General Justice." *The Review of Metaphysics* 71, no. 3 (2018): 517–49.

Finnis, John. "Un ouvrage récent sur Bentham." *Archives de philosophie du droit* 17 (1972): 423–27.

———. *Aquinas: Moral, Political and Legal Theory*. Oxford: Oxford University Press, 1998.

———. "Aquinas on Ius and Hart on Rights: A Response to Tierney." *The Review of Politics* 64, no. 3 (2002): 407–10.

———. *Natural Law and Natural Rights*. 2nd ed. Oxford: Oxford University Press, 2011.

———. "Practical Reason's Foundations." In *Collected Essays*. Vol. 1, *Reason in Action*, 19–40. Oxford: Oxford University Press, 2011.

———. "'Natural Law.'" In *Collected Essays*. Vol. 1, *Reason in Action*, 199–211. Oxford: Oxford University Press, 2011.

———. "A Grand Tour of Legal Theory." In *Collected Essays*. Vol. 4, *Philosophy of Law*, 91–156. Oxford: Oxford University Press, 2011.

———. "On Hart's Ways: Law as Reason and as Fact." In *Collected Essays*. Vol. 4, *Philosophy of Law*, 230–56. Oxford: Oxford University Press, 2011.

———. "Hart as a Political Philosopher." In *Collected Essays*. Vol. 4, *Philosophy of Law*, 257–79. Oxford: Oxford University Press, 2011.

———. "Just Votes for Unjust Laws," In *Collected Essays*. Vol. 4, *Philosophy of Law*, 436–66. Oxford: Oxford University Press, 2011.

———. "Religion and Public Life in Pluralist Society." In *Collected Essays*. Vol. 5, *Religion and Public Reasons*, 43–56. Oxford: Oxford University Press, 2011.

———. "Religion and State." In *Collected Essays*. Vol. 5, *Religion and Public Reasons*, 81–103. Oxford: Oxford University Press, 2011.

———. "Reflections and Responses." In *Reason, Morality and Law: The Philosophy of John Finnis*, edited by John Kecwn and Robert P. George, 459–584. Oxford: Oxford University Press, 2013.

———. "Grounding Human Rights in Natural Law." *The American Journal of Jurisprudence* 60, no. 2 (2015): 199–225.

———. "Aquinas and Natural Law Jurisprudence." In *The Cambridge Companion to Natural Law Jurisprudence*, edited by George Duke and Robert P. George, 17–56. Cambridge: Cambridge University Press, 2017.

Foltzenlogel, Christophe, Claire de La Hougue, and Grégor Puppinck. "La prévention de l'avortement: garantir le droit de ne pas avorter." In *Droit et prévention de l'avortement en Europe*, edited by Grégor Puppinck, 73–105. Bordeaux: LEH Édition, 2016.

Fried, Charles. Review of *A Theory of Justice*, by John Rawls. *Harvard Law Review* 85, no. 8 (1972): 1691–697.

Fuller, Lon L. "Positivism and Fidelity to Law: A Reply to Professor Hart." *Harvard Law Review* 71, no. 4 (1958): 630–72.

———. *The Morality of Law.* 2nd ed. New Haven, Conn.: Yale University Press, 1969.

George, Robert P. "The Unorthodox Liberalism of Joseph Raz." *The Review of Politics* 53, no. 4 (1991): 652–71.

———. "Natural Law and Positive Law." In *In Defense of Natural Law*, 102–12. Oxford: Oxford University Press, 1999.

———. "Religious Liberty and Political Morality." In *In Defense of Natural Law*, 125–38. Oxford: Oxford University Press, 1999.

———. "Public Reason and Political Conflict: Abortion and Homosexuality." In *In Defense of Natural Law*, 196–227. Oxford: Oxford University Press, 1999.

———. "Moralistic Liberalism, and Legal Moralism." In *In Defense of Natural Law*, 300–314. Oxford: Oxford University Press, 1999.

———. "Law, Democracy, and Moral Disagreement." In *In Defense of Natural Law*, 315–34. Oxford: Oxford University Press, 1999.

———. "Kelsen and Aquinas on the Natural Law Doctrine." In *St Thomas Aquinas and the Natural Law Tradition: Contemporary Perspectives*, edited by John Goyette, Mark S. Latkovic, and Richard S. Myers, 237–59. Washington, D.C.: The Catholic University of America Press, 2004.

———. *Conscience and its Enemies: Confronting the Dogmas of Liberal Secularism.* Wilmington, Del.: ISI Books, 2013.

Gilson, Étienne. *Thomism: The Philosophy of Thomas Aquinas.* Translated by Lawrence K. Shook and Armand Maurer. Toronto: Pontifical Institute of Medieval Studies, 2002.

———. *Methodical Realism: A Handbook for Beginning Realists.* Translated by Philip Trower. San Francisco: Ignatius Press, 2011.

———. *Thomist Realism and the Critique of Knowledge.* Translated by Mark A. Wauck. San Francisco: Ignatius Press, 2012.

Gordon, Robert W. "'Critical Legal Histories Revisited:' A Response." *Law & Social Inquiry* 37, no. 1 (2012): 200–215.

Gorsuch, Neil M. "Intention and the Allocation of Risk." In *Reason, Morality and Law: The Philosophy of John Finnis*, edited by John Keown and Robert P. George, 413–24. Oxford: Oxford University Press, 2013.

Green, Leslie. Preface to *The Concept of Law*, by H. L. A. Har, xi–xii. 3rd ed. Oxford: Oxford University Press, 2012.

Gutmann, Amy. "Communitarian Critics of Liberalism." *Philosophy and Public Affairs* 14, no. 3 (1985): 308–22.

Hart, H. L. A. "Are There Any Natural Rights?" *The Philosophical Review* 64, no. 2 (1955): 175–91.

———. *The Concept of Law.* 3rd ed. Oxford: Oxford University Press, 2012. First published in 1961 by Oxford University Press (Oxford).

———. *Law, Liberty and Morality.* Oxford: Oxford University Press, 1963.

———. Introduction to *Essays in Jurisprudence and Philosophy*, 1–18. Oxford: Oxford University Press, 1983.

———. "Positivism and the Separation of Law and Morals." In *Essays in Jurisprudence and Philosophy*, 49–87. Oxford: Oxford University Press, 1983.

———. "Problems of the Philosophy of Law." In *Essays in Jurisprudence and Philosophy*, 88–119. Oxford: Oxford University Press, 1983.

———. "Lon L. Fuller: The Morality of Law." In *Essays in Jurisprudence and Philosophy*, 343–64. Oxford: Oxford University Press, 1983.

Hittinger, Russell. *A Critique of the New Natural Law Theory.* Notre Dame, Ind.: University of Notre Dame Press, 1987.

———. "Varieties of Minimalist Natural Law Theory." *The American Journal of Jurisprudence* 34, no. 1 (1989): 133–70.

———. "Liberalism and the American Natural Law Tradition." *Wake Forest Law Review* 25 (1990): 429–99.

———. Introduction to *The Natural Law: A Study in Legal and Social History and Philosophy*, by Heinrich A. Rommen, xi–xxxii. Translated by Thomas R. Hanley. Indianapolis, Ind.: Liberty Fund, 1998.

———. "Reasons for Civil Society." In *Reassessing the Liberal State: Reading Maritain's Man and the State*, edited by Timothy Fuller and John P. Hittinger, 11–23. Washington, D.C.: The Catholic University of America Press, 2001.

———. "Social Pluralism and Subsidiarity in Catholic Social Doctrine." *Annales Theologici* 16, no. 2 (2002): 385–408.

———. Introduction to *The First Grace: Rediscovering the Natural Law in a Post-Christian World*, xi–xlvi. Wilmington, Del.: ISI Books, 2003.

———. "Natural Law and Catholic Moral Theology." In *The First Grace*: *Rediscovering the Natural Law in a Post-Christian World*, 3–37. Wilmington, Del.: ISI Books, 2003.

———. "Natural Law as 'Law.'" In *The First Grace: Rediscovering the Natural Law in a Post-Christian World*, 39–62. Wilmington, Del.: ISI Books, 2003.

———. "Natural Law in the Positive Laws." In *The First Grace: Rediscovering the Natural Law in a Post-Christian World*, 63–91. Wilmington, Del.: ISI Books, 2003.

———. "Authority to Render Judgment." In *The First Grace: Rediscovering the Natural Law in a Post-Christian World*, 93–112. Wilmington, Del.: ISI Books, 2003.

———. "Natural Rights, Under-Specified Rights and Bills of Rights." In *The First Grace: Rediscovering the Natural Law in a Post-Christian World*, 115–33. Wilmington, Del.: ISI Books, 2003.

———. "Introduction to Modern Catholicism." In *The Teachings of Modern Roman Catholicism on Law, Politics and Human Nature*, edited by John Witte Jr. and Frank S. Alexander, 1–38. New York: Columbia University Press, 2007.

———. "The Coherence of the Four Basic Principles of Catholic Social Doctrine: An Interpretation." In *Pursuing the Common Good: How Solidarity and Subsidiarity Work Together*, edited by Margaret S. Archer and Pierpaolo Donati, 75–123. Vatican City: Pontificia Academia Scientiarum Socialium, 2008.

———. "The Declaration on Religious Freedom, *Dignitatis Humanae*." In *Vatican II: Renewal within Tradition*, edited by Matthew L. Lamb and Mathew Levering, 359–82. Oxford: Oxford University Press, 2008.

———. "The Legal Renaissance of the 12th and 13th Centuries: Some Thomistic Notes." *Doctor Communis* 1–2 (2008): 61–87.

———. "Divisible Goods and Common Good: Reflections on Caritas in Veritate." *Faith & Economics* 58, no. 2 (2011): 31–46.

———. "Political Pluralism and Religious Liberty: The Teaching of *Dignitatis Humanae*." In *Universal Rights in a World of Diversity: The Case of Religious Freedom*, edited by Mary A. Glendon and Hans F. Zacher, 39–55. Vatican City: Pontificia Academia Scientiarum Socialium, 2012.

———. "*Quinquagesimo Ante*: Reflections on *Pacem in Terris* Fifty Years Later." In *The Global Quest for Tranquillitas Ordinis: Pacem In Terris, Fifty Years Later*, edited by Mary A. Glendon, Russell Hittinger, and Marcelo S. Sorondo, 38–60. Vatican City: Pontificia Academia Scientiarum Socialium, 2013.

———. "Polity in Catholic Social Doctrine: Some Recent Perplexities." In *Religion and Civil Society: The Changing Faces of Religion and Secularity*, edited by Mary A. Glendon and Rafael Alvira, 31–51. New York: Georg Olms Verlag, 2014.

———. "An Issue of the First Importance: Reflections on the 50th Anniversary of *Dignitatis Humanae*." *Journal of Law and Religion* 30, no. 3 (2015): 461–74.

———. "Love, Sustainability, and Solidarity: Philosophical and Theological Roots." In *Free Markets with Solidarity and Sustainability: Facing the Challenge*, edited by Martin Schlag and Juan A. Mercado, 19–31. Washington, D.C.: The Catholic University of America Press, 2016.

———. "Religion, Human Law, and the Virtue of Religion: The Case of *Dignitatis Humanae*." *Nova et Vetera* 14, no. 1 (2016): 151–77.

Hoffmann, Tobias, Jörn Müller, and Matthias Perkams. Introduction to *Aquinas and the Nicomachean Ethics*, edited by Tobias Hoffmann, Jörn Müller, and Matthias Perkams, 1–12. Cambridge: Cambridge University Press, 2013.

Koester, Helmut. "ΝΟΜΟΣ ΦΥΣΕΩΣ: The Concept of Natural Law in Greek Thought." In *Religions in Antiquity: Essays in Memory of Erwin Ramsdell Goodenough*, edited by Jacob Neusner, 521–41. Leiden: E. J. Brill, 1970.

Lacey, Nicola. *H. L. A. Hart. The Nightmare and the Noble Dream*. Oxford: Oxford University Press, 2004.

Lamont, John R. T. "Conscience, Freedom, Rights: Idols of the Enlightenment Religion." *The Thomist* 73, no. 2 (2009): 169–239.

Legarre, S. "HLA Hart and the Making of the New Natural Law Theory." *Jurisprudence* 8, no. 1 (2017): 82–98.

Leiter, Brian. "Rethinking Legal Realism: Toward a Naturalized Jurisprudence." *Texas Law Review* 76, no. 2 (1997): 267–315.

———. "American Legal Realism." in *The Blackwell Guide to the Philosophy of Law and Legal Theory*, edited by Martin P. Golding and William A. Edmundson, 50–66. Malden: Blackwell Publishing, 2005.

———. "Legal Realisms, Old and New." *Valparaiso University Law Review* 47, no. 4 (2013): 949–63.

Lisska, Anthony. "Human Rights Theory Rooted in the Writings of Thomas Aquinas." *Diametros* 38 (2013): 134–52.

Long, Steven A. *Minimalist Natural Law: A Study of the Natural Law Theories of H. L. A. Hart, John Finnis and Lon Fuller*. PhD diss., The Catholic University of America, 1993.

MacDonald, Margaret. "Natural Rights." *Proceedings of the Aristotelian Society* 47 (1946–1947): 225–50.

MacIntyre, Alasdair. *After Virtue: A Study in Moral Theory*. Notre Dame, Ind.: University of Notre Dame Press, 1981.

———. *Whose Justice? Which Rationality?* Notre Dame, Ind.: University of Notre Dame Press, 1988.

MacCormick, Neil. *Institutions of Law: An Essay in Legal Theory*. Oxford: Oxford University Press, 2007.

———. *H. L. A. Hart*. 2nd ed. Stanford, Calif.: Stanford University Press, 2008.

Macleod, Alistair. "Rights, Moral and Legal." in *The Cambridge Rawls Lexicon*, edited by Jon Mandle and David A. Reidy, 731–36. Cambridge: Cambridge University Press, 2015.

Maritain, Jacques. "On Knowledge through Connaturality." *The Review of Metaphysics* 4, no. 4 (1951): 473–81.

———. "Quelques remarques sur la loi naturelle." In *Jacques et Raïssa Maritain: Oeuvres Complètes*. Vol. 10. Edited by Jean-Marie Allion et al., 955–74. Fribourg: Éditions Universitaires Fribourg, 1985.

———. *Man and the State*. Washington, D.C.: The Catholic University of America Press, 1998.

———. "La loi naturelle ou loi non écrite." In *Jacques et Raïssa Maritain: Oeuvres Complètes*. Vol. 16. Edited by Jean-Marie Allion et al., 687–918. Fribourg: Éditions Universitaires Fribourg, 1999.

Marmor, Andrei. *Positive Law and Objective Values*. Oxford: Oxford University Press, 2001.

Martin, Rex. *Rawls and Rights*. Lawrence: University Press of Kansas, 1985.

McInerny, Ralph. "The Principles of Natural Law." *The American Journal of Jurisprudence* 25, no. 1 (1980): 1–15.

———. "The Basis and Purpose of Positive Law." In *Lex et Libertas: Freedom and Law According to St. Thomas Aquinas*, edited by Leo J. Elders and Klaus Hedwig, 137–46. Vatican City: LEV, 1987.

———. "Natural Law and Human Rights." *The American Journal of Jurisprudence* 36, no. 1 (1991): 1–14.

———. "The Primacy of Theoretical Knowledge: Some Remarks on John Finnis." In *Aquinas on Human Action: A Theory of Practice*, 184–92. Washington, D.C.: The Catholic University of America Press, 1992.

———. "Natural Law and Natural Rights." In *Aquinas on Human Action: A Theory of Practice*, 207–19. Washington, D.C.: The Catholic University of America Press, 1992.

————. "On Natural Rights and Natural Law." Review of *The Idea of Natural Rights: Studies on Natural Rights, Natural Law and Church Law 1150–1625*, by Brian Tierney, and *Liberty, Right, and Nature: Individual Rights in Later Scholastic Thought*, by Annabel S. Brett. *Modern Age* 41, no. 2 (1999): 174–78.

Michelman, Frank. "Constitutional Welfare Rights and *A Theory of Justice*." In *Reading Rawls: Critical Studies on Rawls's A Theory of Justice*, edited by Norman Daniels, 319–46. New York: Basic Books, Inc., 1975.

Miller Jr., Fred D. *Nature, Justice, and Rights in Aristotle's Politics*. Oxford: Oxford University Press, 1995.

Minda, Gary. *Postmodern Legal Movements: Law and Jurisprudence at Century's End*. New York: New York University Press, 1995.

Minnerath, Roland. *Pour une éthique sociale universelle: La proposition catholique*. Paris: Les Éditions du Cerf, 2004.

————. "The Fundamental Principles of Social Doctrine: The Issue of their Interpretation." In *Pursuing the Common Good: How Solidarity and Subsidiarity Work Together*, edited by Margaret S. Archer and Pierpaolo Donati, 45–56. Vatican City: Pontificia Academia Scientiarum Socialium, 2008.

————. "La doctrine sociale de l'Eglise et les droits subjectifs de la personne." In *Catholic Social Doctrine and Human Rights*, edited by Roland Minnerath, Ombretta Fumagalli Carulli, and Vittorio Possenti, 49–59. Vatican City: Pontificia Academia Scientiarum Socialium, 2010.

Newman, Jeremiah. *Foundations of Justice: A Historico-Critical Study in Thomism*. Cork: Cork University Press, 1954.

Pakaluk, Michael. "Is the New Natural Law Thomistic?" *The National Catholic Bioethics Quarterly* 13, no. 1 (2013): 57–67.

Pieper, Josef. *Four Cardinal Virtues: Prudence, Justice, Fortitude, Temperance*. Translated by Richard and Clara Winston, Lawrence E. Lynch, and Daniel F. Coogan. New York: Harcourt, Brace & World Inc., 1965.

Pihlajamäki, Heikki. "Against Metaphysics in Law: The Historical Background of American and Scandinavian Legal Realism Compared." *The American Journal of Comparative Law* 52, no. 2 (2004): 469–87.

Pink, Thomas. "The Right to Religious Liberty and the Coercion of Belief: A Note on *Dignitatis Humanae*." In *Reason, Morality and Law: The Philosophy of John Finnis*, edited by John Keown and Robert P. George, 427–42. Oxford: Oxford University Press, 2013.

————. "The Interpretation of *Dignitatis Humanae*: A Reply to Martin Rhonheimer." *Nova et Vetera* 11, no. 1 (2013): 77–121.

Popović, Petar. "Securing the Foundations: Karol Wojtyła's Thomistic Personalism in Dialogue with Natural Law Theory." *Nova et Vetera* 16, no. 1 (2018): 231–57.

———. "The Concept of 'Right' and the Focal Point of Juridicity in Debate between Villey, Tierney, Finnis and Hervada." *Persona y Derecho* 78, no. 1 (2018): 65–103.

———. "A Hervadian Realistic Argument for the Juridical Status of Natural Law." *Ius Ecclesiae* 31, no. 2 (2019): 567–88.

———. *The Goodness of Rights and the Juridical Domain of the Good: Essays in Thomistic Juridical Realism*. Roma: EDUSC, 2021.

Popović, Petar, and Piotr Maj. "The Personalostic Value of the Human Act in the Philosophy of Karol Wojtyła." *Anthropotes* 32, no. 2 (2016): 357–84.

Popper, Karl R. *Open Society and Its Enemies*. Vol. 1, *The Spell of Plato*. London: Routledge, 1945.

Porter, Jean. "The Virtue of Justice (IIa-IIae, qq. 58–122)." In *The Ethics of Aquinas*, edited by Stephen J. Pope, 272–86. Washington, D.C.: Georgetown University Press, 2002.

———. "Natural Law, Legal Authority, and the Independence of Law: New Prospects for a Jurisprudence of the Natural Law." In *Searching for a Universal Ethic: Multidisciplinary, Ecumenical, and Interfaith Responses to the Catholic Natural Law Tradition*, edited by John Berkman and William C. Mattison III, 146–55. Grand Rapids, Mich.: William B. Eerdmans Publishing Company, 2014.

———. *Justice as a Virtue: A Thomistic Perspective*. Grand Rapids, Mich.: William B. Eerdmans Publishing Company, 2016.

Puppinck, Grégor. "Abortion and the Eurospan Convention of the Human Rights." *Irish Journal of Legal Studies* 3, no. 2 (2013): 142–93.

———. "Abortion in European Law: Human Rights, Social Rights and the New Cultural Trend." *Ave Maria International Law Journal* 4, no. 1 (2015): 29–43.

Rabbi-Baldi Cabanillas, Renato. "Michel Villey et la question des droits de l'homme: Une critique à partir de ses écrits et de ses sources intellectuelles." In *Michel Villey: Le juste partage*, edited by Chantal Delsol and Stéphane Bauzon, 157–75. Paris: Dalloz, 2007.

Rawls, John. "Justice as Fairness." *The Philosophical Review* 67, no. 2 (1958): 164–94.

———. *A Theory of Justice*. Cambridge, Mass.: Belknap Press of Harvard University Press, 1971.

———. "Kantian Constructivism in Moral Theory." *The Journal of Philosophy* 77, no. 9 (1980): 515–72.

———. "Justice as Fairness: Political, not Metaphysical." *Philosophy and Public Affairs* 14, no. 3 (1985): 223–51.

———. "The Priority of Right and Ideas of the Good." *Philosophy and Public Affairs* 17, no. 4 (1988): 251–76.

———. *Political Liberalism*. Expanded ed. New York: Columbia University Press, 2005.

———. "Justice as Reciprocity." In *Collected Papers*, 190–224. Cambridge, Mass.: Harvard University Press, 1999.

———. "Themes in Kant's Moral Philosophy." In *Collected Papers*, 497–528. Cambridge, Mass.: Harvard University Press, 1999.

———. "The Law of Peoples." In *The Law of Peoples: with The Idea of Public Reason Revisited*, 1–128. Cambridge, Mass.: Harvard University Press, 1999.

———. "The Idea of Public Reason Revisited." In *The Law of Peoples: with The Idea of Public Reason Revisited*, 129–80. Cambridge, Mass.: Harvard University Press, 1999.

———. *Lectures on the History of Moral Philosophy*. Cambridge, Mass.: Harvard University Press, 2000.

Raz, Joseph. *The Morality of Freedom*. Oxford: Oxford University Press, 1986.

———. "Liberalism, Scepticism and Democracy." In *Ethics in the Public Domain: Essays in the Morality of Law and Politics*, 97–124. Oxford: Oxford University Press, 1994.

———. "The Problem about the Nature of Law." In *Ethics in the Public Domain: Essays in the Morality of Law and Politics*, 195–209. Oxford: Oxford University Press, 1994.

———. "Authority, Law and Morality." In *Ethics in the Public Domain: Essays in the Morality of Law and Politics*, 210–37. Oxford: Oxford University Press, 1994.

———. *Practical Reason and Norms*. 2nd ed. Oxford: Oxford University Press, 1999.

———. "The Argument from Justice, or How Not to Reply to Legal Positivism." In *Law, Rights and Discourse: Themes from the Legal Philosophy of Robert Alexy*, edited by George Pavlakos, 17–35. Portland, Ore.: Hart Publishing, 2007.

———. "About Morality and the Nature of Law." In *Between Authority and Interpretation: On the Theory of Law and Practical Reason*, 166–81. Oxford: Oxford University Press, 2009.

———. Preface to *The Authority of Law: Essays on Law and Morality*, v–viii. 2nd ed. Oxford: Oxford University Press, 2011.

———. "Legal Positivism and the Sources of Law." In *The Authority of Law: Essays on Law and Morality*, 37–52. 2nd ed. Oxford: Oxford University Press, 2011.

———. "Legal Reasons, Sources and Gaps." In *The Authority of Law: Essays on Law and Morality*, 53–77. 2nd ed. Oxford: Oxford University Press, 2011.

———. "The Functions of Law." In *The Authority of Law: Essays on Law and Morality*, 163–79. 2nd ed. Oxford: Oxford University Press, 2011.

Rhonheimer, Martin. "Benedict XVI's 'Hermeneutic of Reform' and Religious Freedom." *Nova et Vetera* 9, no. 4 (2011): 1029–054.

———. "The Liberal Image of Man and the Concept of Autonomy: Beyond the Debate between Liberals and Communitarians." In *The Common Good of Constitutional Democracy: Essays in Political Philosophy and on Catholic Social Teaching*, 36–71. Washington, D.C.: The Catholic University of America Press, 2013.

———. "The Political Ethos of Constitutional Democracy and the Place of Natural Law in Public Reason: Rawls's '*Political Liberalism*' Revisited." In *The Common Good of Constitutional Democracy: Essays in Political Philosophy and on Catholic Social Teaching*, 191–264. Washington, D.C.: The Catholic University of America Press, 2013.

———. "Rawlsian Public Reason, Natural Law, and the Foundation of Justice: A Response to David Crawford." In *The Common Good of Constitutional Democracy: Essays in Political Philosophy and on Catholic Social Teaching*, 265–91. Washington, D.C.: The Catholic University of America Press, 2013.

———. "*Dignitatis Humanae*—Not a Mere Question of Church Policy: A Response to Thomas Pink." *Nova et Vetera* 12, no. 2 (2014): 445–70.

Rommen, Heinrich A. *The State in Catholic Thought: A Treatise in Political Philosophy*. St. Louis: B. Herder Book Co., 1950.

———. *The Natural Law: A Study in Legal and Social History and Philosophy*. Translated by Thomas R. Hanley. Indianapolis, Ind.: Liberty Fund, 1998.

Rowland, Tracey. "The Role of Natural Law and Natural Right in the Search for a Universal Ethic." In *Searching for a Universal Ethic: Multidisciplinary, Ecumenical, and Interfaith Responses to the Catholic Natural Law Tradition*, edited by John Berkman and William C. Mattison III, 156–66. Grand Rapids, Mich.: William B. Eerdmans Publishing Company, 2014.

Russell, J. Stuart. "The Critical Legal Studies Challenge to Contemporary Mainstream Legal Philosophy." *Ottawa Law Review* 18, no. 1 (1986): 1–24.

Saccenti, Riccardo. *Debating Medieval Natural Law: A Survey*. Notre Dame, Ind.: University of Notre Dame Press, 2016.

Sandel, Michael J. "A Response to Rawls's Political Liberalism." In *Liberalism and the Limits of Justice*, 184–218. 2nd ed. Cambridge: Cambridge University Press, 1998.

Sanguineti, Juan J. *Logic and Gnoseology*. Translated by Myroslaw A. Cizdyn. Bangalore: Theological Publications in India, 1988.

Schindler, David L., and Nicholas Healy. *Freedom, Truth and Human Dignity: The Second Vatican Council's Declaration on Religious Freedom*. Grand Rapids, Mich.: William B. Eerdmans Publishing Company, 2015.

Schouppe, Jean-Pierre. *Le réalisme juridique*. Bruxelles: E. Story-Scientia, 1987.

———. "Réflexions sur la conception du droit de M. Villey: une alternative à son rejet des droits de l'homme." *Persona y Derecho* 25 (1991): 151–69.

———. "El realismo jurídico de Javier Hervada." In *Natura, Ius, Ratio: Estudios sobre la filosofía jurídica de Javier Hervada*, edited by Pedro Rivas, 35–55. Lima: Ara Editores, 2005.

Shackleton, Stewart R. "La pensée juridique de Michel Villey dans le monde Anglophone." In *Michel Villey et le droit naturel en question*, edited by Jean-François Niort and Guillaume Vannier, 105–34. Paris: Éditions L'Harmattan, 1994.

Shaffer, Gregory. "The New Legal Realist Approach to International Law." *Leiden Journal of International Law* 28, no. 2 (2015): 189–210.

Simon, Yves R. *Philosophy of Democratic Government*. Chicago: University of Chicago Press, 1964.

———. *The Tradition of Natural Law: A Philosopher's Reflection* New York: Fordham University Press, 1992.

Sol, Thierry. "La notion de droit subjectif chez Villey et Hervada." *Ius Ecclesiae* 28, no. 2 (2016): 323–44.

Tamanaha, Brian Z. "Pragmatism in U.S. Legal Theory: Its Application to Normative Jurisprudence, Sociolegal Studies, and the Fact-Value Distinction." *The American Journal of Jurisprudence* 41, no. 1 (1996): 315–55.

———. "The Third Pillar of Jurisprudence: Social Legal Theory." *William & Mary Law Review* 56, no. 6 (2015): 2235–277.

Taylor, Charles. "Atomism." In *Philosophical Papers*. Vol. 2, *Philosophy and the Human Sciences*, 187–210. Cambridge: Cambridge University Press, 1985.

Tierney, Brian. "Villey, Ockham and the Origin of Individual Rights." In *The Idea of Natural Rights: Studies on Natural Rights, Natural Law and Church Law 1150–1625*, 13–42. Atlanta: Scholars Press, 1997.

———. "Natural Law and Natural Rights: Old Problems and Recent Approaches." *The Review of Politics* 64, no. 3 (2002): 389–406.

Torrell, Jean-Pierre, OP. *Saint Thomas Aquinas*. Vol. 1, *The Person and His Work*. Translated by Robert Royal. Washington, D.C.: The Catholic University of America Press, 1996.

———. *Aquinas's* Summa: *Background, Structure, and Reception*. Translated by Benedict M. Guevin, OSB. Washington, D.C.: The Catholic University of America Press, 2005.

Tuck, Richard. *Natural Rights Theories: Their Origin and Development*. Cambridge: Cambridge University Press, 1979.

Tushnet, Mark V. "Critical Legal Theory." In *The Blackwell Guide to the Philosophy of Law and Legal Theory*, edited by Martin P. Golding and William A. Edmundson, 80–89. Malden: Blackwell Publishing, 2005.

Tzitzis, Stamatios. "Controverses autour de l'idée de natures des choses et de droit naturel." In *Michel Villey et le droit naturel en question*, edited by Jean-François Niort and Guillaume Vannier, 29–46. Paris: Éditions L'Harmattan, 1994.

Unger, Roberto M. *The Critical Legal Studies Movement: Another Time, A Greater Task*. London: Verso, 2015.

Vallançon, François. "In Memoriam." In *Michel Villey et le droit naturel en question*, edited by Jean-François Niort and Guillaume Vannier, 13–17. Paris: Éditions L'Harmattan, 1994.

———. "Réflexions biographiques sur Michel Villey." *Droits* 29 (1999): 119–24.

Veatch, Henry B. "Natural Law: Dead or Alive?" *Literature of Liberty* 1, no. 4 (1978): 7–31.

———. Review of *Natural Law and Natural Rights*, by John Finnis. *The American Journal of Jurisprudence* 26, no. 1 (1981): 247–59.

———. "Natural Law and the 'Is'—'Ought' Question." *Catholic Lawyer* 26, no. 4 (1980–1981): 251–65.

———. *Human Rights: Fact or Fancy?* Baton Rouge: Louisiana State University Press, 1985.

———. "On Taking Rights Still More Seriously: Comment." *Harvard Journal of Law and Public Policy* 8 (1985): 109–19.

Waldron, Jeremy. *Law and Disagreement*. Oxford: Oxford University Press, 1999.

———. "What is Natural Law Like?" In *Reason, Morality and Law: The Philosophy of John Finnis*, edited by John Keown and Robert P. George, 73–89. Oxford: Oxford University Press, 2013.

———. "Jurisprudence for Hedgehogs." New York University Schools of Law, Public Law and Legal Theory Research Paper Series. Working Paper No. 13–45, July 5, 2013. http://dx.doi.org/10.2139/ssrn.2290309.

Walzer, Michael. *Spheres of Justice*. New York: Basic Books, 1983.

West, Robin. *Normative Jurisprudence: An Introduction*. Cambridge: Cambridge University Press, 2011.

Wojtyła, Karol. "Subjectivity and the Irreducible in the Human Being." In *Person and Community: Selected Essays*. Translated by Theresa Sandok, 209–17. New York: Peter Lang, 1993.

Index

</pre>

Natural Law & Thomistic Juridical Realism: Prospects for a Dialogue with Contemporary Legal Theory was designed in Minion with Open Sans display type and composed by Kachergis Book Design of Pittsboro, North Carolina. It was printed on 55-pound Natural Offset and bound by Maple Press of York, Pennsylvania.